A QUESTION OF LIFE

A Question of Life

ITS BEGINNING AND TRANSMISSION

A Moral Perspective of the New
Genetics in the West, the USSR, Poland and
East Germany

Patrick J. O'Mahony

Sheed & Ward
London

First published 1990. ISBN 0 7220 7120 5 (Sheed & Ward) and 0 87061 175 5 (Christian Classics)

Book production Bill Ireson

Photoset by Fakenham Photosetting Limited, Fakenham, Norfolk

Printed and bound in Great Britain for Sheed & Ward Ltd, 2 Creechurch Lane, London EC3A 5AQ and Christian Classics Inc, 70 West Main Street, Westminster, Maryland 21157 by BPCC Wheatons Ltd, Exeter

Contents

Acknowledgements

In any research, one is indebted to many people. I have listed in the Introduction over forty experts who kindly helped to explore various aspects of this very specialized subject. To all of them, I am most grateful.

I also thank Jenny Brine, Eva Sawicka and the late Len Corfan, who gave me prolonged and generous assistance with the Soviet, Polish and German sources.

Peggy Hirons, my secretary, organized and typed the manuscript and spent unlimited effort and time in this work. Colette Ware read the manuscript and made helpful suggestions.

Finally, it is difficult to find words to express my gratitude adequately to Walter Hollenweger and his assistants for their invaluable direction and inspiration. Without him, this book would not have been attempted.

Introduction

The recent technological breakthrough in the area of human embryology and fertilization is an epoch-making event and raises new questions about the beginning of human life, sexuality and the role of the family in human maturing. *In vitro* fertilization (IVF), embryo freezing, experimentation, donation and abortion, as well as egg and semen transfer, are largely inter-connected and cause new bio-medical problems, especially at the beginning of human life and its transmission. Like abortion, embryo manipulation forces us to try to clarify our views regarding the values at stake in human life and reproduction, and how the embryo or foetus should be treated. The latter is central to most of the issues caused by the new forms of reproduction. It was, for example, the development of IVF that gave rise for the first time to the possibility that human embryos might be brought into existence which might have no chance to implant because they were not transferred to a uterus, and hence they would have no opportunity to be born. This inevitably leads to the question about the moral status of the human embryo which will be analysed in the first chapter. Our concern is not only with the application of these new techniques but their extension and possible abuse outside their narrow field of application.

As we have come to gain greater control over our physical nature, that nature is rendered an object of manipulation and, therefore, becomes a singular vehicle for our own self-creation or destruction. In some studies a line is presupposed between human life and personal life. In other places, it is assumed that what is human and alive is personal. Again personhood has taken on so many definitions that it has become difficult to use with any precision. Not all persons, it is said, are humans. This is particularly manifested in the Holy Trinity. On the other hand, Lady Mary Warnock (1983, p.241) suggests that when reflecting on the status of the human embryo it is more helpful to abandon the whole concept of personhood altogether.

This book examines the ethical implications of the new reproductive developments. Attention is given to the various responses to them and particularly the Warnock Committee of Inquiry and the reactions that followed publication of its Report (Warnock Report 1984.) Of particular interest is the comparison between the perspective here in the West and some countries in Eastern Europe. A comparison between the Secularist and Utilitarian views is made with the Marxist approach. Both Marxism and Utilitarianism are consequentialist philosophies. Consequently, the question naturally arises as to whether there can be any real difference in their ethical perspective at the beginning of human life, as well as of the new reproductive techniques.

According to the Warnock Committee, people generally want some limits on the development of the new techniques but this, itself, is a problem in a pluralistic society – a point recognized by the Committee. Different countries are at different stages in reproduction developments. Yet, it will be demonstrated that there is a case, as in so many of the great questions of our time, for an international approach, and it is hoped that this would be ecumenical and international. Few will doubt that the development of science and medical technology in the field of human fertilization opens up many new issues, especially for the law. Unless science is to proceed without restriction, which would incur the gravest risks, new laws and priorities will be necessary, especially where scarce resources are involved, because medical science is advancing with startling rapidity. Furthermore, we know from the nuclear question, and indeed the recent report of the British Medical Association (1986), that scientists, medical and otherwise, can fall into the same destructive and inhuman attitudes as the rest of men.

There is, of course, a close link between the modern developments of bio-technology and the age-old problem of abortion. Ever since pre-Christian times, right down to the nineteenth century, the question of unborn life has been consistently explored. The argument amongst the moralists regarding ensoulment was classified as the Immediate and Delayed Hominization Debate, though in Christian tradition unborn life was always protected. The debate flared up again in the 1960s when legislation on abortion was made more permissive, although this trend had already begun in the 1950s in the Eastern European countries. The argument is now more intense than before because of the development of IVF. This inevitably raises questions about the status of the unborn, discarded embryos, embryo research and experimentation. All these areas are essentially linked with the beginning of human life and the respect that should be given to it. Hence the debate regarding the unborn is now extended to the very early weeks of human existence. Again, with the new medical technology, more information is available about human life and sometimes there is an impetus towards abortion when possible anomalies and malfunctions are diagnosed. Once again, the complex question about the moral status of the embryo cannot be circumvented.

Connected with these problems is the issue of the transmission of human life and how far marriage and the meaning of parenthood are affected. More particularly, the security of the child will be affected for better or worse by all these new techniques. Not only that, but the identity both of future generations, and of our future society as a whole, is now very much in question because of donor assisted reproduction and anonymity. The recommendation by some that the genetic source of individuals should be systematically concealed, not only from them, but also from future generations by being omitted from public records, demands serious reflection. It betokens a massive shift in the social concept of parenthood and a mentality of social acceptance of bonding rather than genetic descent as the central reality of parenthood. My claim is that what is being countenanced is a certain element of biological rootlessness in the human race, and that it is an infringement of a child's right to be denied the access to identity of his or her genetic parents. What is suggested is that behind all these new techniques and attitudes is the belief that all have an absolute right to have a child and there is a tendency, therefore, to favour the interests of the adult over the interests of the child, and the liberty of the individual over the values of marriage, the family and the future of society.

It is also my argument that artificial insemination by donor (AID) egg and embryo donation are an intrusion into marriage and deprive the child of the right to be born of parents who will bring him/her up. In Britain every year 1,500 to 2,000 babies are born from AID. This number becomes highly significant over a period of years in a time of falling birth rate and there is now the added danger of transferring acquired immunity deficiency syndrome (AIDS) to the mother and child. In a word, the child and his rights are used as a means to an end. His life and wellbeing are subordinated to the parental desire for a child. So these human beings become instruments to the service of others.

In Chapter II, the new techniques are considered and evaluated. The Report of the Warnock Committee and responses to it are analysed in Chapters III and IV. Special consideration is also given to the mainline churches – the Catholic Church, Church of England, Church of Scotland, Baptist and Methodist Churches.

In Part II, the attitudes and responses to these questions in three Eastern European countries are compared with those of the West. Poland has been chosen because of its Catholic tradition, East Germany because of its Protestant tradition and the USSR because of its Marxist ideology, though containing religious collectivities. All three are Socialist countries. It is argued that in the basic questions regarding reproductive techniques and decisions about unborn life, there is little, if any, difference between the Marxist approach in the East and the Secularist/Utilitarian view in the West. In both philosophies, individual human life is expendable and all values can be "traded off" because, in this thinking, individual human life is not of paramount moral value. Consequently, there is a serious threat to create another apartheid in humanity when some human beings are treated as sub-human or properties that are disposable in a "throwaway" society. It will be demonstrated in this book that nowhere is this more evident that in the case of unborn life, where even religion and ideology fail to act as a brake. The role religion plays in determining attitudes, therefore, and moral behaviour is explored. Until very recently, in East Germany the Church exists *within* Socialism, whereas in Poland it is *against* Socialism. In the USSR the official ideology stresses "this world orientation". In considering the part played by ideology and religion, and its influence on moral behaviour, it is shown that, in some instances at least, religious affiliation is an important variable in determining peoples' attitudes to unborn life. But the evidence will suggest that, in fact, final choices and moral behaviour are determined by other factors. This is indicated by shifts of opinion regarding unborn life, both in the West and in the East European countries.

Finally, it is contended that the new modern techniques benefit the few at grave risk to many in the present and in future generations. IVF is accomplished at enormous wastage of human life and scarce resources. Would it not be better to use these scarce resources on the causes of infertility, which are often self-inflicted? Would it not be better to direct limited money to other necessary forms of medication, where vast numbers of the human community are suffering from diseases caused by poverty, hunger and deprivation?

At present, in Britain, a human embryo can be frozen, manipulated, sold, experimented upon and killed without any infringement of law, and genetic engineering can be practised without limitation, legislation, or even adequate supervision. This is a grave threat to humanity with the possibility of horrific consequences. Secrecy in science is an enemy to safety and wisdom. Moreover, these challenges cannot be met by outmoded regional and national categories. The introduction of international legislation is imperative to handle international problems. Genetics can be no nation's monopoly – too much is at stake for the international community.

PART I

The Perspective in Western Society

CHAPTER I

The Beginning of Human Life

The attempt to grasp the definition of the human being is a complex exercise. Yet it is a necessary one. It has occupied generations of philosophers from the time of Plato and Aristotle. Today the search for clarification is as urgent as ever. The pertinent question is when does human life begin and what respect should it receive? The object of this chapter is to examine this question and to analyse the recent criteria that have been put forward. The modern debate can, in general be grouped under five headings or schools of thought and these are discussed below.

The Genetic School

Under this school are all those who argue that human life begins at fertilization. One of the best known proponents is Dr T. Iglesias, the Research Officer of the Linacre Centre, London. In a well-argued article she concludes that a new human person comes into existence at fertilization (Iglesias 1984, pp. 32–7). In another article she asks: Who counts as a human? (Iglesias undated). The question, she says, has two perspectives: Who is a member of the human species?; And who enjoys moral status with inviolable human life? Both questions are distinct, but inter-connected. Judged solely from the evidence submitted by the Royal College of General Practitioners (1984) to the Warnock Committee of Inquiry, the embryo should be treated with respect from fertilization. For Iglesias, it is at fertilization that a being of human material unity, organization and constant dynamism of intrinsic self-development of a human kind – and only of a human kind – comes into existence. The soul, the principle of life, the *anima* is the form of the human organism from its beginning. That is to say, it makes it what it is – giving it existence, a new being, a new organism – a member of the human species (Iglesias 1984b, p. 78). The development of this new human being and its finality is inbuilt in the power of the new organism itself and can be described as a process of becoming the one he or she already is. Humanity is, for Iglesias, the universal ground of our equal status and membership of the human species and is acquired at fertilization, no matter how incipient or vulnerable that organic development may be.

She reasons that to disregard humanity as the basis of moral status is to depart from the tradition and the ideas that rejected slavery. It would also depart from the medical traditions and codes of practice which respected human life from the time of conception. She proceeds to say

> It is a departure from the non-instrumental vision of life inherent in traditional morality as opposed to the instrumental view of life defended by Utilitarianism. (Iglesias 1984b, p. 81.)

A further explanation is given when she insists that human beings are just one entity and not a composite of two. They are not human organisms first and persons later when the advent of the soul or consciousness takes place. If we can attain self-consciousness at some stage, we must already be the kind of beings that can attain it:

> The inseparability of what a thing is and its capacities is particularly manifested in its organic contents, in its being always the same organism.

Whatever capacities we have now, have developed, she contends, from what we were from the beginning. These abilities, like self-awareness and choice, are only explicable if there was always the presence of the inherent capacity for those abilities from fertilization. Hence the kind of life a zygote has, because of the capacity it has, is a personal life, which at a later stage in development will be exercisable. But the ultimate ground of value is being *per se* not the passing state of being-like activities of choice and awareness.

Another well-known proponent of the Genetic School is the Harvard professor, John T. Noonan, who believes that

> once conceived, the being was recognized as man because he had man's potential. The criterion for humanity thus was simple and all-embracing: If you are conceived by human parents, you are human. (Noonan 1970, p. 51.)

The positive argument for conception as the decisive moment of humanization is that at conception the new human being receives the genetic code:

> It is this genetic information which determines his characteristics which is the biological carrier of the possibility of human wisdom which makes him a self-evolving being. A being with a human genetic code is man.

Noonan rejects viability, experience, feelings and social visibility (perceived as human) as criteria. This then is his answer to the question: Where does human life begin?

Since Noonan's writings have been circulating for a number of years, he naturally has more critics than Iglesias. For example, he has been criticized by Pastrana (1977, p. 249) for jumping from arguments based on biological data to ethical demands. However, it is difficult to see what other data could be used to determine how the embryo should be treated. Callahan (1972, p. 381) feels that Noonan's argument fails because if we are seeking a test for humanity, both the sperm and the ova separately pass the test. This does less than justice to Noonan. First the genetic constitution of the zygote (embryo) is not that of the sperm or ovum. The 46 chromosomes in the zygote are a new kind of reality and distinct from the 23 in the sperm or the ovum. Again the zygote is from the very beginning a genetically complete, organized unique individual organism in the species. However, Callahan admits later that Noonan does stipulate that the being must be conceived by human parents. But he returns to the subject with another objection, namely that it begs the question as to whether a conceived being is in fact a man. The conceptus might not develop, he says, because of various factors like abnormalities:

> The potentiality of a zygote to become a human being may not necessarily be fulfilled.

People like Iglesias will, of course, reply that the zygote is already a human person and that accidents and diseases can happen to all of us at any stage of development and, of course, the biological data support her contention. Therefore, the way a zygote develops does not negative what it is already.

Germain Grisez (1970, p. 274) asserts that it is certain that the conceptus is a living human individual from fertilization. Nevertheless, he is faced with the problem of twinning and recombination, a problem which I introduced into the theological debate some years ago. However, it is reasonable to suggest that recombination, according to the literature – O'Mahony and Potts (1967, pp. 45–51); Ford (1969, pp. 104–9); McLaren (1976, p. 125); O'Mahony (1977, p. 400) – is not really a big problem since such examples recorded seem to be the result of abnormalities in fertilization. Grisez answers that in the conceptus there are two types of individuation; one at fertilization but, in the case of twins, there is further individuality established when this second event occurs. He then proceeds to enquire if all human beings should be treated as persons and if so does this include the human embryo? He, like Iglesias, believes that freedom, choice, knowledge are not to be considered as separated from the *capacities* in which they are rooted because they are not separate entities but products of the continuous progression of the capacities which were present at the beginning of the embryo's existence when fertilization occurred. Nevertheless, Grisez (1970, p. 307) freely admits that we can never be absolutely sure. But there are no compelling arguments to deny that the embryo is a person:

"We must admit that the embryo can as well be considered a person as not." Grisez is criticized by Pastrana (1977, pp. 252–3) for his concept of individuation and for introducing two kinds of individuality. Pastrana feels that Grisez should have analysed the meaning of personhood more carefully and argues that until absolute incommunicability is achieved it is not possible to talk of individuality.

Albert Moraczewski claims that the embryo is a person because it possesses the essential requirements. He believes that the conceptus embodies absolute "intelligent freedom". The embryo is *radically* capable of rational thought though this power need not be actually exercised here and now, just as a person in sleep or in a coma. Therefore, a human person requires, first of all, that the individual has the appropriate biological make-up. Secondly it must have the *radical* capacity of development into a human being with characteristics such as rationality, choice, etc.:

> In brief, the human foetus is a person from the moment of the individual's first cell, the zygote, which results from the fertilization of the egg by the sperm. The pronuclei of each gamete unite to form the new nucleus, complete with a unique set of genetic information necessary for the consequent growth, differentiation and development of the new individual. (Moraczewski 1983, pp. 302ff.)

He faces the argument of embryo wastage, which is sometimes placed at 50 per cent and upwards, and points out that one contemporary physician (William Bucham) is cited as saying "that one half of the human race ... die in infancy."

Moraczewski observes: "I would find it difficult to argue that because of all these wasted human lives, these were not human persons."

Perhaps Moraczewski is weakest when he tries to explain the phenomena of twinning and recombination (1983, p. 307). He claims that he does not see the process of twinning as being incompatible with the incommunicability of the human person and he quotes the example of organ transplants from living donors which does not violate the incommunicability of the donor's personhood:

In the case of the very young embryo, the state of the cell being "donated" and the environment in which it occurs permits a new human individual to be constituted.

It might be worth noting here the remarks of the Anglican, J. Fleming. He rejects the contention that there is a distinction between human beings and human persons in the sense that the embryo is first a human being and later a human person (Fleming 1986). A person is someone, he says, who has certain human functional abilities – talking, choosing, awareness and suchlike. People, he says, have argued that personhood is achieved. He feels that this is a flawed argument. If personhood is something achieved, it can be lost. What if the individual becomes mentally disabled? Does that individual cease to be a person? Again, "nature does not revolve round function, rather function revolves round nature." I communicate, he says, because I am a human person. I am not a human person simply because I communicate. If the person were illiterate or dumb, he remains a person. Communication is the result of his personhood. He, therefore, suggests that personhood is an endowment, rather than an achievement which is present at fertilization. It is curious that Fleming's claim about the human individual being synonymous with personhood does not find support where one would expect, namely in the *Declaration on Abortion*, the Vatican's Acta Apostolicae Sedis 66 (1974, p. 738). In this declaration, it is possible to have a human life without soul. The official teaching is that we cannot be absolutely sure when the soul is present or when the human conceptus has personhood – it could well be at the moment of fertilization. But whatever about the personhood or soul, the Vatican declaration does believe that there is incipient biological human life and it should always receive the benefit of the doubt.

EVALUATION
The attractions of the Genetic School are evident but it is not without its difficulties. There is, as already mentioned, the high percentage of fertilized ova that do not implant but are simply

lost. Such loss raises the question as to whether each embryo was a person with an immortal destiny. Or, as some would put it, did each have an immortal soul? However, this problem does not appear to be different from the problem of infant mortality in poor countries. The second difficulty arises from the development that can occur to the embryo during the first two weeks of its existence. As already mentioned, this can happen in the form of twinning, and as some would indicate recombination, although as I have already suggested, the latter is not a serious problem. In the first week the embryo can divide into two and each continues to develop independently. The contention that the embryo at fertilization has sufficient individualisation for a personal being is, therefore, under strain. It is even more difficult if one speaks in terms of immediate ensoulment at fertilization. What has happened to the soul, one may ask, when splitting takes place? It would also appear that, in some cases, embryos can subsequently combine into one which proceed to develop as if nothing had occurred. If previously there were two or more embryos, what precisely has happened from the point of view of personhood or indeed the soul? Against this it is argued that one cannot reason from the particular to the general and that these are exceptional cases and that twinning and recombination are very exceptional and rare cases. And in the case of the latter, abnormality at fertilization is suggested. But there is a further problem because it appears that this is a phenomenon which can be brought about by IVF and, therefore, appears to indicate that it is inherent in all embryos. Other objections to the Genetic School can be found amongst some medical experts like Dr R. Edwards who rejects fertilization as the unique moment when life begins because of the various occasional abnormal products such as the hydatidform mole (Edwards 1983, p. 78). In reply, it can be stated immediately that because there is a structural defect or some other abnormality, the claim for fertilization, as the beginning of human life, is in no way negatived because the hydatidform mole is not a human embryo and the question does not arise.

Another writer, J. J. Thomson (1971, p. 48) criticizes the

Genetic School because it claims too much: "Fertilization of the egg or the implantation of an assemblage of cells is no more a person than an acorn is a tree." But this criticism is based on an incorrect metaphor because the acorn, when planted in the earth, has started the process of vegetation and is, in fact, an oak in *statu nascendi*, and the destruction of the developing acorn is the destruction of the young oak. Another objection which is levelled at the Genetic School is that each animal has its own genetic code and by giving the human a special moral status, one proclaims species prejudice or the racism of the human species. It is generally admitted, however, that while one does respect the animal species, which is required by our stewardship in Genesis, man is, nevertheless, the steward made in *Imago Dei* and different in kind from the rest of creation. As Mary Warnock (1983, p. 242) would say: "A preference for humanity does not stand in need of justification."

Perhaps the strongest argument against the Genetic School is, as I stated above, the phenomenon of twinning. The fact that the foetus is not definitely one for the first two weeks, or that it is possible that two or more embryos can become one in this period, demonstrates for many that individuation is not finally determined till after the primitive streak (14th or 15th day after fertilization) and, therefore, the embryo cannot be seen as an individual human being or person. Without this stable individuation there is no personhood. But it should be said here that the reason for twinning is imperfectly understood. There is evidence that the determinant – the "thing" that triggers the separation has been present at least from fertilization. Some very interesting work has been done on this subject by Wilder (1904, pp. 387–472), Corner (1955, pp. 933–51), Bulmer (1970, *passim*), Allen and Turner (1971, pp. 538–42), and O'Rahilly (1973, p. 631). In 1985 research was published by Dr Philippe of the University of Montreal which supports a genetic origin for both monozygotic and dizygotic twins (Philippe 1985, pp. 97–105). He compares his results with work done in 1981 by Carmelli *et al.* There were remarkable constants in the research though several new factors emerged in Philippe's work, which quite clearly supports a genetic origin for twinning. It could, therefore, be argued that twinning becomes *observable* later on but does not occur at that point. The fact that IVF may artificially play a part in twinning suggests, at first sight, that the twinning factor is something inherent in all embryos which can develop in certain circumstances, including deliberate human intervention. However, IVF constitutes a significant departure from the norm and clearly other factors could be operative during the IVF process that could never be operative during *in vivo* fertilization. These include the use of hormones to induce super-ovulation which also alter the internal environment of the female reproductive tract. This latter aspect may also be affected by the absence of seminal fluid which is specifically excluded from the whole IVF process. Additionally, the ova and early embryo are "handled" and cultured in artificial media before insertion. In the embryo of small rodents, such as rats and mice, these factors are known to induce altered patterns of development. The claim, therefore, that genetic makeup could determine identical twinning in normal circumstances does not exclude such an event being artificially induced by other extraneous factors in the absence of genetic determinants. Again, some would argue, if twinning does occur after the event of fertilization, it merely demonstrates that somehow or other one becomes two. Put in another way, the twins presuppose that there is already one from which they came, whereas in the Warnock Report (as we shall see later) the impression is given that the twins were proceeded by none. Always it is a case of a human individual or individuals that is or are in the process of development.

Before proceeding to consider the other schools of thought, it is well to remark that there is a massive amount of medical literature supporting the Genetic School. For example: Tuchmann-Duplessis *et al* (1972, p. 8); O'Rahilly (1973, p. 631); Warwick and Williams (1973, p. 71); Gasser (1975, p. 1); Longman (1975, p. 3); Basmajian (1976, p. 8); Scothorne (1976, p. 19); Philipp *et al* (1977, pp. 175–252); Harrison and Romanes (1981, p. 15); and Fox (1984, p. 1).

(The Genetic School also claims the favour of many proponents of high standing in their own disciplines. For example:

the Paris University geneticist, Professor Lejeune; one time Master of the Rolls, Lord Denning; and the legal expert of Oxford University, Dr Finnis.)

If there is a doubt, the fact that the embryo is in the state of becoming what it really is cannot be ignored. The least that can be said, therefore, is that the benefit of the doubt must be given in favour of the embryo as the consequences are unthinkable if risks are taken.

The Developmental School

This group of proponents require further development of the conceptus before it can be legitimately said it is an individual human being. There are, of course, differences of opinion within this school about how much development is required. Indeed there are those who sympathize with the Genetic School but endeavour to avoid the problems of twinning and recombination by placing the beginning of the human individual after the time when it is settled that it will be one or two, or more embryos. That is to say after the possibility of twinning and recombination. Well-known names support this view of development, such as Curran (1973, pp. 180ff), Ramsey (1973, pp. 174ff), McCormick (1981, p. 249), and Mahoney (1984, pp. 52ff). However, there are others who prefer a later stage of development. Some view the formation of the cerebral substance as a critical event in hominization. Without the presence of the cerebral cortex, they claim, no personal life is possible. But personal life manifests its nature through consciousness. A parallel is sometimes drawn with the increasing acceptance of "brain death" of the human person (Harvard Medical School 1968, p. 339). If, it is argued, brain death is the death of the human person, however much cellular activity may survive it, then the onset of brain life must be the life of the human person, however much cellular activity may precede it. This is seen as confirmation of the more general argument that for personal human life to be present, there is need of a human biological substratum which can only be the development of the cerebral cortex during the period of about 25 to 40 days into pregnancy. This theory has its own difficulties. It is not clear what is needed. Is it the first development of the nervous system for electrical activity in the brain (about 8 weeks) or the completion of the brain structure (about the 12th week)? In any case, an analogy of brain death is not that helpful. In the case of irreversible coma (indicated by flat electrocardiograph) it is not the coma as such but the irreversibility which is the critical factor. With the death of the brain comes the loss of all potential for personhood – its physiological basis is *irreversibly lost*. In the case of the *conceptus*, however, even before the event of the brain waves, at least the potential for personhood exists. There is no irreversibility. On the contrary, there is present a process of progressive development and cumulative integration essentially unlike the process of dissolution and disintegration.

Another argument against the analogy of brain death is put in the following way: It is an abuse of the clinical understanding and determination of death as "brain death" to claim that human death ensues when "personal identity" or "self-consciousness" is lost because the brain is dead regardless of the rest of the state of the organism. What the new understanding of death as "brain death" establishes is precisely that we know that the *human organism as a whole* is dead when the brain stem is dead; we know that without brain stem functioning, the unity of the organism collapses, so that breathing, blood circulation and heartbeat also stop. Hence it is the organic death of the body as the unified whole, as a unified living being, which is at stake in brain death and not merely the death of one of its organs or the loss of conscious personal identity (Schenk 1968, p. 16; Iglesias (undated); Häring 1972, pp. 81ff). Consequently, the analogy of brain death is misunderstood because too much emphasis is placed on a part of the body rather than the total individual and body as a whole. There is no more comparable criterion for determining who counts as a living human being than the criterion of the living human body, the living human organism. That is why clinicians claim that the end of the life of the organism as a whole is to be determined by empirical organic and bodily criteria; no other extraneous considerations are required. The body criterion, so the argument goes, is used to determine the beginning of human life, that is to say where the new entity, i.e. the fertilized ovum, is a total reality of humanness – a living bodily being of the human species.

All the same the analogy of the brain death school is popular amongst many thinkers. For example, Fr Bernard Häring claims that the basic structure of the human cerebral cortex is outlined between the 15th and 25th day. By 12 weeks, he says, the brain structure is complete and he asks:

> Can it then be said that at least before the 25th and 40th day the embryo cannot yet (with certainty), be considered a human person, or to put it differently, only about that time the embryo becomes a being with all the basic rights of a human person. (Häring 1972, p. 84.)

But he proceeds with a caution because this is merely an opinion, he says, that requires serious consideration but does not provide ground "for depriving the embryo of the basic human right to live."

But this approach incurs the risk of disregarding the findings of genetics for it can be argued that the human biological substratum, which personhood or animation requires, is none other than the human conceptus itself

> composed as it is of cells which are genetically human through and through, and which in its turn, requires only irrevocable stability in the human genetic material to constitute a developing individual sufficiently predisposed to receive the infusion of its human and rational soul. (Mahoney 1984, p. 66.)

Indeed the Genetic School would reply that irrevocable stability is already sufficiently present in order to constitute an individual.

Another objection to the "brain death" theory is its unreliability. Dr Szawarski, of the Philosophical Department of Warsaw University, argues that this is not a definite criterion of cessation of humanity (Szawarski 1978, p. 60). But I have already referred to this point and I have also developed it elsewhere (O'Mahony 1978, p. 381).

The criterion of the ability to lead an independent life is a sufficient stage of development for other writers. That is to say: "When it is capable of independent existence at 28 weeks then it should have the same rights as a newly born child." (Potts 1969, p. 75. See also Engelhardt 1983, pp. 183ff.)

The problem about this theory is the fact that capability for an independent existence depends on various factors which do not have a single meaning. The healthier and the more developed the embryo, the greater are its chances of surviving premature birth. But this state is connected with a number of factors – the health of the mother, the progress of medical science, new incubation methods, and new ways of keeping the embryo alive *in vitro* from the earliest moments, which is a possibility in the future, make the criterion of independent existence an unreliable guide. Again this kind of thinking is a threat to all who are not capable of independent existence, such as the mentally handicapped, the paralysed, those who are artificially sustained in life, and even the new born child.

The Animation School is another classification within the Developmental School. It is as old as Aristotle and its theory has been held for a number of years by many Christians. This maintains that the embryo or foetus attains humanity at a certain stage in its development when the organism is properly organized or suitably disposed. These writers, who include Aristotle and Aquinas, see the developing zygote as first vegetative then animal and finally human, i.e. hominized. Donceel is one of the modern exponents of what is now called the Delayed Animation Theory (Donceel 1970, pp. 76ff). He argues that the human soul can only exist in a properly disposed human body, which he claims is in keeping with the philosophical theory of hylomorphism. Some degree of bodily organization must be present, he says, for animation. Just as death occurs when the body is no longer sufficiently organized to retain its soul (substantial form) so also the body cannot receive the soul until it is properly disposed. Therefore, since soul and matter are strictly complementary, the fertilized ovum is not ready because the matter is not organized or properly developed. Or, to quote his own words (Donceel 1970, p. 83): "There can be an actual human soul only in a body endowed with the organs for the spiritual activities of man." Donceel strives gallantly to demonstrate that this theory avoids dualism and concludes

> that the least we may ask before admitting the presence of a human soul is the availability of these organs: the sense, the nervous system, the brain and especially the cortex. (Donceel 1970, p. 101.)

Curiously enough, it seems that although Donceel strives to avoid dualism, it is, in fact, latent in his writing. Moreover, it is easy to slip from hylomorphism into a Platonic-Cartesian conception of man which denies his unity. It sees the human being as a union rather than a unity, a couple rather than an individual where body and soul are linked together like Gilbert Ryle's *Ghost in the Machine*.

Another difficulty about this theory, and indeed the whole Developmental School, is that there are different stages of development that claim serious attention, i.e. fertilization, implantation, quickening, brain structure, viability and birth. Embryonic development is a continuum and every phase is a definite and important characteristic. Any of these might be chosen and the choice is slippery and uncertain. That so many points are suggested as the beginning of a human individual underscores the hazards of the Development School. In a very real sense, we are all developing in potentiality from conception to adulthood. How much actualisation should count before we are classed as individuals or human persons?

The Relational School

This approach, which is sometimes referred to as the French School or the Theory of Humanisation, is unwilling to accept merely physical criteria and argues for what is called more personalistic criteria in determining the beginning of human life.

The first factor of the Relational School is their unwillingness to assess the beginning of human life on biological evidence alone. The destination of the embryo to become a human being is not something which is simply in the flesh and in biological terms but is inscribed also in the relation of acceptance and of recognition by the parents and others. Biological life is not then the most important criterion; without the will of the parents there can be no humanization, a view vigorously supported by Bernard Quelquejeu (1972, pp. 57–71). For him, the conceptus is humanized only through the procreative will expressed by the mother, the father and in some way by society itself. Louis Beirnaert (1970, p. 522) points out that contemporary epistemology shows the participation of culture and of a knowing and recognising element in the very essence of discourse. He adds that this is symbolized when the child is given a name and thereby recognized by the parents. That is to say, the unborn must be admitted to the family and indeed the human family. To be refused recognition is to be unwanted. In other words, it must be humanized. (Beirnaert 1970, pp. 522ff.)

Other writers reflect on different aspects of the same approach. Antoine (1974, p. 573) says that, in certain tribes of Eskimos, because of their severe winter and lack of food, the child is not accepted by the local community; rather he is sacrificed because the survival of the group is threatened. On the other hand, when the child is accepted, he becomes a brother. This is a decisive moment for the tribe and the infant. His life must now be defended at all costs. So also, in the case of the unborn. Without relationship and recognition, it lacks humanization until such time as it is adopted by parents and society.

Against this reasoning of Beirnaert, Antoine and others, it could be argued that many children already born or about to be born are not humanized and have no hope of obtaining human status. So their argument seems to prove too much. Other supporters of the Relational School are Jacques-Marie Pohier (1970, p. 179) and Bruno Ribes. Ribes (1970, p. 202) argues that there are economic, psychological, cultural and even religious aspects of human life as well as biological aspects, and he adds that where humanization does not exist either before or after the birth, one has to ask about the legitimacy of allowing such a child to be born. Quelquejeu calls into question the method of applying general principles to particular cases, such as the question of the unborn. A new methodology is needed. One should start with the existential situation, or the particular case, and discover if there is a *locus theologicus*, a moral experience, or a rational basis, for a new moral attitude to this problem.

Two articles by the Jesuit writer and philosopher, Fr V. Fagone, appeared in a quasi-official Roman journal during 1973. He examines carefully the question of humanization as distinct from hominization and gives a detailed analysis of Quelquejeu's views. He feels that Quelquejeu's reasoning is faulty. If the conceptus, he argues, is a child it has priority over the parents' decision which is external to the actual life of the embryo (Fagone 1973). Fagone insists that the life of the unborn is independent of society and other parental relationship. It is true, and acceptable to contemporary philosophy, that communication with others is an essential part of human existence. It is a fact that we are humanized by the web of relationship in which we are involved, but this, says Fagone (1973a), must not be confused with the *ontological capacity* to communicate or enter into a relationship. There is a distinction between the *capacity* and the *exercise* of the capacity. Where the unborn is concerned, it is a human individual irrespective of the parents and society. Perhaps Fagone failed to state that the embryo has already acquired a relationship with those whose union brought him/her into being, namely with this mother who carries, feeds, shelters him, and with the human family because of the end to which he or she is ordained. Indeed the words of Adam could be applied here: "This is bone of my bone, flesh of my flesh." (Genesis 2:23.) There is no need to place the ontological argument against the relational aspect. They are not mutually exclusive.

Professor Curran, of Washington University, states that none of these authors is willing to apply their criteria to the born child (Curran 1973, pp. 177ff). But he feels that their reasoning is defective because one cannot logically draw the line at birth. Relationships can deteriorate after birth and if they do disappear, what happens to the individual's life in this case? And what happens at the other end of life when people are unconscious and relational criteria have disappeared? They are still human beings. Furthermore, it can be asked whether the relational criteria must be mutual – the child would then need to acknowledge and recognize the gift of the parents before a human relationship is truly present. Like Fagone, Curran freely admits the importance of relationship in human existence, but he states that at the beginning and end of life "we are not dealing with human life in its fullest actuality." (Curran 1973, p. 117.)

The Social Consequences School

These authors base their theory about the beginning of human life on psychological or moral factors. Emphasis is placed on the "manifestations" of human life. In a very thoughtful analysis, Dr Sissela Bok attempts to find new criteria by understanding why human life is sacred and the "harm that comes from taking human life." Dr Bok believes that a concern for human life is more important than the definition of humanity and places great emphasis on the feelings people experience when life is destroyed. She lists four reasons as underlying the sacredness of life (Bok 1981, pp. 55–60):

1. Killing is viewed as the greatest of all dangers for the victim.
2. Killing brutalizes the killer.
3. Killing causes grief and a sense of loss in the family of the victim.
4. It is a threat to the whole of society.

Bok adds that clearly most of these criteria for protecting human life are absent in the early stages of pregnancy, while infanticide is definitely excluded (Bok 1981, p. 59). She asserts that quickening and viability provide the best guidelines because, before quickening, the reasons to protect human life are negligible "perhaps absent altogether."

Between quickening and viability, reasons for protecting human life increase. After viability, the reasons to protect human life may now be thought to be partially present and, therefore, the killing of the unborn should be prohibited save on the rarest occasions, such as saving the mother's life. Against this it must be noted that the problem of viability is its definition which varies from one child to another and depends on our state of knowledge concerning life support. As technological progress pushes back the time of independent survival, viability as the cut-off point also moves back. Bok replies to this by reminding us that viability was thought to be a good guideline. Not so much because the child could survive outside the mother, but because the reasons for protecting human life seems to be more present at that stage. At present the two coincide but, if in the future, the two diverge, Bok claims that even when the embryo could be kept alive without its mother, the reasons for protecting it would still be absent (Bok 1981, p. 60).

Now this type of reasoning, in my opinion, is not very convincing. It can also be argued that the thesis is unsound because it is based on feelings that are subjective and notoriously individual.

Glanville Williams (1964, p. 20) believes that social practices and attitudes indicate that zygotes are not considered human beings. People do not feel the same way about the zygote as the born child. Death certificates are not required for each aborted foetus, nor is there a form of burial service for them, which seems to confirm and reflect the common attitude. This approach, as Callahan contends, is open to serious objection in that it totally neglects the biological data. It makes no place for the concept of development which in reality cannot be removed from any serious treatment of the unborn. "Becoming" is something that must be conceded to the developing embryo (Callahan 1972, pp. 392ff).

The Potentiality School

This approach is linked closely to the modern development of bio-technology. Because it was at issue, more than any other, it first caused the prolonged debate on the status of the unborn. Ever since Aristotle, right down through Aquinas to the nineteenth century, the status of the unborn has been debated. Over the centuries – as Connery (1977, p. 467) has so painstakingly pointed out in his historic study of abortion – some theologians spoke of three different categories of abortion: prevention of conception, abortion of the inanimate foetus and abortion of the animated foetus. The argument regarding the ensoulment of the foetus and the kind of protection that should be accorded to the unborn human child was classified as the immediate and delayed hominization debate. The former supported ensoulment at conception, the latter claimed that ensoulment occurred between conception and birth when the body was sufficiently organized to receive the "infusion" of the soul. By the nineteenth century there was little dialogue between science and theology. The theory of immediate ensoulment eventually gained support. Hence, apart from sporadic discussions by people like Professor de Dordolot of Louvain and the Jesuit, Dr Messenger, in the 1930s and 1940s, the issue became obsolete (Messenger 1949, pp. 219–333). Nearer to our time, the debate regarding the status of the unborn flared up again and this was a result of the passionate controversy in country after country about abortion and legislation (O'Mahony and Potts 1967, pp. 45–51). It has evoked an immense and diverse literature as we have already seen in this chapter. Today, because of *in vitro* fertilization, the issue is even more acute than ever. Indeed as Mary Warnock noted when reflecting on the Warnock Inquiry:

> All the other issues we had to consider seemed relatively trivial compared with this one, concerned as it is with a matter which nobody could deny is of central moral significance." (Warnock 1985, p. xvi.)

The precise point of dispute within the Inquiry, as we shall see later, was not on the value that should be attached to human life in general, but rather at the earliest stages of its development. Consequently, the debate about the moral status of the unborn was again revived with more renewed vigour. Mary Warnock was mistaken in describing the situation as "wholly unfamiliar matter" when, in fact, the argument dates right back to pre-Christian times (Connery 1977, pp. 1–46). This demonstrates that abortion is clearly connected with the central question in the bio-technological discussion.

Again, from another aspect, abortion is also closely associated with the new bio-medical technology because pre-natal diagnosis provides more precise and early information about possible anomalies and malfunctions. This new knowledge is often an additional impetus for abortion, so much so that it creates this *de facto* link between bio-medical technology and the abortion problem. But even here, the matter of abortion is clearly opposed by writers like Professor John Marshall, of the Institute of Neurology, London.

With this background, it is now appropriate to introduce the argument from potentiality. Exponents of this position, like Marshall (a member of the Warnock Inquiry, and a signatory of Expression of Dissent "B" on embryo experimentation), contend that the case does not rest on the view that the embryo is a person from the moment of fertilization. Such a view, they say, is difficult to sustain in the light of traditional Christian teaching and the current knowledge of embryo development. Even the official teaching of the Catholic Church, Marshall would claim, is at one with Warnock in deciding that the time a person comes into existence cannot be determined. The tradition that ensoulment might occur later in development of pregnancy "has a long and respectable history in the Church." (Marshall 1984, pp. 787ff.).

But Marshall states that there can be no doubt that the cluster of multiplying cells derived from the union of the sperm and ovum is from human species and alive. In that sense the life of the human embryo begins at fertilization, but this is not equivalent to saying a *person* begins at that time. Personhood is not an event that can be observed scientifically. It is a philosophical and theological concept. Marshall develops his argument carefully and logically. The case rests in the end on the embryo being alive and having the *potential* to become a human person. The potential is of such importance that it would be wrong to deliberately destroy it. To bring an embryo into existence, with a view to implantation, as a way to relieve the burden of a couples' infertility is one thing; to bring it into existence with a view to its destruction through experimentation, although albeit in the pursuit of useful knowledge, is something quite different. As to the consequences on research, he believes that we could still be where we are but with greater risk. He adds, there is no doubt that this stance would handicap the progress of scientific work but, nevertheless, experimentation on embryos leading to their destruction, cannot be justified (Marshall 1984, pp. 787ff).

Szawarski also supports this argument but draws different conclusions. Again, it was in the light of the abortion debate that this Polish philosopher wrote his analytical article on the status of the unborn (Szawarski 1978). I have been fortunate to exchange numerous letters with Dr Szawarski, not only on this question but on different aspects of Marxism in regard to life and the status of the unborn. Some of these factors will be considered later. In the meantime, it is of interest to note that Szawarski, like Marshall, favours the potentiality argument and yet forms different conclusions. He reasons that there is no significant moral difference between an adult and a child, and between a zygote and an eight month foetus. Put in another way, there is no moral difference between a zygote and a human adult. Therefore, he says, it is morally wrong to kill the potential of a human individual conceived by human parents. A human zygote, therefore, he says, even though opponents of potentialism claim there is a tremendous difference in quality and quantity, is not different from the adult and both can have the same moral rights. He refers to Tooley (1971) and Hare (1975) in presenting his argument.

Thomson (1971, pp. 47ff) indeed asserts, as we have already seen, that the zygote is no more a person than the acorn is an oak tree. Against this, Szawarski retorts than an acorn in the earth is, in fact, an oak tree in becoming, just as a zygote is an adult in the state of development. Therefore, says Szawarski, because of the potential embedded in the zygote "it is morally wrong to kill it." However, in his conclusion, he differs from Marshall in that he argues: "The only justification for killing a conceived human individual is the potential of another individual, which is either not conceived as yet or is in existence." (Szawarski 1986–88.)

Hence Szawarski would argue that abortion could be justified for medical reasons, such as German measles and in the case of using national population policies, and it is precisely here that the principle of choosing the lesser evil is relevant, namely that one chooses abortion rather than over population.

Professor Ian Kennedy, of Kings College School of Medical Law and Ethics, London, looks favourably on the potentiality argument and subjects it to a number of tests (Kennedy 1984, p. 6). He asserts that one form of the argument is difficult to sustain because embryonic development can fail to become human as scientists have pointed out. They indicate various occasional abnormal products such as the hydatidform mole. Therefore, he puts the alternative form of the argument – to assert that something has the potential to develop is not necessarily to assert that it has the necessary and sufficient conditions to do so. It may merely mean that it has a good chance of becoming that thing; that is given the opportunity to do so. In the case of the embryo, certain criteria are present. It has the genetic package "to enable it to participate in the lottery which nature contrives for the continuation of existence till birth." Embryonic development, therefore, without fertilization can, he claims, be discounted. Even if it is argued that the fertilized ovum does not always succeed in nature's lottery, this is no reason for man to imitate nature. Indeed, says Kennedy, it is the aim of medical science to come to terms with nature rather than be subject to its whims.

But Kennedy tests the potentiality argument still further. If the fertilized ovum is not potentially human, can one make the claim for protection for it against research? The fact that we are sufficiently concerned, he says, and exercised about the early embryo that we need to justify our behaviour towards it, self-demonstrates the plausibility of the potentiality argument. If it were the moral equivalent of a hamster our concern would be less or of a different order. And here Kennedy subjects the argument to further tests. Let us accept, he says, for the moment, the minimum criterion of humanness now commanding agreement, namely the capacity for sentients or the development of the central nervous system. Let us imagine that a technique was developed which would prevent the development of the brain or the nervous system, but otherwise allowed for the normal development of the embryo. Would it, he questions, be morally licit to experiment on such embryos intentionally crippled so that they can never meet the criterion of humanness? The response to this would be one of moral outrage and that outrage can be seen to rest "on the wrongness of interference with the potentiality of the embryo to develop further."

But the Templeton Prize Winner, Professor T. F. Torrance, believes that there is a serious ambiguity about the use of the world potential in relation to the embryo (Torrance 1984, p. 3). He would disagree with the above thinkers in that he claims that potentiality in this context is not that "of becoming something else but of becoming what it essentially is." In this way, Torrance sees the embryo, not as a potential human being but a human being with potential. Being a scientist as well as a theologian, he has no hesitation in stating that the embryo must be respected for what it is in itself and in its own right. There is no scientific doubt, he says, about the fact that from the moment of conception, the human embryo is genetically complete and unique and must be treated as such, as distinctively human and not just a mere biochemical episode:

> If the human embryo is genetically complete and distinctively human from the very beginning, then arguments allowing for scientific experiment or genetic manipulation after a certain period, 7, 14 days or whatever, are scientifically and morally specious. (Torrance 1984, p. 2.)

Later in his work, he urges that Parliament should be

influenced to accept this scientific fact without "any of the fudging that appears in the Warnock Report, in subordinating the rights and claims of the individual human embryo to other social or technological ends." (Torrance 1984, p. 6.)

EVALUATION

The "body soul" question which has dominated much of Christian thinking seems to assume a thoroughgoing dualism, seeing the human being as a union rather than a unity. Whether in the context of immediate or delayed ensoulment, it is difficult to conceive of the "infusion of souls" by the Creator in the light of modern science (Towers 1964, pp. 25ff; Hick 1976, pp. 35–54). It seems more realistic to envisage the developing embryo as the human individual becoming what it already is by self-propulsion. The development of this new human being has an inbuilt finality; it is a genetically unique organism with an independent life, as IVF demonstrates. Moreover, it appears to be a dynamically organized coherence of matter-spirit whereby it is genetically programmed to be not just a human individual, but this particular human being – Tom, Dick or Mary and in relation to God, and the parents.

Nor does it seem necessary to postulate a body-soul union or to claim that matter and spirit in the human being are disparate. Indeed it seems more in line with the new genetics to think of matter and spirit as two aspects of the one human unity. It would also seems reasonable to suggest that whenever this genetically unique organism is set in motion, whether by the union of gametes as in conception, or by some other form of fertilization as might be possible in nucleus substitution, there is present a human unity with its own ongoing principle which could be described as a person at least in capacity and becoming, if not already in actuality. Accordingly as this unity develops, the individual would become capable of transcending the limitations inherent in its physical composition. It will then surpass, because of its spiritual dimension, the merely biological, so that in the future it will not be the "soul" of that individual that actually thinks, chooses or prays, but the whole individual that is becoming what he already was essentially, namely a complete individual, matter and spirit, in development.

It seems inappropriate to try to visualize God as creating souls *ab extra* and also to speak of the infusing of souls in each conception somewhere between fertilization and birth, which was the traditional thinking (Aristotle; Aquinas; Hewson 1975, chapter 4). In this case, the soul is considered as an extra-terrestrial reality which God adds to each human conceptus. It would seem more fitting and adequate to claim that God acts through secondary causality and therefore through the parent or parents as agents. It is true that Tertullian, because of his theory of Traducianism, was unpopular in early Christianity. But there seems to be no intrinsic reason why the Creator, as in other processes, should not work through his creatures to create the whole individual, matter and spirit, and to empower his creatures to act, as it were, above and beyond their power as secondary causes (Rahner 1965, pp. 98–9; North 1967, p. 247; Lonergan 1975, p. 664). By sharing in God's concursus, they could be enabled to transcend themselves. The result would be that the Creator's eternal act would be effective in time due to his use of creative agents. I would suggest tentatively that the embryo, from the first moment of its existence, with its millions of molecular items of information dynamically organized to control itself till death, is in the act of becoming what it already is, a total human individual – a psycho-physical unity. This is a continuous process during which the embryo itself has the only active role, abstracting all that it needs from a tissue fluid environment. It is true that this development is incomplete; it is still incomplete at birth. But the embryo is a living human separate individual in a process of continuous development to adulthood with the power within itself to produce the enormous number and variety of cells and organs leading to the human adult. It is, as Torrance claims, "becoming what it essentially is."

CHAPTER II

The Reproduction Revolution

In this chapter, we will discuss the beginning and the transmission of human life as well as the procedures that replace partly or totally the natural process of conception and *in utero* gestation. The chapter will, therefore, include what is a reality at the present moment, that is to say, human artificial insemination, *in vitro* fertilization, surrogacy and embryo experimentation. The chapter will also look at future possibilities in genetic engineering such as cloning. It will be argued that, while there are some advantages in the new techniques, there is concomitantly a threat to human life at its weakest state and to the traditional concept of marriage as a stable, loving, exclusive relationship in which children are begotten and reared.

Background to Human Fertility Techniques

Success in implanting an ovum, fertilized *in vitro*, and in bringing it to term now makes technically possible a number of reproductive variants, opening up new social horizons. Human artificial insemination has, of course, made it possible for a wife to conceive by her husband (AIH) despite certain incapacities on his part or indeed in his absence (or even after his death, through freezing and banking of sperm). In the case of total infertility on the part of the husband, or where there is no husband, the practice of artificial insemination of a woman by a donor (AID) is also growing. In the past AID has been held to be morally unacceptable by some writers (Acta Apostolicae Sedis 41 1949, pp. 559–60; Mahoney 1984a, p. 285). The objection is largely based on the fact that the semen is obtained by masturbation. Additionally, it is contended that it is morally unacceptable to separate the intrinsic relationship between loving marital intercourse and the emergence of a new human being as the expression of such love. Put in another way, it is said that it is wrong to disrupt the procreative and unitive element – though not all would accept this point of view.

The first success in alleviating female infertility has been the by-passing of bilateral fallopian tube occlusion. However, other applications are possible. If, for some reason, a woman is incapable of producing her own ova, it will be possible to implant in her an embryo derived from another woman's ovum and fertilized *in vitro* by her husband's semen or by another donor's semen, and either singly or in batches for monitoring and possible selection, before insertion into the womb for pregnancy to result. If a woman is able to produce her own ova for fertilization, but is incapable of carrying an embryo or infant to term, then another woman can act as a host mother for her, at least until such time as the artificial womb can be successfully developed. In this case, the husband and wife are the genetic parents of the child, contributing the egg and the semen to be fertilized *in vitro*, but the gestating mother is simply acting in this case as the human incubator. This is called IVF surrogacy as distinct from AID surrogacy, where the child is the genetic offspring of the husband but the host mother is the genetic parent of the child. This distinction is made by Mary Warnock (1985a, pp. 2–4). However, it should be noted that normally AID refers to donor sperm and not, as in this case, the husband's. Various time factors arising from the female cycle, the availability of suitable sperm, eggs or embryos, or the wish to time pregnancy, can be met by developing "techniques of freezing and storing such material" (Mahoney 1984a, p. 285).

Further progress from *in vitro* fertilization, lies in the possibility it gives for research into the early development of the fertilized ovum and experimentation upon human embryos "whether spare embryos found defective or surplus to reimplantation requirements or embryos produced and grown specifically for such research and development." (Mahoney 1984a, p. 285.)

Behind some of this thinking, and indeed much of the discussion that surrounded the Warnock Report, is the belief that every woman has an absolute right to have a child but this, in fact, argues for a principle of self-fulfilment to the exclusion of other moral considerations. For example, and on the contrary, a woman may be morally obliged not to have a pregnancy if she can foresee that the result would be a severely abnormal child. To argue that every woman has an absolute right to a child could also incur the danger of seeing the child not as an end, but as a means to an end (Curran 1973a, p. 212; Mahoney 1984b, p. 10).

AIH

In the case of artificial insemination by the husband, the semen is inserted by means other than sexual intercourse. The semen is collected by masturbation and the technique is used by some couples who cannot conceive but where the man is not totally infertile. Where, in some cases of AIH, the semen is deposited as a result of sexual intercourse because the act of intercourse is assisted in some way, from that aspect there are no moral difficulties whatsoever. But where insemination has been used outside of the marital action then some find such a technique to be unacceptable (Healey 1956, pp. 154ff; Marshall 1960, p. 75). In objecting to artificial insemination, even by the husband, and where the gametes are obtained exclusively from husband and wife, the case is also put forward that masturbation is a frustrating action which essentially contradicts the purpose of human reproductive organs and, for those who believe in God, some will hold that it is, therefore, an attack on the divine built-in purpose of the procreative faculty. In this case AIH is not connected with the marital action; moreover it depersonalizes human sexuality because of the separation which is said to be involved between the procreative and the unitive aspects. Not all are convinced by the argument against masturbation because the production of the semen is directed precisely towards procreation. As regards the question of the disruption in the procreation action itself, it is one thing to state that the child must be the expression of marital loving actions

> but quite another to state that only through the marital act itself may loving union be expressed and made effective and if science can now bring to birth this living expression of the love between husband and wife, which would otherwise simply not exist, this too it would appear must be seen as part of the Creator's loving plan for all his children. (Mahoney 1984, p. 17.)

AID

Artificial insemination by a donor (a man other than the husband) is used when investigations have shown that the husband is sterile or has seriously reduced fertility. Despite the comparatively extensive use of human insemination through-out the world, judicial regulation and public control of this activity is entirely lacking in most countries including all Western Europe. In some states of the United States and in Canada there exists certain legislation governing AID. The purpose of these statutes is mainly to give an insemination child the same legal status as a child born in matrimony. Artificial insemination and its implications have been dis-cussed in the Council of Europe but nothing has resulted from these discussions nor is there any agreement in regard to future strategy. The practice of AID in animals was carried out in the USSR in the 1900s and reintroduced humanely in 1952. The most informed country, in my opinion, is Sweden. The Swedish government set up an enquiry on this question and introduced law which became effective in March 1985.

In Britain the first formal public comment on AID came in 1948 with publication of the Archbishop of Canterbury's report on the subject (Archbishop of Canterbury 1948). The archbishop, himself, was critical of AID but not of AIH. The report failed to refer to an excellent article by a former Minister of Health on the legal aspect of AID (*The Practitioner* 1947, pp. 349ff).

In 1960 the Faversham Committee reported its findings. It accepted AID but believed that the majority of society and indeed the medical profession were opposed to its practice (Faversham Committee 1960). Evidence from various bodies had been submitted to this Government-appointed committee; for example, the Catholic Union of Great Britain (1960) published a statement under the title *Artificial Insemination*. They too found AID morally unacceptable. Prior to this, continuous discussion had taken place in the *British Medical Journal* in 1944 ranging over a period of six months. However, in 1969, the Minister of Health decided that AIH and AID should be available within the National Health Service (NHS), provided that techniques were recommended on medical grounds. In 1971, under the chairmanship of Sir John Peel (formerly President of the Royal College and the Queen's gynaecologist), a panel was set up to examine the medical aspects of AID. It reported in 1973 and it recommended that the practice should be available where appropriate within the NHS at accredited centres (Peel 1973, pp. 3–5). In the years since Peel, demand for AID has increased.

A child born of AID, under the existing law, is illegitimate and the husband has no rights or duties where the child is concerned. Nevertheless, in law, AID does not constitute adultery. In 1982, the Royal College of Obstetricians and Gynaecologists knew of 1,000 pregnancies conceived and 780 live births as a result of AID in Britain (Warnock Report 1984, p. 19). This would be considered an understatement as NHS centres are not required to identify themselves in any of the returns that health authorities make to the Government health department, though there are several centres where AID is provided under NHS auspices. In the United States it was estimated that 100,000 AID children had been born by 1957 and the total must now be several times that figure (Singer and Wells 1984, p. 72).

It is of interest to note here that much of the AID practised in France is controlled by an organisation known as Centre d'Etude et de Conservation du Sperme Humaine (CECOS). It is managed by a Board of Administration with representatives from the Ministry of Health, as well as the medical disciplines, and has been formed to control the majority of AID clinics in France. Some distinctive features are (Council for Science and Society 1984, p. 82):

(a) Only married men, having at least one healthy child, are used as donors. The consent of the wife must be obtained and there is no payment.
(b) Only five or six semen samples are given by each donor and all within one month.
(c) A high degree of centralization and government involvement allows AID to be closely regulated.
(d) The donation of sperm is to a childless couple and there is always extensive counselling of the donors and the recipients.

In the United States, Joseph Fletcher, the Utilitarian and moral philosopher, Ethics Department of the University of Virginia, believes that sperm and ova should be made available for others; sperm banking, he contends, gives many wonderful opportunities. He considers the exclusive relationship of marriage to be based on selfishness (Fletcher 1974, p. 69). Hermann Muller (1967, p. 532) recommends sperm and ovum banks which contain the material of outstanding people to improve the genetic pool.

SWEDEN

By a decision of 3 December 1981, the government of Sweden set up the Statens Offentliga Utredningar (SOU), a national public enquiry, to investigate the question of AID. A special examiner was appointed, Mr Tor Sverne, the Parliamentary Commissioner for the Judiciary and the Civil Administration. To assist him in an advisory capacity, twelve other experts were appointed and a committee formed.

The enquiry noted that AID has been undertaken in Sweden since 1920. As already mentioned, in the 1900s it had been practised on animals in Moscow and spread rapidly to many countries including Sweden. During the period 1945 to 1948 there were 95 inseminations resulting in seven pregnancies in Sweden (SOU 1983: 2).

In 1953 a Swedish government committee had submitted recommendations on AID. This did not result in legislation but since then the interest in AID has increased. (About 250 children are born annually in Sweden of AID conception. In all Europe about 2,000 are now born as a result of AID annually and in the United States 10,000 are born each year.)

Draft proposals for new and amended statutory provisions were submitted by SOU. The basic consideration underlying their recommendations was the best interest of the child. They stated:

> If AID is considered from the viewpoint of the prospective child, there are weighty reasons in favour of a decision – despite the risk that in an initial stage the activity would decrease in hospitals – to demand that only such sperm donors are used who do not oppose that their identity may subsequently be disclosed to the child. Such a decision would hopefully lead to that it would be possible in the long term to obtain only donors with a responsible and mature attitude to their co-operation. When evaluating the reasons for and against, the Committee has arrived at the opinion that the consideration to the best interests of AID children must – also in the matter of their origin – be given preference over considerations to other parties involved. Due regard to the AID children requires that these children – like all other children – have in principle the right to be informed at adult age of the identity of the natural father. We are aware of the possibility that an openness like this will – at least during a transitory phase – entail problems for the AID activity. It is our hope, however, that this openness will entail that the activity will in the long term be to the benefit of all parties involved. (SOU 1983: 15.)

As a result the Swedish Law on Insemination came into effect in March 1985. The law does say that when a child has reached adult age, it has the right to receive: "Information about the donor from the hospital journal." Although the law is weighted in favour of the child, it does seem to be somewhat qualified (in comparison with SOU 1983: 42). It does not say, explicitly, like the draft proposals, that the child has the right to be informed at adult age "of the identity of the natural father." This point was raised with the Swedish Embassy and clarification was sought. The embassy consulted the Ministry of Justice of Sweden and (in a letter to me, dated 6 June 1985) confirmed that, in fact, there was no difference between the law and SOU 1983: 42. It was "just a question of wording."

EVALUATION

On the whole, the Catholic response to AID is hostile, mainly because it is seen as violating the marriage covenant wherein exclusive, non-transferable rights to each others bodies and generative acts are exchanged by the spouses. There are, as we have seen, other reasons given by some, such as severing of procreation from sexual intercourse and also the means of obtaining semen by masturbation. There is, it is contended, an inseparable link between the unitive significance and the procreative aspect which are inherent to the marriage act. Professor Paul Ramsey is the noted Methodist defender of this attitude (Ramsey 1977, p. 128). (Further comment on this argument will be made when IVF is being discussed later in this chapter.) Protestant appraisals of AID reveal diverging viewpoints from Ramsey, on one extreme, to Joseph Fletcher, on the other. The latter would support most of the new techniques. It is also of interest that the Board for Social Responsibility of the Church of England (1984, pp. 10–11) having conceded the force of the opposing arguments, see AID as an acceptable practice. Much of the Catholic thinking is connected with the argument against disruption of the marriage act, as instanced in the teaching of Pius XII (Acta Apostolicae Sedis 41 1949, pp. 559–60) and Paul VI (1970).

However, others with a different set of presuppositions argue differently. They believe that the demand of love in regard to parenthood is fulfilled by ensuring that all children born of whatever means be reared in a family (Hamilton 1969, p. 743). Others would argue that sexual love and procreation are, and should be, distinct human acts (Francover 1970, p. 109). The point is also made (McCormick 1981, p. 318) that parenthood, in its deepest sense, is not merely a matter of biological begetting but "a more broadly human function – a man and a wife accepting responsibility for caring and rearing a child." McCormick contends, however, that the sexual love which generates ought to become, in *principle*, the parental love that nurtures. Parents don't love children just because children need love. They ought to love the children because they have parentally loved each other. The children are expressions of this love. Therefore, to separate the act of nurturing and generating and then to associate parental love only with the former is to "undermine the very foundation of the love that nurtures and is an attack on several values, such as the meaning of human sexuality, marriage and indeed parenthood." The argument, therefore, is that, in principle, the acts that generate ought not to be separated from the acts that nurture. To do otherwise, it is claimed, is to introduce a destructive dualism according to McCormick's thesis.

This line of reasoning is not accepted as convincing by Mahoney who candidly asks: "Why is it that only loving marital intercourse may be the context and the cause of human procreation." (Mahoney 1984, p. 16.)

It will be necessary, of course, to return to this discussion about sexual love and generation in Part II. Meanwhile, Karl Rahner adds another dimension when he fears that the sperm donor in AID rejects his responsibility and his name as a father. He hides from the prospective mother and child in his anonymity. If this kind of genetic manipulation (Häring 1975, p. 197) should become ingrained in the public conscience, according to Rahner (1972, pp. 246–8) then we should have two quite different human races "the one a technically manipulated 'chosen race' and the other a non-selected 'lower race' reproduced in the old fashioned way."

Many arguments against AID are based on its possible consequences. It is suggested that the wife would see the child as hers but not that of her husband and that the husband may experience a sense of inadequacy and exclusion because he had not participated in the creation of the child. Again, if the child is desired to preserve the marriage, the outlook for the child may be very poor. It is also suggested that AID is shrouded in secrecy and the falsification of public records, and would undermine the whole network of family relationship. Secrecy may be difficult to maintain and the impact of disclosure could be devastating for the child. Nor can it be predicted in every case that the psychological effects on the partners will be beneficial when they have mutually sought aid. One cannot be sure that this deception does not cause grave harm and it is argued that it places strain on family relationships because of the endeavour to keep the truth from the child. Nevertheless, against this it can be argued that some of these difficulties could be overcome by telling the facts to the child but this, in turn, raises another problem as frequently children will wish to know about their genetic fathers and, if left unfulfilled, this could be a major source of unhappiness.

Other problems connected with AID are the possibility of incestuous relationships or marriage within the forbidden degrees. This argument, however, is not as forceful as it appears, though it does exist.

Recently another problem has arisen that is connected with AID and also IVF when a third party is involved. In 1985, the *Observer* (3 October) reported that four Australian women had been infected with the killer virus AIDS through artificial insemination with donated semen. Earlier, the *Irish Times* (22 August) had carried a report in which specialists had alleged that there is no method at present which can establish the absence of AIDS virus from semen.

Finally, there is the argument that the biological and relational imbalance between the genetic parent and the social parent is the major objection to AID. This is not necessarily true. There are parallel cases in a second marriage where one parent may bring children of a previous marriage and in the case of these step-parents, there are instances of success. However, the argument against AID can still be based on the harmful consequences. Again, it is a grave consideration to introduce a third party into an exclusive marriage relationship or covenant which God has established between man and woman, which reflects the union between God and his people and for Christians is a sign of the union between Christ and his

Church. Ideally, it is only in this context and, as an expression of such unions, that children should be brought into existence in the Image of God as the effects of his creative love and of the co-creative mutual love of husband and wife. This, of course, is not to say that every marriage meets the requirements that are necessary for love and life. On the contrary, and in practice, the ideal has not been fulfilled. Although the exclusive relationship of one man and one woman is the ideal which Jesus, the early Church and official Christianity have always upheld, the opposite has frequently been the case. Nor should this ideal be imposed on others with opposite and sincerely held beliefs. But what can be said is that, in spite of its weaknesses, the institution of marriage and the family continues to provide the most favourable circumstances for the loving, begetting, transmitting and nurturing of human love and, therefore, should be supported and strengthened rather than weakened.

In Vitro *Fertilization*

Unlike AID, IVF is very much a new development in the West. The concept is straightforward. A ripe human egg is extracted from the ovary just before it would have been naturally released. It is mixed with semen of the husband or partner so that fertilization can occur. The embryo, once it has started to divide, is then transferred back to the mother's uterus under carefully controlled conditions. The technique for extracting eggs is through laparoscopy. It is called *in vitro* as distinct from *in vivo* (normal conception) because it is accomplished in a glass tube. Because of the difficulties, it is common to transfer more than one embryo to the potential mother whenever possible. The eggs are achieved by super-ovulation of the ovaries and this ensures the production of more than one egg. There is an argument that two or more embryos are transferred to help each other towards implantation. If too many eggs are transferred, there is a risk of multiple pregnancy with all the risks of miscarriage, premature delivery and resulting immaturity.

In the West, IVF was first reported by J. Rock and M. F.

Menkin in the 1940s (Rock and Menkin 1944, pp. 105–7). Iglesias divides the history of IVF in the West into three periods (Iglesias undated):

(a) 1950–1968. A period of intense research and study on the process of mammalian-egg maturation, which was achieved by the method of *in vitro* maturation of the eggs of various animals as well as the human egg. Significant discoveries were achieved in that field by Dr R. Edwards who, in 1965, reported the identification of the first meiotic division of the human egg. So the process of egg maturation had been observed in England.

(b) 1968–1978. This decade saw IVF begin a collaborative endeavour between scientists and clinicians. They were now attempting to effect human IVF to alleviate some forms of infertility and to study the origin of inherited defects. The result was the birth of the baby, Louise Brown, conceived *in vitro* and born July 1978. Soon after Louise's birth more fertilizations were achieved quite quickly in Britain, Australia, France and the United States.

(c) 1978–1983. Two fundamental developments took place, namely the opening of Bourn Hall Clinic by Dr Edwards and Mr Patrick Steptoe in 1980 and the emergence of countless centres all over the West where IVF is practised.

There is little doubt that the technique is necessarily implemented at the expense of thousands of embryos that are directly used and destroyed, either in or because of the process. It has been claimed, however, that IVF compares in efficiency with the natural method of conception and continuation of pregnancy in which nature economically provides just one egg for fertilization. But, on the basis of some findings, the wastage of human embryos by nature is very high. Some evidence indicates that it can be as high as 30 to 60 per cent. James (1970, p. 241) for example, analysing studies by Hertig and Rock (1949) concluded that one embryo in three perishes before pregnancy is realised and one in every four or five is lost after the diagnosis of pregnancy is established. In total, he estimated, that one fertilized ovum in two is aborted spontaneously.

However, Whittaker *et al* (1983, pp. 1126–7) have demonstrated an unsuspected pregnancy loss incidence of 8 per cent showing that nature is far more efficient than had previously been asserted. Their paper points to methodologic shortcomings in earlier work. Whittaker *et al* used normal healthy women in their research project.

Additionally, some experts (Fleming and Iglesias 1985, p. 168; Yavich 1985, pp. 283–4) estimate that in the IVF process only 40 per cent of embryos have the capacity to implant which means an inviability of 60 per cent and, according to the Medical Research Council (1985, p. 270) only one in ten embryos transferred to the womb survives, leaving a total loss rate of 96 per cent. Consequently, it would seem from modern research, as reported in 1985 in *The Times* (13 February), that IVF is very wasteful of human life and does not favourably compare, contrary to previous claims, with nature, especially when one takes into account that the number of embryos born by the end of 1985 was about 1,000.

In view of this, the question of the status of the embryo returns. If one believes that human life begins at fertilization and that the embryo has the status of an individual human being, then the case of embryo wastage is a very serious moral problem with the gravest implications. Regardless of doubts about the personhood of the embryo and ensoulment, there is little doubt, as I have shown, that human life begins *in vitro* (by fusion of sperm and ovum) in the same way as it is conceived *in vivo*. The very probability, and certainty for some, that a human being exists constitutes an absolute veto against this kind of experimentation or wastage (Häring 1975, p. 198). It is freely admitted that in the IVF process, more than one ovum is fertilized. Whether this is based on economic or scientific reasons is not very clear, not does it seem to be absolutely essential to the process as such. In 1984, an interesting letter, signed by Dr Edwards and Mr Steptoe, appeared to this effect in *The Times* (11 February) where doubt was expressed as to the number that should be implanted:

> We believe that replacing three embryos is sufficient to avoid most of the pitfalls of multi-pregnancies while at the same time increasing the chance of pregnancy adequately.... Surely the number of embryos replaced in a mother should be restricted until the consequences of replacing two or three are known. Some guidelines are clearly necessary. This could be another topic for reference to the Warnock Committee.

Consequently, embryos not used will perish which is not a problem for those who claim that the embryo is mere biological material, nor does it constitute a very serious problem for some who claim that the embryo is something other than a human individual because of its lack of stability to possess the human soul and be identified as a person, even though it has an intrinsic promise for personal development. In any case, some would say that despite the great loss of embryos, the technique is doing no more than imitating nature. But this type of argument does not take seriously the fact that there are many things that happen naturally, that ought not to be effected deliberately. As McCormick (1981, p. 330) says: "We may not produce by artifice everything that happens in nature."

Perhaps a more solid argument could be based on replicating nature's achievements and not its disorders; that is to say achieving artificially what nature achieves naturally. Therefore, it might be argued that if normal sexual relations inevitably mean a certain loss of fertilized ova, this is also permissible when achieving pregnancy artificially. One, of course, understands the argument that the value and interest of science and society are of the greatest importance but the point at issue is whether they override the interest and value of the new human being, if that is what is present.

The Marxist-Leninist philosophy, as we will see later (Part II) gives preferential treatment to society and this follows from a materialistic philosophy. Secularist, and indeed some theological, approaches, however, differ in that the definition of the human being varies from fertilization up to birth. Some arguments that are put forward could equally justify infanticide, and the reasoning of the secularists at times is not very different from Marxist thinking (a point that I put to Lady Mary Warnock, and which will be considered later). This is not surprising since both philosophies are committed to a materialistic concept of man.

One of the main arguments against IVF is the divorce of the generating of human life from human sexuality, as I have already mentioned, and ultimately from the confines of the body itself. Writers like Ramsey (1977, p. 87) and Kass (1972, pp. 18–56) believe that IVF is unacceptable because of this disruptive factor and in consequence causes a laboratory production of human beings which is not human procreation. It is a "making" not a "begetting". Procreation is, itself, a human activity: an activity of an embodied man and woman. They, therefore, would claim that IVF depersonalizes and dehumanizes the process of human procreation and, thereby, is another assault on marriage (Rahner 1972, pp. 225–52; McCormick 1981, p. 295. f.3). Some have difficulty in accepting this argument without qualification because it excludes a procedure that can extend the marriage covenant and achieve an essential end of marriage, which is the *bonum prolis*. (*Bonum prolis* has always been seen as one of the primary ends of marriage and has been listed under the New Code of Canon Law.) For example, it would be acceptable to transfer the fertilized ovum from the womb to an incubator before gestation is completed if this were for the good of the mother and the child. The use of such a resource in circumstances where, for whatever reason, a woman's womb was unable to function properly and safely, would be similar to the generally accepted and morally routine recourse to kidney or heart/lung machines to supply for a failure of other bodily functions. The whole process, it is argued, is no more than an extension of the marriage covenant where husband, wife and child are included. There is also, a significant distinction between this and the use of a host mother for the latter is once again the introduction of a third party, which would infringe the exclusive covenant of marriage.

The disruptive argument was also made by the Catholic Bishops' Conference of England and Wales when its Joint Committee on Bioethical Issues (1983, p. 19) submitted evidence to Warnock that IVF was a technique that is morally flawed for this purpose whereas its Social Welfare Commission (1983a, pp. 17ff) saw the IVF technique as morally acceptable. The latter opinion was also that of the Catholic doctors who submitted evidence to Warnock (Guild of Catholic Doctors 1984). The Board for Social Responsibility of the Church of England (1984) had also recommended IVF though it referred in passing to the separation of the unitive and procreative functions of marriage. It is interesting to note that later the Joint Committee on Bioethical Issues, in their *Comment on the Warnock Report* (1984), found the simple case of IVF was morally unacceptable.

SWEDEN – SURROGACY AND IVF

The committee of SOU, consisting of the same membership as that which had reported on AID in 1983, presented firm recommendations on IVF and surrogacy in 1985. The committee regarded surrogate motherhood as "an undesirable phenomenon" and, therefore, would not recommend it. (SOU 1985: 5.)

As to IVF when the couple concerned are the biological parents, and there are medical obstacles against fertilization *in vivo*, this method is acceptable for "remedying involuntary childlessness." Moreover, there was nothing against the well-being of the child in this method.

SWEDEN – IVF WITH AN UNRELATED SPERM DONOR

The committee did not recommend this procedure and "thinks a limit should be set to how far to go regarding manipulations to limit childlessness." Indeed it makes the interesting remark "that nature's insufficiencies must be accepted sometimes." In the committee's view, the combination of sperm donation and IVF goes beyond this limit and should not be allowed in Sweden and, therefore, children can never be an unconditional human right.

Consequently, it was not surprising to find that egg dona-tion was not recommendable as it goes, according to the committee, "against the natural process of life." In fact, they consider it "ethically indefensible" and should not be allowed in the country.

EVALUATION

Because of the reasons stated above, some thinkers find IVF morally unacceptable. Even as a technique they would claim it is morally flawed; others, because of the problems connected with it, such as the wastage of human life, spare embryos, masturbation and severing of the unitive and procreative aspects, find it reprehensible and a very radical solution to a problem that pertains to the few here in the rich industrialized countries. It may be useful to conclude this evaluation with a quotation from the famous French geneticist who in 1959 discovered the cause of Down's Syndrome, Professor Lejeune (1984, p. 32):

> If our only goal is to help women who cannot procreate because of tubal difficulties, have we chosen the right track? Let us return to technicalities. If, in reality, the early embryo is not an experimental material to be split, mixed and manipulated, what is the interest of this trip of a few days in the outside world?
>
> Doctor Craft and his colleagues [1982] have already shown that the fertilized ovum can be implanted in the womb right away. Could we not get even closer to physiological process? Possibly the egg could be placed in the uterus during laparoscopy with the sperm already being supplied by normal intercourse. Why not study more closely the fluids of the fallopian tube? Would it not be the best medium for early development? Research workers would be very wise to explore new avenues rather than automatically following the wrong detour of *in vitro* fertilization.

Developments in Human Fertility Techniques

The point made here by Lejeune seems to be a very valid one as a new method of aided conception is at the moment being developed. Babies were conceived recently in San Antonio, Texas using a method developed by Dr Richard Asch of the

University of Texas. The method is called Gift (gamete intra-fallopian transfer) and is potentially less expensive than the classic IVF technique. It is true that both techniques start with the surgical removal of a ripe ovum from the mother-to-be. In normal IVF, as we have seen, the ovum is fertilized in a tube before implanting it into the womb and allowing nature to take over. Gift is much simpler. The selected ovum is taken from the ovary and put together with semen outside the body; this is then injected into the fallopian tube – fertilization occurring inside the body. The baby then develops in the normal way and begins the journey to the womb and eventual birth. In 1985, *The Times* (31 March) reported that, according to experts, this is a less dramatic intervention in the natural process than IVF but it can't be done with bilateral tubal occlusion, which suggests its limited application.

There is no doubt that there has been a variety of theological opinions on the morality of IVF. Thomas Shannon (1978, p. 20) faults it on several accounts. A great deal of money is spent, he says, for the benefit of the few. The procedure involves risks of harm to an unconsenting third party. And he asks, what is to be done about mistakes? Others, like the Bishop of Cork, Cornelius Lucey, cannot see anything wrong when used by childless couples (Lucey 1978 *passim*). The argument, based on introducing too much technology into a highly personal context (parenting, family) and thereby mechanizing and depersonalizing the context, could be classed as a prudential caution rather than a moral judgement. However, there are thinkers, like the Bishop of Augsburg (1979, p. 100) who compare what they term as "technical manipulation" of human eggs and sperm with the atom bomb. The Sacred Congregation for the Doctrine of the Faith (1987, p. 30) have listed all forms of IVF, even "the simple case", as morally unacceptable because they deprive human procreation of the dignity that is proper and connatural to it.

EMBRYO EXPERIMENTATION

It was the development of IVF that, for the first time, gave rise to the possibility that human embryos might be brought into existence which would have no chance to implant because they were not transferred to the uterus and hence had no chance to be born. Embryo transfer (ET) inevitably leads to an examination of the moral rights of the embryo (a question that has been discussed already in Chapter I).

It is the normal practice, when treating infertility by this method, to extract a number of ova from the would-be mother's ovaries and mix all of them with sperm. This increases the chance of obtaining at least one promising embryo for transfer to the womb. It is also common procedure, as I have noted, to replace in the womb more than one embryo – from two to five or even more. It is said, though no clear reason is given, that this procedure increases the chance of implantation of at least one embryo (Edwards 1983, p. 78).

Up to now there has been much discussion about experimentation on spare embryos, that is to say those surplus to therapy. But, more recently, most spare embryos are frozen for future use and will not be available for research as *The Lancet* reported (2 February 1985). No doubt volunteers will be sought to supply ova donated for this purpose, which will be fertilized to provide embryos simply for experimentation. Indeed, *The Lancet's* report noted that the Medical Research Council recommended such a procedure that same year (1985). In the past, spare embryos were either discarded or used for research, for freezing, thawing and implanting. IVF as a treatment for infertility has a background of years of experimentation with animals and human embryos (Edwards 1983, p. 12). It is claimed that while some knowledge is gained from animal experimentation, the species differences are such as to require the testing of any technique with human ova before it is applied clinically.

Understandably there is much controversy over embryonic research as understood in the non-therapeutic sense, that is research which is not intended to benefit the embryo as such and is, therefore, carried out with the ultimate intention of discarding the embryo. The Warnock Report (as we shall see later) recommends research up to the fourteenth day. It also recommends that it would be a criminal offence to transfer to the womb an embryo which had been the subject of experimentation.

THE BENEFITS OF RESEARCH

The possible benefits of research are broadly of two sorts. First there is the increase of scientific knowledge for its own sake. If such research adds to our understanding of embryonic development, that is classed as a good thing even if it confers no practical benefits. But there is also, it is claimed, a number of practical benefits that might be expected such as detecting of new contraceptive techniques, the treatment of infertility, prevention of congenital disorders and creation of cell lines for therapeutic use.

IMPROVEMENTS IN THE TREATMENT OF INFERTILITY

Most obviously this could come from improvements in the IVF technique itself. Overall, it is said, as we have seen, there is a wastage of 96 per cent. With further research the reasons for this may become better understood and the success rate improved. Studying contraception in the laboratory is likely to improve the understanding of infertility generally, including male infertility. Enhanced understanding is likely to mean more effective treatment. It is also claimed by some that research on human embryos may make it possible to prevent miscarriages.

PREVENTION OF CONGENITAL DISORDERS

Studying human embryos in the laboratory may lead, it is said, to the prevention of chromosomal abnormalities such as Down's Syndrome and perhaps eventually congenital abnormalities such as spina bifida. Also experiments on embryos may make it possible to detect an ever-growing number of genetic defects such as give rise to thalassaemia, cystic fibrosis and the like. Parents at risk of giving birth to babies with these defects could then be asked to conceive by IVF. The embryos could be screened for such defects before being transferred to the womb. At the moment, such parents might rely on anti-natal diagnosis which, it is pointed out, could result in a late abortion of a foetus believed to be suffering from a congenital disorder.

CREATION OF CELL LINES FOR THERAPEUTIC USE

If it becomes possible to keep human embryos alive in the laboratory to the point at which cells begin to differentiate, one might for example, be able to create cultures of insulin-producing cells to insert in the pancreas of diabetics or dopamine-producing cells to insert in the brains of those suffering from Parkinson's Disease. There are indications from animal studies that embryonic cells tend not to be rejected by the recipient's immune system and continue to function in their new environment. It is claimed that would-be foetal cells can be cultured in the laboratory and these can be obtained from the embryo or foetus without damage to it. On the other hand, the notion that whole embryos might be grown for use as replacement tissues in adults is much more unacceptable from a moral point of view.

In fact, the critical question is, just how beneficial these experiments are likely to be and the medical experts are very divided in their replies. In 1985, in a letter to *The Times* (13 February), twenty-one Fellows of the Royal College of Obstetricians and Gynaecologists rejected any experimentation on human embryos because "it reduces the embryo to an experimental animal" and "contravenes the code of medical ethics and must be rejected." This rejection is implicit, the Fellows claimed, in the code of professional ethics pertaining to all human experimentation

> which from time immemorial has been endorsed by the medical profession and repeatedly confirmed by the World Medical Association and other professional bodies. The central principle of this code is that concern for the interest of the subject, namely the patient, must always prevail over the interests of science and society.

This point, of course, is also outlined by the Helsinki Declaration. The Fellows went on to state that the human embryo, conceived by IVF, is the doctors' concern, just as an adult patient and should not be put at risk for any reason other than to enhance his or her wellbeing, i.e. therapeutic treatment. The effective investigation, they claim, of pathological conditions developing during pre-natal life should not require the killing of the embryos:

> Indeed primary prevention of many such conditions, as opposed to their secondary prevention, by killing those who suffer from them, is more likely to be achieved by applying new techniques of research to human gametes and not human embryos.

This statement was also signed by Sir John Peel. Prior to this letter, Dr Stephen Hillier, Senior Lecturer at Hammersmith Hospital, London, had stated "the embryology side of IVF is totally overrated.... Everyone seems to have missed the point; it's the egg that's important." (Hillier 1984.)

Addressing that very point in a BBC interview, Professor Lejeune, one of the world's greatest experts on chromosomes, strongly rejected the usefulness of embryo experimentation: "Experimentation on an embryo would tell us nothing." Having been asked why "so many of your professional colleagues in research science want to be able to experiment on embryos?" he replied that he honestly could not understand this attitude but disagreed that there was a large number of scientists performing experimentation. Indeed the

> majority of research work around the world, dealing with genetic diseases and with chromosomal abnormalities, are not all thinking about manipulating, about tampering with human embryos.

Lejeune went on to claim that any experimentation could be done equally effectively on the monkey embryo (Lejeune 1985). The same attitude was supported in 1985 by Dr James Le Fanu, whose letter to *The Lancet* (23 February) concluded:

> The main purpose of defending the right to experiment on human embryos seems to have less to do with a realistic belief in the

benefit that would result than with the concern of the scientific community to preserve its freedom to pursue its own narrow interests unfettered by moral or legal constraints.

All the same there are equally eminent scientists who would claim that experiments are necessary. The well-known scientists Edwards and Steptoe are among them as we have seen. The claim that embryo research would be of medical value was further advanced in 1985 by eight geneticists in their letter to *The Times* (19 March). The geneticists – Martin Bobrow (Guy's Hospital Medical School), Malcolm Ferguson-Smith (University of Glasgow), Peter Harper (Welsh National School of Medicine), Rodney Harris (University of Manchester), Michael Lawrence (Welsh National School of Medicine), Marcus Pembrey (Institute of Child Health), Paul Polani (Guy's Hospital Medical School), David Weatherall (University of Oxford) – were quite explicit in their claims:

> Mr Enoch Powell, in introducing his bill to prohibit medical and scientific research on post-fertilization stages of human development obtained by *in vitro* fertilization, concedes that this may retard potentially valuable medical advances. Whether or not this price is worth paying is for Parliament and the nation to decide.
>
> In contrast, many of Mr Powell's supporters have obscured this issue by suggesting that no important lines of research are at stake.
>
> In an attempt to portray major disagreement among experts on this issue, no fewer than six speakers in the parliamentary debate quoted the negative views of Professor Jerome Lejeune, who had been invited by the anti-research lobby to come from Paris to speak to parliamentarians.
>
> As practising medical geneticists in this country, concerned for the impact that this issue and its wider implications may have on the wellbeing of our current and future patients, we wish to draw to public attention the virtually complete isolation of Professor Lejeune's views on this point.
>
> Despite his illustrious early discoveries, Professor Lejeune's later hypotheses on the treatment of Down's Syndrome and other forms of mental retardation have failed to convince the vast majority of his colleagues.
>
> There are few, if any, serious practising medical geneticists in this country, or abroad, who would have been willing to express

the views which have been given so much weight by so many parliamentarians.

In the early detection of genetic defects and in understanding the origin of some forms of childhood disability, as well as in the area of fertility, and its disorders, it seems more probable that research on very early post-fertilization stages will be of medical value. This is one factor which should be given due weight in the public debate on this issue.

Or, as Dr Edwards had written the year before, 1984, in his letter to *The Times* (26 June): "The need for knowledge is greater than the respect to be accorded the early embryo."

Professor Lejeune was quick to reply to the geneticists. He wrote to *The Times* (26 March):

It is a great honour and great surprise for a research worker to learn in *The Times* (letter, March 19) that his name has been quoted by "no fewer than six speakers in the parliamentary debate". It is no surprise and no dishonour to learn at the same time that his work has "failed to convince that vast majority of his colleagues", as undersigned by eight of them.

But such a personalization of a scientific debate is a surprise and hardly an honourable one. Fame, names and authority should not interfere with matter-of-fact discussions.

Having had the privilege of investigating the grave issue of experimentation upon human embryos, at the request of some members of Parliament, I addressed two questions:

First, is it demonstrated that no equivalent research could be performed in laboratory animals instead of experimenting upon early human embryos? The answer is no, because already very refined protocols have been used in mice experiments, leading to great achievements.

Second, is this type of experiment on early embryos the most appropriate way of learning about the causes, the mechanisms and possibly, the prevention and/or cure of genetic disabilities like haemophilia, muscular dystrophies or Down's Syndrome (to take examples quoted in the Warnock Report)?

The answer is again no. Maturation of the blood, of the muscles or of the brain cannot be achieved in human embryos less than 14 days old. Hence troubles affecting these tissues must be studied in subjects having already developed the relevant organs.

Apparently I failed entirely to convince the vast majority of my eight distinguished colleagues and I apologize for that. I am so much the more thankful to the six speakers in the parliamentary debate.

Moral Objections

OBJECTION I: THE WRONGNESS OF EXPERIMENTING ON HUMAN SUBJECTS WITHOUT THEIR CONSENT

The ordinary man or woman may think that the question hinges on when human life begins. If it begins at conception then experimenting on a human embryo is to be condemned on essentially the same grounds as the Nazi doctors at Auschwitz were condemned who performed experiments on concentration camp victims without their consent. Some may retort that it is irrational to feel outrage at experimentation on embryos of two weeks or less while our abortion law allows the destruction of foetuses up to 28 weeks. Whatever the force of this retort, it does not meet the thrust of the argument. In any case, it could easily be claimed that two wrongs do not make a right.

Rejoinder

This, as we have seen, rejects experimentation on the grounds that life begins at conception. I reflected on the complications that arise under this heading in Chapter I, but possibly the most frequent rejoinder is that human embryos, unlike Nazi experimentations, will feel no suffering. Moreover, the Nazi experiments were done not merely without the subject's consent but against their will. But, we would still have condemned the Nazi doctors had they confined their experiments to infants too young to have a view on the matter who were kept anaesthetized or later painlessly killed.

OBJECTION II: DEPRIVATION OF LIFE

What upsets some people about research on human embryos is that the embryos are being denied any chance of normal development and are doomed to be destroyed. This concerns many who would not accept that the human individual or person begins at conception. It is enough, they argue, that the potential for human life is there and is denied any possibility of being realised. Indeed this, as we have indicated, was the claim of a minority report to Warnock where special status is claimed for the embryo because of its potential to become a human person: "It is, in our view, wrong to create something with a potential for becoming a human person and then deliberately to destroy it." (Warnock Report 1984, p. 90.)

No doubt, as has been shown, it can be retorted that 30 to 60 per cent of all naturally produced embryos fail to achieve their potential for human life, although this is now challenged. However, there is a significant moral distinction between deliberately creating embryos that are given no chance of life because they are destined for experimentation, and creating embryos that have some chance of life, albeit a low one. Indeed this would seem to be the rationale behind Enoch Powell's Unborn Children (Protection) Bill, which would make it a crime to create a human embryo for any other purpose than insertion in the womb of a named woman.

Rejoinder

It is sometimes argued that even sperm and ova have the *potential* for human life. What is so special about the embryo? In the case of sperm and ova, such potential will not be realized unless and until fertilization occurs. The rejoinder, therefore, is that the potential in the human embryo likewise will not be realized unless and until it implants in the womb and so where is the difference? But this argument fails because it can be argued that, in the case of the human embryo, an ongoing independent human life has already begun, unlike the sperm or ovum taken separately. It will, unless anything untoward happens, develop into childhood and, therefore, should not be cut short or frustrated. Some argue that the potential for human life does not apply to spare embryos that are a by-product of IVF treatment for infertility and if they are destined to be discarded in any case, there can be, in this view, no objection to experimenting on them first. This was the view taken by another minority view of the Warnock Committee who did not want embryos created *specifically* for the purpose of research (Warnock Report 1984, p. 94.)

Finally, it is asserted that, any one for whom the deprivation of life is the central objection to embryo research, in consistency, ought to object to abortion and other devices which work by preventing implantation. Perhaps, also they should oppose the practice of discarding spare embryos created as a by-product of IVF, though some recent writers tentatively suggest that this might be justified under the traditional distinction between killing and letting die (Mahoney 1984, p. 100).

OBJECTION III: THE SLIPPERY SLOPE ARGUMENT

Whether or not there is anything intrinsically objectionable about experimenting on human embryos, some fear that to permit this procedure might contribute to undermining respect for human life generally and help to create an ethical climate that would encourage other practices such as involuntary euthanasia.

Rejoinder

The rejoinder to that objection is that it underestimates a person's ability to judge each individual issue on its merits. The very fact of such widespread public opposition to experiments on human embryos, it is claimed, might itself be thought to give the lie to the slippery slope argument after eighteen years of virtual abortion on demand.

OBJECTION IV: PUBLIC SENTIMENT

Even if the other moral objections to experimenting on human embryos are acceptable, the fact remains that polls show most members of the public are opposed to such experiments and some feel that this, in itself, is a sufficient reason in a democracy for outlawing the practice. What is behind much of this thinking, is the claim that it is unacceptable to carry out research on a human embryo which, by its very nature, cannot give consent.

Rejoinder

Someone might reply that the role of Parliament is not merely to reflect public opinion but to provide moral leadership. Members of Parliament are, as Edmund Burke stated, properly regarded as representatives rather than delegates

> but his unbiased opinion, his mature judgement, his enlightened conscience ... are a trust from providence, for the abuse of which he is deeply answerable. Your representative owes you, not his industry only, but his judgement ... (Mill 1973, p. 157).

They are chosen for their supposed judgement and have a duty to exercise it. The claim, therefore, is that in the case of human embryo research, it would be wrong for law-makers to allow themselves to be dictated to by public sentiment.

Child Experimentation

The subject of experiments directs consideration to a further field of research and introduces new questions when such experimentation is conducted on children or other human individuals who may be incapable of consent. Mahoney (1984, p. 102) makes the distinction between therapeutic experimentation and that which is directed "at more long term and far reaching findings" though he admits this distinction is not clear cut. But even when one is considering the former in regard to those incapable of consent, the experimentation should be in the best interest of the patient and only when it is clear that more established, tried and tested forms of treatment are, for some reason, unavailable. There is also need to estimate the benefits desired from such a procedure and to offset them against risks involved, undesirable side-effects or the overall final state of the patient which will result. At best, only the patient can take the decision but, in the case of children and other incompetents, presumed consent is acceptable. The basis for this can be the knowledge of the patient himself/herself and what decision he/she would be likely to make in these circumstances. This is known as interpretative consent. On the other hand, the consent may be based on what any reasonable person would do in his/her own best interest in these circumstances. This is called constructive consent. The latter would be reasonable in the absence of interpretative consent and would apply specifically to children. The whole matter, both the dilemma of necessary experimentation on children and lines towards a responsible solution, is well expressed in the proposed international guidelines of the World Health Organisation and Council for International Organisations of Medical Sciences (CIOMS) which refine the revised Helsinki Declaration on bio-medical research by stating that there are many individuals who are incapable of giving adequate consent: "For such groups in particular, independent ethical review is imperative." (CIOMS 1982, p. 24.)

The discussion on child experimentation is also prevalent in the United States between Professors Ramsey and McCormick. Ramsey refuses any experimental procedure that involves a degree of risk or harm, however minimal, where incompetents are concerned. Therefore, those incapable of consent are out-of-bounds for non-beneficial research as distinct from therapeutic (that carried out for the best interest of the subject). Any other view, according to Ramsey, involves using the patient as a means only and not as an end. Ramsey is, no doubt, mindful of Kant (1959, p. 47).

> The practical imperative, therefore, is the following. Act so that you treat humanity, whether in your own person or in that of another, always as an end and never as a means only.

This approach, which is also accepted by Birch and Cobb (1981, p. 162), is challenged by Professor Joseph Fletcher (1971, p. 777). He labels it "apriorist" – that is starting with moral principles to make a judgement; whereas he would decide the morality of an action by its consequences. Ramsey seemed to modify his view later. McCormick (1981, p. 88) suggests, however, that there are things that a child ought to choose simply as a human being. A minimum would be a procedure which would not benefit the child but rather, at no cost to himself/herself, he/she would contribute to the benefit of others. If this is true of adults, it is no less true of infants, McCormick claims, because the infant is a member of the human race and has some responsibility like the rest of us to it. McCormick's argument is based on *sociality* not *age*. The good of infants is inseparably interlocked with the good of others for, in fact, they are social human beings. McCormick (1981, p. 92) rounds off his position:

> At some point, then, our willingness to experiment on children (and foetuses) when risk, discomfort and pain are at a minimal or non-existent, points to a duty that we all have to be willing to bear our fair share that all men may prosper.

The problem about McCormick's position is the difficulty of defining limits. Additionally, high motives cannot be presumed on behalf of young children. Later McCormick (1981, p. 329) addresses the question of embryo experimentation and argues that as a general rule embryos should not be used merely for experimentation. However, he is much more tentative and indeed ambiguous when it is a question of discarded foetuses (1981, p. 330). The argument is that the very procedure that gives life is inseparable from risks.

Mahoney (1984, p. 97) also seems to favour limited experimentation on embryos if it can be described as

> a human organism not yet sufficiently stable to possess the human soul and be identified as a person, but none the less charged with remarkable promise for the future, then it might be possible to conclude that the sacrifice of such promise could be justified in the interest, not just of "pure" research (if such there be), but of other human beings, whether now fully alive or as yet non-existent.

Later, the same writer states that

> perhaps, then, one may conclude that, given sufficient reason, it is morally justifiable to decide not to bring a child into existence, even from a fertilized egg or what might be termed a biological node, however regrettable one may consider this, in view of what might have been.

In this line of argument, experimentation on embryos which is

> directly relevant to clinical problems, as the Medical Council stipulates, may be seen as contributing to human biological life and to the wellbeing of such individuals as do develop.

And so Mahoney seems to justify tentatively non-therapeutic (non-beneficial) experimentation on embryos. However, this procedure was emphatically condemned (Acta Apostolicae Sedis 75 1983, pp. 35–9) by John Paul:

> I condemn, in the most explicit formal way, experimental manipulations of the human embryo since the human being, from conception to death cannot be exploited for any purpose whatever.

On Mahoney's reasoning, creating embryos simply for experimentation could be justified because his argument is based on the ontological status of the embryo, as he sees it, and not the purpose for which it was brought into existence. (In correspondence during March 1985, I put this point to Fr Mahoney. He replied: "If one were to agree that the status of the early embryo were such that experimentation could be justified, then would not this apply not only to 'spare embryos' but also to others?")

EVALUATION

Consequently, there is conflict amongst scientists as to the benefits of embryonic experimentation. There is also difference of opinion in regard to the moral status, as we have seen, of the fertilized ovum and, therefore, with what respect it should be treated. What cannot be doubted is the fact that human life is present from the moment of conception. We are, therefore, faced with a human life, a live entity with its own ongoing existence; this apart altogether from the question of ensoulment, personhood and human rights, is a human life that demands corresponding respect and, therefore, should have protection in law. It has been suggested that, from a legal aspect, the least that should be required is that surplus embryos should not be researched without explicit consent of the donors. This should also apply to gametes. This kind of legislation would give society more control of embryo research. However, I believe that, taking all the factors into consideration, the embryo should always be given the benefit of the doubt, and therefore, only therapeutic research, that is research performed in the best interest of the individual embryo, should be permitted. In a word, the embryo should receive the same respect as the adult, as was indicated in the last chapter.

Surrogacy

SURROGACY IN THE BIBLE

Cases of surrogacy can be found in the Old Testament: in Genesis (16:6) for example there is the story of Abram and his wife, Sarai, who requested that Hagar, her slave girl, is used as a surrogate mother in place of Sarai herself who is childless. As a result, Ishmael was born and there is friction between Sarai and the surrogate mother.

Another case arises (Genesis 30:1–24) when Rachel asks Jacob to let Bilhah, the slave girl, act as a surrogate as Rachel, herself, is childless and is jealous of Leah, her sister. Two sons are born. Jacob's second wife, Leah, even though she had given Jacob four sons, asked Jacob to allow Zilpah to act as a surrogate. The point of mentioning these events is not to make a case for surrogacy, but to demonstrate that Abram and Jacob were ahead of modern technology.

It is also worth recalling here that polygamy was practised by the Jews. When Christ came on earth, he restored marriage to its monogamous state; a point that was also emphasized by Paul (Romans 7:2). That is why so much emphasis has been placed, down through the centuries, by Christianity on monogamous marriage (Joyce 1948). It is also the reason why some writers consider that surrogacy and AID are an infringement of the exclusive monogamous covenant.

KINDS OF SURROGACY

Surrogacy is the practice where one woman carries a child for another with the intention that the child is handed over after birth. Surrogacy can take different forms. The commissioning mother may be the genetic mother in that she supplies the ovum, or she may make no contribution. The genetic father may be the husband of the commissioning mother. Therefore, there are various combinations and if there are various forms, the most likely occur where surrogacy involves AID or IVF as we have already seen. In the case of AID, a third party is used; therefore, the child is the biological offspring of the third party and the surrogate mother. Sometimes, however, a woman is inseminated by the commissioning husband and, in this case, the child is the biological offspring of the commissioning husband and the surrogate mother. The child is conceived by ordinary sexual intercourse or by artificial insemination – the semen donated by the husband. So, in this case, the wife is not biologically related to the child. In the case of *in vitro* surrogacy, the couple who commission the child are its biological parents, contributing ovum and semen to be fertilized *in vitro*; the resulting embryo then being implanted in a different woman who has lent her womb for the purpose. "She is, in such cases, simply acting as a human incubator." (Warnock 1985a, pp. 2–4.)

Baby Cotton was a case of AID surrogacy where the semen was transmitted to the surrogate by artificial insemination. Baby Cotton was, therefore, a child genetically related to the husband and the surrogate mother but not to the wife. The Cotton baby was the first AID surrogate baby in England and was born for a fee of £6,500. Another form of surrogacy, less well known in Britain but now practised in the United States, is where the husband fertilizes another woman and after five days, with special syringe, the tiny embryo is flushed out of the womb of the surrogate mother and placed in the womb of the husband's wife who carries and gives birth to the child. The advantage of this technique, it is claimed is that it is non-surgical and the embryo is more mature than the IVF embryo (Buster 1984).

There are certain cases where surrogacy would be an option, as we have seen, for the alleviation of infertility. Examples are where the wife cannot carry a child or has no womb or where medical conditions would make pregnancy dangerous. Surrogacy might also be sought for less serious reasons when pregnancy is not desired because it is simply inconvenient. Moreover, if surrogacy does take place, it can involve payment for the carrying mother. It is said by Warnock (Warnock Report 1984, p. 44), and others (Singer and Wells 1984, p. 115) that the weight of public opinion is against surrogacy. According to the Morgan Gallup Poll, 44 per cent in Australia and 55 per cent in Britain were against it.

The new possibility of separating genetic parenthood from social parenthood and of separating both from physiological parenthood, as in the case of the host mother, or womb leasing, raises serious questions for society. One recent study has reflected on this question and compares surrogacy with the case of the artificial womb, where the use of such a method would merely be supplying for the failure of the natural function. If a woman's womb cannot function properly it would be morally acceptable, it is contended by Mahoney (1984, p. 24), to supply for that function as in the use of kidney or heart machines. However, to introduce apparatus into a monagamous marriage is one thing; to introduce a third party is quite another. This attitude is out of line with the same writer's contention when he speaks of a third party "who trespass upon the covenant of marriage and exclusive relationship between husband and wife, who are, as Genesis describes 'one flesh'."

It should also be remembered that the capacity to conceive is not synonymous with the capacity to procreate as the latter includes carrying a child to successful delivery. That is to say the process of procreation entails both fertilization and carrying a child to term. The objection, therefore, about exclusiveness, extends to the introduction of a third party into the whole process of procreation, whether it means fertilization, carrying or both.

This is not the only problem raised by surrogacy. What if the surrogate mother were to become disenchanted with pregnancy and desire an abortion? What if the genetic parents decided upon abortion and tried to force the surrogate mother to undergo it? What if the genetic parents are determined to have a healthy child and refuse a handicapped or retarded one? In the United States there is the case of Baby Doe, born 10 January 1982 to a 26-year-old surrogate mother. The baby was born with severe congenital abnormalities – the father refused to accept it. The questions must be asked: Who is truly the mother of the child? Who has rights and responsibilities regarding the child? Suppose the surrogate mother attempts to extort extra payment beyond the agreed fee and threatens either to keep the baby or abort it? These, and many other questions, are linked with the technicalities of surrogacy.

No doubt there can be cases of surrogacy where the host mother is motivated by extraordinary generosity as could happen when the gametes are supplied by the husband and wife in the case of a sister who volunteers to carry for the wife. In this case, because of some medical reason, the wife is incapable of carrying a child and the sister acts in her place. But even here, there can be problems as Häring (1975, p. 201) recognises:

> What if the host mother (whether mercenary or unpaid volunteer) becomes psychologically attached to that which is physically attached to her?

Again, there is the question of whether the genetic mother will be able to achieve the same mother-child relationship as if she herself had carried the child. This is apart altogether from a consideration for the child and how he/she will relate to the surrogacy situation. These are deep and perplexing questions where answers are not readily known. Behind all these questions there seems to be a lack of consideration regarding the child and how these techniques will effect him. There is also the question, where donor parties are involved, that the child will be deprived of knowledge regarding his origin. Again, there is a deep and widely held belief that the relationship of a child to the woman who carries and gives birth to it is a very special one indeed, and this relationship may be gravely distorted by the technique of surrogacy.

EVALUATION

In my opinion, surrogacy for convenience alone is ethically unacceptable. Those who argue that the unitive and procreative aspects of the marital action should not be separated will reject surrogacy on this basis.

While there are many questions and problems regarding surrogacy, as outlined above, the objection against it is based on some of its consequences, and also on the fact that it introduces a third party into the process of procreation, which process should be ideally confined to the marital covenant and the mutual loving relationship of the husband and wife. Additionally there is the danger of making the child the means rather than an end in itself.

Cloning

The reproductive technology known as cloning represents the most intense intervention of all. Clone is a botanical name meaning twig (cutting) and the word "colony" is one of its cognates. Cloning means asexual reproduction and were it to occur, it would remove completely insemination and fertilization from the marriage relationship. It could also remove one of the partners from the entire process of procreation. Its supposed advantages are eugenic such as removing unacceptable or inferior material from the gene pool and maximizing desirable traits.

DIVISION OF CELLS

The simplest form of cloning can occur in IVF. At the two-cell stage, both cells are separated (twins). Each cell is placed in suitable conditions for growth. It is possible that both could grow to childhood and would be equivalent to identical twins with common genetic constitution. This form of cloning has already been achieved in animals. There would appear to be no technical reason why it cannot be accomplished in humans. It has been suggested that the advantage is that one half could be examined to type the other. Embryos carrying defective genes could then be aborted *in vitro* at five days of gestation and a non-defective embryo replaced in the mother. Again it has been mentioned that embryos could be grown to provide tissue or organs and thereby avoid the common problem of rejection which does not occur in donations from identical twins and would not occur with the donation from one's own clone. In the case of two-cell division, one cell could be frozen, therefore, and kept as a replacement organ or tissue for the other when childhood and adulthood have been reached and should replacement ever be required. The logistics of such a policy are horrendous.

CARBON COPY CLONING

This is, essentially, nucleus transplantation or substitution. The nucleus of a mature fertilized egg is removed and replaced by the nucleus from a somatic cell (an intestinal or skin cell). For some strange reason, the egg with its transplanted nucleus appears to embark on a normal development. The parent of the offspring would be the one from whom the nucleus was taken in the first place. Moreover, if it is taken from a woman, the offspring will be female and if it is taken from a male, the offspring will be male. The parent and the offspring would be genetically identical, that is to say the offspring would be the identical twin of the parent. In this case the clone is incubated in surrogate mothers or indeed the mother parent of the clone. Many reasons are given for this procedure.

(a)   Replication of people of genius, beauty or intelligence.
(b)   Determination of sexes in the future.
(c)   Improvement of the gene pool.
(d)   A solution for infertile couples.

The technique has been successfully achieved only in frogs, but obviously the situation would be more complicated where humans are concerned.

EMBRYONIC BIOPSY

The embryo, in this case, is allowed to develop until it is possible to remove one or more cells without putting the embryo at risk. The cells of the biopsy would be allowed to develop while the rest of the embryo is frozen. Once it is determined from the biopsy that the embryo is free from abnormality, a decision could be taken as to whether or not to thaw the frozen embryo and transfer it to the mother's uterus. The technique, of course, requires the use of IVF.

One of the main concerns about genetic engineering in the human context is about the human gene pool which could be altered deleteriously. The anxiety really arises in regard to eugenic genetics which is practised to produce new qualities so as to improve the species by breeding programmes. It is not yet practised on people, though in a bizarre sort of way the Nazis took some crude and horrifying steps to produce a super race.

It is feared, nevertheless, that a substitution programme of eugenic genetics could, in fact, reduce the variety of genes in the genetic constitution of the human species. Moreover, there is no such individual as the perfect genotype – no one is perfect. Every person, genius or otherwise, carries genes for undesirable traits. Evidently it is one thing to arrange breeding programmes, say, to increase the milk yield of cows, it is another and more difficult thing to breed for several diverse traits at the one time.

The concept of achieving superior humans by eugenic engineering or by cloning is based on a non-ecological model of human existence. It sees humans as largely what they are by virtue of genetic inheritance. Environment, the community in which we live, our various relationships, including those *in utero*, in a phrase "the ecology model" are all of prime importance and this is not included in eugenic engineering. Again, to produce physical qualities is one thing, to produce interrelated balanced mental products is quite another.

Another concern about genetic engineering was the matter of Recombinant DNA. (Recombinant DNA equals a hybrid molecule containing a DNA sequence (gene) from one species (such as humans) inserted in the genetic material of another. This is often achieved through the intermediary of a bacteria or other virus. DNA is Deoxyribonucleic acid – linear molecule made from four different nucleotides arranged in varying proportion.) While the possible advantages appeared to be considerable, the main anxiety was the possible escape of micro-organisms that would be gravely damaging to the human race. An international conference was called for this very purpose in 1975. It was named the Asilomar Conference and was held in Pacific Grove, California. (Amongst other experts attending, were members of the scientific community of the USSR, a matter we will return to in Part II.)

Another object is that research and development in genetic engineering directs scarce resources away from areas where more people could benefit. It develops expensive technology for the few and deprives others of basic health care (King 1980, p. 271; Birch and Cobb 1981, p. 228).

EVALUATION

Needless to say, this procedure raises all sorts of agonizing questions and causes public anxiety about selective breeding. Some authors find the idea of cloning morally unacceptable (Häring 1975, p. 203; Cass 1972, p. 53; Corkery 1983, pp. 106ff). They believe, if it became widespread practice, amongst other effects, it would undermine the stability of marriage and the family. Man needs to belong and be accepted. Moreover, cloning poses problems about the ethical and social ability of one group of people manufacturing another group with pre-established genetic characteristics. It is also difficult to assess what effect it would have on the parent-child relationships, where a child has been deliberately chosen to duplicate the parent rather than be an individual with his/her own unique personality. Above all, according to some, to limit the notion of parenthood to caring for and rearing a child is a radical attack on several human-Christian values – the meaning of human sexuality, marriage and parenthood where children should be the expression of human love, the meaning of man as an embodied spirit, to mention but few. To exclude these essential dimensions of humanity is to dehumanize and fragment man. To exclude the genetic aspect from parenthood, and see the latter solely in terms of rearing a child, is to reduce the biological, the bodily dimension of man to the non-human. Another fear about cloning is the effect it could have on a human relationship. Does not our sense of belonging stem in a very real way from our knowledge that we are the result of a parental union? It provides a sense of continuity with them and well-being; an expression of our parent's affection. Man is an embodied person that needs to belong, to trust and be accepted.

The total by-passing of the marriage relationship and the rupture of the unitive and procreative aspects have been mentioned already in regard to other techniques that equally apply in cloning, where the by-pass is total. Though no element from outside the couple is introduced, however, genes come from only one parent. Moreover, by abolishing the normal relationship between parents and children, the irreversible commitment of specific adults to specific children will be endangered – the begetting and carrying would be at a minimum. It would mean reproduction without human love, the family, the wider human community and more significantly mans' corporeality (Corkery 1983, p. 111). In short, the manifoldness of nature would be replaced by the discriminating replication of cloning which, in turn, would reflect a diminished humanity. There are some writers, of course, and even moralists, who see cloning as desirable in terms of consequences and advantages. Professor Fletcher (1974, p. xiv) believes that the more planned, controlled, contrived, produced and designed man is, the more human the result will be. So he concludes that normal procreation is less human than laboratory reproduction. Fletcher, of course, is a consequentialist and measures rightness and wrongness exclusively in terms of results. Yet these are but one determinant of the moral quality of human conduct.

It is interesting to note that some moralists claim that a form of cloning, in exceptional circumstances, would be acceptable even though like IVF, it circumvents the natural mode of parenthood. If there were sufficient reasons, they believe, it could be justified. Professor Curran lists the *bonum prolis* as one of the goods of marriage, and he writes that if there is infertility, a possible procedure for such a case could be cloning or nuclear substitution where the mother supplies the ovum and its nucleus is replaced by a nucleus from the father's organism (Curran 1973a, p. 217). One can see this is a technical possibility in the future in certain cases of tube blockage, sterile semen or difficulty in carrying a child, and artificial placenta could be used. This procedure would certainly be unacceptable for some because it by-passes completely the sexual act of marriage. For others, however, since, no element from outside the couple is introduced, it is, at least, a pastoral solution where other possibilities do not exist. However, the genes, as we have said, come from the husband only.

Conclusion

The problems facing society, marriage and parenthood in particular, in the light of these new techniques, are immense but nothing as severe as those facing the child. Society has learned to appreciate the importance of knowing its origins. This knowledge is essential for our stability because it tells us who we are and appreciates our dignity. Yet, in some of these new techniques, children will be denied the information about the circumstances of their origin from donor material. So it is that the self-identity both of future generations, and of future society as a whole, could be in question if techniques such as AID, ET and cloning, as well as forms of surrogacy, encourage the concealment of the individual's genetic source. What is being encouraged is a certain element of biological rootlessness in the human race. Concealment would extend not only to individuals but to future generations by the falsification of public records or omissions therein. Perhaps Sweden has acted wisely in legislating that all children have a right to the knowledge of their parenthood. Britain might be wise to follow this example. On the other hand, it has been argued by some that for the child or individual, the social parents are more important than genetic origin, at least where psychological and emotional development is concerned. Indeed they would say that from the point of view of the individual, at any rate, too much emphasis is placed on the knowledge of his origin. (This point will receive further treatment in Part II, Chapter VIII.)

The impression also comes over that every individual has a moral right to have a child. There is a real tendency to favour the adult at the expense of the child and to favour the liberty of the individual at the expense of marriage and the family. This is to advocate a principle of self-fulfilment against parenthood. If we see procreation as merely biological, there is also the real danger that the result of conception will be seen as something merely biological – a product rather than the loving, personalized expression of husband and wife.

The exclusiveness of the marriage covenant, which God has established, is endangered by the introduction of a third party into the procreation process. The couples' desire for a child, would not, in my opinion, be sufficient to circumvent it. The covenant of marriage, in spite of its limitations, should continue to be the most favourable organization for the loving transmission and nurturing of human life. I see no substitute for monogamous marriage. Therefore, it should be strengthened as far as possible.

As regards embryo experimentation, one's evaluation depends very much on one's view of the status of the embryo. However, while noting the admonitions of Helsinki and realizing the debate regarding the moral status of the embryo, perhaps the most prudent and morally acceptable position is to give the benefit of the doubt to human life, rather than the advancement of science and the wellbeing of society because the case for human life, beginning at fertilization, is very strong indeed.

One other feature about these new infertility techniques is, as we have seen, that they benefit the few. The needs of the vast majority of people are not addressed and frequently, as in the case of the nuclear bomb, the energies of science and technology are misdirected, a point underlined by the large percentage of the world's scientists involved in the arms race. A science that is orientated to the needs of few, diverts resources and energy from areas where the majority could benefit. Indeed by redirecting the resources of science into less manipulative channels calculated to prevent disease and improve the quality of human life, the world community as a whole would be better served without introducing gravely disturbing risks. This does not mean that risks should not be taken; rather it is a case of where to draw the line. In the questions of the marriage covenant and of the transmission of human life, it is, in my opinion, more prudent to draw the line to protect the mutual marriage relationship and prevent the eugenic manipulation of human life. As the great physiologist, Claud Bernard said: "Science teaches us to doubt and in ignorance refrain."

It would seem clear that we have neither the knowledge nor the wisdom for such undertakings.

CHAPTER III

The Report of the Warnock Committee

In response to considerable public concern throughout late 1981, when the medical, legal and ethical implications of assisted reproduction were revealed through the mass media in Britain, the Government appointed a Committee of Inquiry into Human Fertilization and Embryology. The Committee was chaired by Lady Mary Warnock and began taking evidence in July 1982. Its Report was published in July 1984.

Most of the Report deals with the techniques for alleviating infertility. Since the evaluation of the Report on AIH and AID differs from mine (as stated in Chapter II) I shall give the Report's arguments in detail supporting these two practices. While the findings of the Report against surrogacy are, in the main, in agreement with my argument, it will be more appropriate in this case to state the counter-arguments in favour of surrogacy. As to IVF, there were certain qualifications in my assessment; therefore, the argument for both sides has been listed. Again in embryo experimentation both the arguments and counter-arguments are listed. Finally, consideration will be given to the findings of the Committee on cloning, transspecies fertilization and freezing and storage of semen, ova and embryos.

Presenting the Report, Lady Warnock observed that the issues raised by the Inquiry "reflect fundamental moral, and often religious, questions which have taxed philosophers and others down the ages." (Warnock Report 1984, p. iv.) We are told that the Inquiry was set up to "examine, among other things, the ethical implications of new developments in the field." (Warnock Report 1984, p. 1.)

The new developments themselves have been described in the last chapter and these were mainly the questions that the Warnock Committee was invited to consider both in themselves and their legal and social implications. The Committee had to direct its attention not only to future practices and possible legislation but to the principles on which such practices and legislation would rest. While arguing in favour of the position adopted by the members of the Committee, due weight would be given to counter-arguments where they existed. However, as Mary Warnock herself says, in reality, "our personal feelings and reactions have been as diverse as those presented in the evidence."

Some members of the Committee had a clear perception of the family and its role within society; in considering the various techniques, their focus was on upholding family values and on the primacy of the interest of the child. But other members felt equally strongly about the rights of the individual within society. While Mary Warnock claimed their views were based on argument, sentiment or feelings were not excluded as "reasons and sentiment were not opposed to each other in this field." Nor should Utilitarianism be the moral system of assessment. Questions, such as these, concerned not only "a calculation of consequences, but also strong sentiments with regard to the nature of the proposed activities themselves."

However, Lady Warnock did write later (Warnock 1985, p. xvi) that "the Committee was obliged to use a mixture of utilitarian considerations and of judgement."

The General Approach

The membership of the Committee reflected a range of lay professional interest, totalling sixteen members which included doctors, lawyers, social workers, scientists and a theologian. The Committee's terms of reference were to consider:

Recent and potential developments in medicine and science related to human fertilization and embryology; to consider what policies and safeguards should be applied, including consideration of the social, ethical and legal implications of these developments; and to make recommendations. (Warnock Report 1984, p. 4.)

The Committee invited and received a considerable amount of evidence from individuals and interested bodies. There was a sense that events were moving too fast for their legal implications to be assimilated. It was well realized that the techniques opened up new horizons for infertility and embryology:

> Society's views on the new techniques were divided between pride in the technological achievement, pleasure at the new-found means to relieve, at least for some, the unhappiness of infertility, and unease at the apparently uncontrolled advance of science, bringing with it new possibilities for manipulating the early stages of human development.

While there was diversity in the Committee arising from religious, philosophical and humanist beliefs, nevertheless, there was in common, and this was confirmed by the evidence, the awareness that the public wanted "some principles or codes" to govern the development and use of the new reproductive techniques: "There must be some barriers that are not to be crossed; *some* limits fixed beyond which people must not be allowed to go." In a pluralistic society, there were difficulties as any one set of principles cannot be accepted. But Lady Warnock claimed there could be a shared morality beginning with the law itself which binds everyone and embodies a common moral position within society: "Within the broad limits of legislation, there is room for different, and perhaps much more stringent, moral rules." (Warnock Report 1984, p. v.) Consequently, it was agreed that barriers must be set up but there was not universal agreement on where these barriers should be placed.

THE SCOPE OF THE INQUIRY
It was recognized that the Committee was considering a sphere of activity which was developing and rapidly changing. A common factor linking all developments was the anxiety which

was caused in the public mind. Hence the new processes of assisted reproduction, including surrogacy, were considered. Also included was artificial insemination, which though practised in Britain for some years, was not universally accepted ethically nor indeed regulated by law. Abortion and contraception were outside the terms of reference.

Within the terms of reference, two words were given for clarification. The first of these was embryology and the second was potential. While the term embryo had been defined variously, the Committee took as their starting point the meeting of egg and sperm at fertilization. The embryonic stage was regarded to be the first six weeks following fertilization. The second word that needed clarification was potential and here the Committee was much more vague. It recognized the unpredictability of the scientific pace. It took the pragmatic view that it could react only to what it knew and what was realistically foreseen but no further attempt was made to define potential.

METHOD OF WORKING

The task was divided into two parts. The first concerned the *individual* who faced the problem of infertility. The second concerned *society* and the pursuit of knowledge for its benefit rather than that of the individual. The two, of course, cannot be absolutely separated. Hence the Report dealt first with the alleviation of infertility and, secondly, with scientific developments.

The Committee invited evidence; submissions were received from over 300 organizations, 24 Community Health Councils, 11 Regional Health Authorities, 22 Universities and 695 letters were received. Some individuals were invited to give oral evidence. The recommendations of the Committee were made as applicable to Britain, though the members accepted there was a case for an international approach.

Infertility

The Inquiry recognised that infertility can be a source of stress. It is a malfunction. Arguments were put forward against the treatment of infertility, such as over-population. If a couple cannot have children without intervention, they should not be helped to do so, the argument ran. Secondly, there was a body of opinion that held such interventions as the new techniques were unnatural or against God's will. Desire for a child was a wish not a need. Therefore, genuine needs of other people should have priority. The Committee attempted to answer these questions. On the first point, the reply was based on the claim that the number of children born from infertility techniques was insignificant. The Committee held that the second objection was not convincing owing to the ambiguity of the worlds "natural" and "unnatural". Finally, in regard to the idea that to have children was a wish and should not be satisfied at the expense of more urgent needs, the Committee held this could be answered in many ways. Several other treatments, even at present, were not designed to satisfy absolute needs. The Committee also added that infertility may be the result of a disorder which needed treatment for the patient's health. It was a malfunction and should be considered in the same way as any other.

TECHNIQUES FOR THE ALLEVIATION OF INFERTILITY

Some techniques, as we have seen, involve a third party: in AID semen is provided; in egg donation, another woman other than the spouse provides the egg; in embryo donation, both another man and woman contribute; in surrogacy, another woman provides the womb for the duration of the pregnancy. The question then is whether it is better that a third party who helps should be known to the couple. The Committee recommended that any party donating should be "unknown to the couple before, during and after treatment and equally the third party should not know the identity of the couple." (Warnock Report 1984, p. 15.)

AIH

The practice of artificial insemination has been known for years. However, in the case of AIH, the practice takes place within the marriage and for many this is most acceptable. However, the Committee does admit that there are arguments against AIH and acknowledges the sincerity of the views that support these arguments. The majority of views expressed saw no moral objection to the practice and believed that it simply entailed the assistance of *in vivo* fertilization. However, there were grave misgivings about one type of AIH where semen is placed in a bank and, after the husband's death, a widow may seek to be inseminated. The Committee felt that this could give rise to profound psychological problems for the child and the mother.

AID

The arguments for and against AID are clearly outlined in the Report:

> Many of the arguments against AID can be countered, as we have shown. In addition to these counter-arguments, however, there are several points directly in favour of AID. AID enables couples to have a child whom they can bring up as their own and who is biologically the wife's. It is not a particularly invasive process. It is essentially simple and painless: no anaesthesia or surgery is required. It is an out-patient treatment requiring only regular visits to the clinic. If a woman continues AID treatment for a period of time, the success rate is similar to that of natural insemination, and this may be very important for a couple already in their thirties, or suffering acutely from the distress of childlessness. An AID child is a child very much wanted: a couple may have had to endure years of waiting and consequently cherish the child. The fact that the couple share the experience of pregnancy, in the same way as any other couple does, may strengthen their relationships as joint parents. Many of the submissions made to the Inquiry were strongly in favour of AID. (Warnock Report 1984, pp. 22–3.)

The Warnock approach has been criticized for rejecting surrogacy and accepting AID. In both cases a third element is introduced into the marriage. Therefore, sanctioning AID and rejecting surrogacy indicates an inconsistency, according to some. Strangely, Mary Warnock observes

> that we did not treat the two practices in the same way, may partly reflect the fact that AID is pretty common, several thousand AID children being born each year and it would be difficult to stop something so widespread. (Warnock 1985a, p. 3.)

IVF

Unlike AID, IVF, as we have seen, is very much a new development. I need now to address the arguments for and against as presented by the Report.

The argument *against* IVF (Warnock Report 1984, pp. 31–2) was:

> Although many people regard IVF as an exciting new possibility for helping the childless, there are those who are deeply worried by its development. This opposition can be categorized as opposition either based on fundamental principles, or based on the consequences of the practice of IVF. The fundamental arguments against IVF are the same as those against AIH – that this practice represents a deviation from normal intercourse and that the unitive and procreative aspects of sexual intercourse should not be separated. Those who hold this view believe that this is an absolute moral principle which must be upheld without exception. This view is sincerely and strongly held. As a question of individual conscience, there will be those who will not wish to receive this form of treatment nor participate in its practice, but we would not rely on those arguments for the formulation of a public policy.
>
> The arguments against IVF based on a consideration of the consequences are more varied; but those who put forward such arguments may take as their starting point the acceptance of IVF as a legitimate form of treatment for infertility. Their reservations start when IVF results in more embryos being brought into existence than will be transferred to the mother's uterus. They argue that it is not acceptable deliberately to produce embryos which have potential for human life when that potential will never be realized. As we have noted above the opinion of the medical profession on the whole is that in the present state of knowledge superovulation is very desirable. But if more embryos are brought

into existence than are transferred, it is held to be morally unacceptable to allow them to die.

Another argument against IVF is that which draws an analogy between IVF and heart transplants, or other forms of "high technology" medical care, and asks whether the country can afford such expensive treatment which benefits only a few, and whether money could not be "better spent", that is, with beneficial effects for more people, elsewhere. While we accept that questions about the use of resources are proper questions, deserving serious consideration, essentially they relate to the extent of provision, not to whether there should be any provision at all. Further, without some provision of a service there can be no opportunity to evaluate the real costs and benefits of a technique, nor can the technique be refined and developed so as to become cost-effective. The priorities argument is, in our view, an argument for controlled development, not an argument against the technique itself.

The argument *for* IVF (Warnock Report 1984, pp. 31–2) was:

The positive argument in favour of IVF is simple: the technique will increase the chances for some infertile couples to have a child. For some of these couples this will be the only method by which they may have a child that is genetically entirely theirs.

Surrogacy

Surrogacy, Warnock points out, can take a number of forms:

The commissioning mother may be the genetic mother, in that she provides the egg, or she may make no contribution to the establishment of the pregnancy. The genetic father may be the husband of the commissioning mother, or of the carrying mother; or he may be an anonymous donor. There are thus many possible combinations of persons who are relevant to the child's conception, birth and early environment. Of these various forms perhaps the most likely are surrogacy involving artificial insemination, where the carrying mother is the genetic mother inseminated with semen from the male partner of the commissioning couple, and surrogacy using *in vitro* fertilization where both egg and semen come from the commissioning couple, and the resultant embryo is transferred to and implants in the carrying mother.

Later, Mary Warnock (1985a) agreed that the Committee did

not perhaps make enough of the distinction between AID surrogacy and IVF surrogacy and admits that their position would have been clearer if they had discussed each separately. She agreed also that some people feel very strongly that it is inherently wrong for a third party to intervene in the birth of a child "to be brought up as the child of a couple who are not both of them the genetic parents." She spelt out very clearly that in IVF surrogacy, the couple who commission are the child's biological parents, whereas in AID surrogacy the husband of the commissioning couple and the surrogate mother are the biological parents of the child.

The argument *for* surrogacy (Warnock Report 1984, pp. 45–6) was:

> If infertility is a condition which should, where possible be remedied, it is argued that surrogacy must not be ruled out, since it offers to some couples their only chance of having a child genetically related to one or both of them. In particular, it may well be the only way that the husband of an infertile woman can have a child. Moreover, the bearing of a child for another can be seen, not as an undertaking that trivializes or commercializes pregnancy, but, on the contrary, as a deliberate and thoughtful act of generosity on the part of one woman to another. If there are risks attached to pregnancy, then the generosity is all the greater.
>
> There is no reason, it is argued, to suppose that carrying mothers will enter into agreements lightly, and they have a perfect right to enter into such agreements if they so wish, just as they have a right to use their own bodies in other ways, according to their own decision. Where agreements are genuinely voluntary, there can be no question of exploitation, nor does the fact that surrogates will be paid for their pregnancy of itself entail exploitation of either party to the agreement.
>
> As for intrusion into the marriage relationship, it is argued that those who feel strongly about this need not seek such treatment, but they should not prevent others from having access to it.
>
> On the question of bonding, it is argued that as very little is actually known about the extent to which bonding occurs when the child is *in utero*, no great claims should be made in this respect. In any case, the breaking of such bonds, even if less than ideal, is not held to be an overriding argument against placing a child for adoption, where the mother wants this.

While the question of surrogacy presented the Committee

with some of the most difficult problems, nevertheless, the Committee rejected surrogacy from a moral point of view and recommended that legislation be introduced to render criminal the creation or operation in Britain of agencies whose purposes included the recruitment of women for surrogate pregnancy, and such legislation should be wide enough to include both profit and non-profit making organizations.

Cloning

The Report mentions a number of techniques which are "well into the future" (Warnock Report 1984, p. 74). One such procedure is called cloning. Unfortunately, the Report has little guidance to give on this matter and simply concludes by recommending

> that the proposed licensing body promulgates on what types of research, apart from those precluded by law, would be unlikely to be considered ethically acceptable in any circumstances and therefore would not be licensed.

Human Embryos and Research

The Report gives a very clear description of the early development of the embryo but seems to fail when it comes to the moral status of the fertilized ovum:

> Although the questions of when life or personhood begin appear to be questions of fact susceptible of straightforward answers, we hold that the answers to such questions in fact are complex amalgams of factual and moral judgements. Instead of trying to answer these questions directly we have therefore gone straight to the question of how it is right to treat the human embryo. We have considered what status ought to be accorded to the human embryo, and the answer we give must necessarily be in terms of ethical or moral principles. (Warnock Report 1984, pp. 58–60.)

It is difficult to see how the embryo should be treated without determining first of all the moral status of the embryo. Consequently, the Committee seems to have circumvented this fundamental question by moving to more pragmatic conditions, but then concludes that these will depend not for instance on socially agreed conventions, or legal stipulations but on ethical principles which cannot but have regard to the objective reality of the embryo. Therefore, on this very complex question about the beginning of human life, the Committee rather fudged the issue only to have it appear under the heading "What respect and protection should be given to the embryo of the human species?" Again it is difficult to talk about the kind of respect and protection a human embryo should receive unless one faces the difficult question of where human life begins. Furthermore, the question of human embryos and research hinges on this point. On the one hand the Report accepts that

> once the process has begun, there is no particular part of the developmental process that is more important than another

and, thus,

> biologically there is no one single identifiable stage in the development of the embryo beyond which the *in vitro* embryo should not be kept alive.

Nevertheless, and inconsistently, the Committee settled on the fourteenth day as the limit beyond which experimentation should not be allowed. It did, of course, point out that the formation of the primitive streak begins about fifteen days after fertilization and this marks the beginning of *individual* development of the embryo, and is the latest stage "at which identical twins can occur."

The Report then turned to the argument *against* the use of human embryos (Warnock Report 1984, pp. 61–2):

> It is obvious that the central objection to the use of human embryos as research subjects is a fundamental objection based on moral principles. Put simply, the main argument is that the use of human embryos for research is morally wrong because of the very fact that they are human, and much of the evidence submitted to us

strongly supports this. The human embryo is seen as having the same status as a child, or an adult, by virtue of its potential for human life. The right to life is held to be the fundamental human right, and the taking of human life on this view is always abhorrent. To take the life of the innocent is an especial moral outrage. The first consequence of this line of argument is that, since an embryo used as a research subject, would have no prospect of fulfilling its potential for life, such research should not be permitted.

Everyone agrees that it is completely unacceptable to make use of a child or an adult as the subject of a research procedure which may cause harm or death. For people who hold the views outlined in 11.11., research on embryos would fall under the same principle. They proceed to argue that since it is unethical to carry out any research, harmful or otherwise, on humans without first obtaining their informed consent, it must be equally unacceptable to carry out research on a human embryo, which by its very nature cannot give consent.

In addition to the arguments outlined above, and well presented in the evidence, many people feel an instinctive opposition to research which they see as tampering with the creation of human life. There is widely felt concern at the possibility of unscrupulous scientists meddling with the process of reproduction in order to create hybrids, or to indulge theories of selective breeding and eugenic selection.

Those who are firmly opposed to research on human embryos recognize that a ban on their use may reduce the volume not only of pure research but also research in potentially beneficial areas, such as the detection and prevention of inherited disorders, or the alleviation of infertility, and that in some areas, such a ban would halt research completely. However, they argue that the moral principle outweighs any such possible benefits.

The argument *for* the use of human embryos (Warnock Report 1984, pp. 61–2) was:

The evidence showed that the views of those who support the use of human embryos as research subjects cover a wide range. At the one end is the proposition that it is only to *human persons* that respect must be accorded. A human embryo cannot be thought of as a person, or even as a potential person. It is simply a collection of cells which, unless it implants in a human uterine environment, has no potential for development. There is no reason therefore to accord these cells any protected status. If useful results can be obtained from research on embryos, then such research should be permitted. We found that the more generally held position, however, is that though the human embryo is entitled to some added measure of respect beyond that accorded to other animal subjects, that respect cannot be absolute, and may be weighed against the benefits arising from research. Although many research studies in embryology and developmental biology can be carried out on animal subjects, and it is possible in many cases to extrapolate these results and findings to man, in certain situations there is no substitute for the use of human embryos. This particularly applies to the study of disorders occurring only in humans, such as Down's Syndrome, or for research into the process of human fertilization, or perhaps the specific effect of drugs or toxic substances on human tissue.

Trans-species Fertilization

In my opinion, it was surprising to find that the Warnock Committee allowed this kind of fertilization. It is a test on which human sperm may be analysed where there is a case of sub-fertility of the male. Consequently, the test of the human sperm was carried out on a hamster egg. The resulting embryo does not develop beyond the two-cell stage. This has caused, nevertheless, public concern about the prospects of developing hybrid half-human creatures. It will be seen in the response to Warnock (in the next chapter) that deep concern was expressed about the Committee's recommendation in support of this project.

Freezing and Storage of Semen, Ova and Embryos

The freezing, storage and thawing of human semen and embryos for subsequent use in AID and IVF are already realities. The Committee saw no objection to the use of freezing in principle. There are, however, practical problems because so far no reliable method has been found of freezing and thawing human eggs. However, in 1985, *The Times* (16 March) reported that there has been an advance in this procedure and this could remove the need to freeze human embryos for test tube babies; one of the most controversial areas of the research programme. Doctors and technicians at the Royal Free Hospital, London, have successfully carried out research on improving the freezing process of ova and if the technique proves successful, ova and semen could be frozen instead of embryos.

The Committee recommended the use of frozen semen in artificial insemination but that the use of frozen ova should not be undertaken until research has shown that no unacceptable risk is involved. It also recommended that the clinical use of frozen embryos may be continued to be developed under review by a licensing body. Needless to say the argument in regard to embryo freezing continues although few would see a problem if the undamaged embryo was used by the contributing couple in some future cycle. This could be an asset where there have been fertility difficulties and where a couple wish to time pregnancy by freezing and storing their own embryo. This is an entirely different matter from the case of the embryo or gametes stored for donation to a third party. Moreover, the Report recommended "the sale or purchase of human gametes or embryos ... under licence." (Warnock Report 1984, p. 79.)

Possible Future Developments in Research

The Report lists a number of future techniques which have not yet reached the stage of practical possibility. It lists ectogenesis, use of embryos for drug testing, parthenogenesis, cloning and nucleus substitution, trans-species fertilization, gestation of human embryos in other species. It rejects the last mentioned, believes that parthenogenesis will not take place in the foreseeable future and recommends that the growing of a human embryo *in vitro*, beyond 14 days, should be a criminal offence. As to cloning and nuclear substitution, it was disappointing that the Committee had no recommendations to make. The members were satisfied to note that cloning had been used successfully in other species. However, it would have seemed more sensible to recommend legislation for the prevention of cloning and nucleus substitution than to wait until it has taken place.

Expressions of Dissent

There were three expressions of dissent. The first in regard to surrogacy: the second and third in regard to embryo research.

SURROGACY (Dissent "A")
(Supported by 2 Members.) The dissenters held that, on rare occasions, surrogacy could be beneficial to couples as a last resort. However, they shared their colleagues' concerns about surrogacy. Nevertheless, it would be a mistake, they said, to close the door completely on surrogacy being offered. In this way surrogacy could be more effectively assessed as a treatment for childlessness. The dissenters recognised the need even here for legal and licensing authorities.

USE OF HUMAN EMBRYOS IN RESEARCH (Dissent "B")
(Supported by 3 Members.) The dissenters, in this case, pointed out that the question of where life begins cannot be simply answered nor can it be easily defined as to when a human person comes into existence. Therefore, they ask: "At what stage of development should the status of a person be accorded to an embryo of the human species?"

Whatever the answer may be, the embryo has a special status because of its potential for development "to a stage at which everyone would accord it the status of a human person." Therefore, it is wrong, in the view of the dissenters, to create something with the potential of becoming a human person and then deliberately to destroy it: "We therefore recommend that nothing should be done that would reduce the chance of successful implantation of the embryo." Moreover, the dissenters went on to recommend "that experimentation on the human embryo is not permitted."

Obviously the dissenters agreed that embryos should not be deliberately created for the purpose of experimentation and the numbers of embryos should be the optimum judged clinically to be necessary to secure implantation. That is to say:

> More embryos should not be implanted than is clinically judged to be optimum solely because they have been created and this would diminish the chance of their survival and expose the mother to the danger of multiple pregnancy.

In other words, the people signing this dissent would only support the creation of embryos with a view to their ultimate implantation.

USE OF HUMAN EMBRYOS IN RESEARCH (Dissent "C") (Supported by 4 members.) While this dissent would allow experimentation on embryos that are spare, nevertheless, they dissented from the view that "research should be permitted on embryos brought into existence specifically for that purpose or coming into existence as a result of other research." Consequently, they agreed that research may legitimately be undertaken on spare embryos which are available by choice and not needed for the purpose of treatment. Their problem arose about the generation of embryos brought into being specifically for the purpose of research and where there was no question of their being transferred to the mother. This also excluded embryos which came into existence as a by-product of research on fertilization.

Conclusion

The Inquiry's terms of reference were to consider new developments that related to human fertilization and embryology and also the safeguards and policies that should be applied. However, there is, in fact, a chance of perspective in the Report which really uses more space than one would have expected in considering recent implications about "assisted reproduction" (Warnock Report 1984, p. iv). Much less attention is given to the generation and the development of the conceptus than to assisted methods of reproduction. The result is that the Report is rather dominated by the concerns for adults rather than for the embryo and child.

Furthermore, the Report, while giving much time to the treatment of infertility, is totally silent about its causes. It is said, and there is some evidence for it, that oftentimes, the case of tubal occlusion is self-inflicted. (Baird 1969, p. 828; Bloom and Van Dongen 1972, p. 8; Jeffcoate 1975, p. 585; Llewellyn-Jones 1978 *passim*; International Planned Parenthood Federation (IPPF) 1979, p. 3, 1979a, p. 3, 1981, p. 2, 1982, p. 3; Weiner and Brit, p. 205; Chamberlain and Winston 1982, p.69.) These matters, therefore, should have been given more consideration, especially when we are determining the distribution of limited resources.

The proposal (Warnock Report 1984, p. 15) that the genetic source of individuals should be completely concealed, not only from children, but from future generations by omissions from public records seems to countenance a biological rootlessness of the human race. This is, at best, mistaken kindness. In my opinion, the public good is not well served by the systematic falsification of public records for the years that are to come.

It appears to be inconsistent, as some have asserted, to allow AID and reject surrogacy as both introduce a third element into the marriage. One of the reasons given by Mary Warnock (1985a, p. 3) for this approach, namely "that AID is pretty common" is not a very convincing one.

It was rather surprising to discover that trans-species fertilization between human gametes and animal gametes was recommended under licence. Such procedures seem to reduce humanity to a lower order of being. This can have the gravest consequences and open up horrific possibilities of monsters, hybrids and effects that we can't foresee or imagine.

While the efforts of the Committee were to place "some barriers" on the new methods, it seems, at any rate, that some of the recommendations are more likely to erode family and marital unity, than strengthen it. The Inquiry does not see marriage as the only proper framework within which children should be conceived and reared. Again, one fails to find in the Report, any reference to marital love or the needs of children.

It seems paradoxical for the Report to claim that the embryo deserves some protection on the one hand and to recommend on the other that a human embryo may be sold. This is perilously close to the slave market for those who believe a human embryo is a human being with potential, or at least a potential human being. It is odd, to say the least, that according to the Report, research may be carried out on any embryo resulting from IVF up to the end of the fourteenth day after fertilization. But the embryo which has been used for research should not be transferred to a woman. In other words, newly conceived human beings could be used for experimentation, according to the Report, provided they are deprived of any chance of surviving. This also removes the possibility that the individual used in this way, might, at a later date, seek to vindicate his or her rights and demand compensation for damage that had been done.

The Warnock Report is obscure when it discusses the primitive streak and the question of twinning. As we have seen (Chapter I), why and how twinning occurs is not clearly understood. Hence it is unwise to place too much emphasis on this factor. In the event of twinning, the fact that there are now two, pre-supposes the existence of one and that one becomes two. The Warnock thesis seems to assume that if twinning occurs then, before this event, nobody existed. One other point is worth mentioning; if the fourteenth day were written into a statute, it seems reasonable to forecast that it would be just a matter of time before this event was extended further. Warnock is correct in that the moral wisdom of the past produces no ready made answers to the new scientific questions. It is true that the problems are new but it is unwise to abandon the moral insights of the past from Plato and Aristotle right down through the ages. They took into account the notion of the human person's potential and the goal of human living. They attempted to judge whether a human action or attitude was conducive to that goal. The problem with the Warnock approach is that it is based on the calculation of consequences, feelings and intuition. When one applies the consequential approach there is no room for a distinction between the consequences *intended* and the consequences merely *foreseen*. Intentionality is excluded as if it made no difference whether the man I have killed was a victim of wilful intent, calculable neglect or merely foreseen in a life-saving attempt on behalf of other people. It is rather concluded that if the consequences are similar, the moral judgement is similar.

Human actions are not merely procedures for producing results or consequences nor are they merely measurable in a scientific sense. Indeed this was attempted by Bentham, Mills and the Utilitarians when they tried to make moral reasoning as like "scientific" reasoning as possible. They argued that a good action is one which produces as much happiness and as little pain as possible. Some even spoke about a calculus of pleasure by which the beneficial results could be measured. But the matter is more complicated than that. How is pleasure compared or measured? Again, if killing one innocent person quietens the rioting mob, and thereby saves many lives, then the good consequences are mathematically greater than the evil ones. But if that is the only question, one may rightly ask, what has happened to the rights of the innocent person directly and intentionally killed? I would suggest, therefore, that it is not possible to treat the problems posed in the new kind of scientific knowledge by making moral reasoning as much like "scientific" reasoning as possible.

Warnock (as will be seen in the next chapter) also appeals to sentiments, feelings and intuition. But while these criteria are not to be ignored, they do not reflect what is surely basic to any genuine morality, namely that all people have a fundamental equality as human beings. Feelings and intuition are a consideration that should not be ignored but their role is very limited.

One other point is worth mentioning here. It is true that facts are an essential part of the process of evaluation, but facts, scientific or otherwise, are not the whole of reality. One has to take into account, as we have seen, what a human being is and therefore the goal of human living, and whether a particular action is conducive to that goal. Now this sense of purpose is lacking in judgements which are based on intuitions or on the calculation of the measurable consequences of various courses of action. Murray has observed:

> The facts of experience, whether scientifically verifiable or not, do not alone provide the basis of moral judgements: they do so only when they are seen in the context of the whole truth about humanity. (Murray 1985, p. 12.)

Science, therefore, deals with an aspect of reality and only answers questions formulated in its own terms. The whole of science can only yield measurable truth. Generosity, love, honest, fidelity are not "scientific" or measurable concepts and there is always more to them than science is capable of revealing.

When we are reflecting on the treatment of human embryos and the new reproductive techniques, we are not seeking merely to find how different people feel, nor are we simply analysing or measuring consequences. Rather we are searching for the truth about these actions as *a whole human reality*. This is also the point that Murray and others like Torrance are at pains to emphasize. Indeed it is impossible to understand human life, except in the context of a journey or pilgrimage with a beginning and end. Whole scientific analysis of human beings should not exclude this moral evaluation. Consequently, we argue that human actions cannot be evaluated in isolation from the whole purpose and direction of human life. Hence it is not only a question of what takes place but also the *meaning* of the action and how it relates to life's journey and the goal of human living. Justice is not done to the whole of reality when intuition and feelings do not account for meaning, and when the calculus of consequences omits intentionality and the significance of the action in regard to the purpose of living. Furthermore, the dignity of the human being can only be seen in totality. That is when he/she is considered in his/her own origin, nature and destiny and interrelated with other people of like nature, who are members of a redeemed humanity and who are linked with us in life's journey. This, of course, means that we have a responsibility to the whole of humanity and that includes those who are to come after us and who are called to the universal kingdom. Additionally, it obliges us not to use our fellow pilgrims as a means to an end. Nor should we deny or exploit the dignity of others who are journeying with us.

Finally, the question that can be fairly posed is whether the approaches to moral reasoning in the Warnock Inquiry are, in any way, capable of doing justice to human living and indeed the whole of human dignity. Warnock sums up the Inquiry's position in the following assertion (Warnock Report 1984, p. 2):

> Moral questions such as those with which we have been concerned are, by definition, questions that involve not only calculations and consequences, but also strong sentiments with regard to the nature of the proposed activities themselves.

It has been demonstrated above that neither of these, nor both of them together, can give an adequate basis for moral evaluation. Not only that, but there is no reference whatsoever to people who may be injured by such actions. Again no human being, at any stage of his existence, may be treated in any way that violates his distinctively human nature and status. Nor should a human being ever be subjected to being a means to an end. Hence the Helsinki Declaration states that in research on man, the interests of science and society should never take precedence over considerations related to the wellbeing of the subject (a point we have noted in Chapter II). In Christian thinking the human being is on the path to human fulfilment which is offered by God and in communion with Him, and with the whole of redeemed humanity. It would follow from this that our freedom should be used in harmony with that truth and, therefore, it is not enough to regard human actions as methods of producing results, nor to evaluate them in terms of feelings and intuitions. Love of God and neighbour makes it utterly imperative that our actions should always express and never deny this reality: a reality which is backed by the love incarnated in Christ. Indeed by the Incarnation, the love of

God is embodied in interpersonal relations so that all human behaviour should be subordinated to this truth. It is by true reference to Christ, as the controlling centre of human living, that the decisions and recommendations of the Warnock Report should be assessed, but this is not possible in a pluralist society and Parliament.

The Committee, however, did recognize that there should be some "limits". Indeed it has been said that war is far too serious a matter to be left to the generals. It is equally true that medical research of this nature cannot be totally left to the medical scientist.

CHAPTER IV

The Response to Warnock

Surrogate motherhood had come to Britain having been practised in the United States for about eight years (*The Times* 24
May 1984). Like surrogacy itself, test tube births, embryo
experimentation and freezing were leaping ahead of moral and
legal codes. Hence the complex questions, such as donor and
anonymity, status of the embryo and AID had been under
discussion long before Warnock reported. The public realized
that these were agonizing questions which go to the very heart
of humanity. But the thrust of scientific work outpaced the
public's ability to ask questions about the direction of that
thrust and, if necessary, to set down rules. Hence there were
at least two areas for investigation. The first concerned the
professional environment in which genetic research is to be
conducted. The second concerned the social and ethical accep-
tability of that research in society and outside the laboratory.
Society is slow to evolve attitudes. Science, on the other hand,
acts rapidly. Consequently, Warnock, as we have seen, had to
wrestle with the question of how professional conduct should
be guided and then to devise and recommend some legal
codification, if necessary, for the laity. Indeed it was feared that
the Report would be outdated before it was published. It was
not surprising then that when the Report did see the light of
day (in July 1984) a fascinating debate was set in motion. In this
chapter, I propose to examine some of the principle responses
that resulted after publication, namely the debate in the press,
on television, in the House of Commons, in the House of
Lords, the General Synod of the Church of England, the
Catholic Bishops' Conference of England and Wales Joint
Committee on Bioethical Issues, a Jewish reaction and the

response of other Churches, and the introduction of Enoch Powell's Unborn Children (Protection) Bill.

The Debate in The Tablet

In July 1984, just before Warnock was published, Dr Iglesias wrote an article in *The Tablet* about the "simple" or "straight" case of IVF. She questioned its morality and observed that while the submissions to the Warnock Committee of the five Catholic commissions "have expressed total unanimity on the principle of respect for the sacredness of every human life from its beginning of conception", nevertheless they did not express any explicit objection to the "straight" case of IVF, which is the case of the married couple, who respect life from conception and alleviate infertility through IVF. In her view, IVF itself, as a technique, was flawed morally. (Iglesias 1984a.)

However, in the same issue of *The Tablet*, Mahoney disagreed with Iglesias. As to the beginning of human life and in reply to the above observations, Mahoney stated that Iglesias's argument had no firm basis and that the status of the embryo at conception was not necessarily equivalent to a human individual as it was not sufficiently stable to be considered a person. Mahoney was emphasizing that much of Iglesias's argument was based on the assumption that every fertilized embryo was a human person. In *The Tablet* the following month (4 August) the Australian professor, R. B. Zachary, in reaction to these observations by Mahoney, stressed, however,

> that the zygote has the power within itself to produce the enormous numbers and varieties of cells and organs leading to the human adult. This is a continuous process during which the embryo itself has the only active role, abstracting all that it needs from tissue fluid environment. Nothing is added from outside for this new human individual is complete in itself.

In an earlier issue of *The Tablet* (28 July), and shortly after the publication of the Warnock Report, Professor J. J. Scarisbrick, the chairman of *Life*, had taken Mahoney to task for stating, among other things, that "the human embryo, though human and alive is not yet sufficiently stable and biologically developed to be considered a human individual or person". Scarisbrick considered this reasoning "muddled and muddling". But in the same issue, Mahoney spelt out that the early human conceptus is "more than tissue but ... less than an individual human being" and this applies as long as it remains biologically unstable. He proceeds to assert that the Warnock Report was correct in judging that "the question of when human life or personhood begin ... are complex amalgams of factual and moral judgements". But the Report failed, however, he believed, in abandoning its analysis precisely at that point in favour of more pragmatic considerations, in spite of the fact that, as the letter presenting the Report stated, experimentation on human embryos is a subject which arouses the "greatest public anxiety".

In spite of the lack of consensus in the Warnock Committee with seven of its sixteen members opposed to the creation of embryos specifically for experimentation, it was recommended by a majority of two to approve experimentation on embryos of "whatever provenance up to the end of the fourteenth day after fertilization". It would, according to Mahoney, be fairer and reflect the deep division of opinion in society, as well as the division in its own members on such a fundamental ethical question, for the Committee to have recommended to the Secretary of State the imposition of a moratorium on all experimentation, pending thorough national and Parliamentary consideration of the question. Meanwhile the Master of the Guild of Catholic Doctors, Dr Seymour Spencer, and Professor Scarisbrick, accused Mahoney of reducing the human embryo to a "new inferior class of human organism". A sort of "human being" who is a "non person" like "Jews" and "Blacks".

The *New Scientist* (9 August), referring to the beginning of human life and in response to the Warnock Committee, insisted that "new humans are made when sperm meets egg". A few weeks before that, the same periodical took up the fourteen days limitation on embryo experimentation as recommended by Warnock, and observed that as in Britain, there are no laws banning research on human embryos elsewhere in the world. But most other countries operate some sort of voluntary code of practice. In the United States, the National Institute of Health (NIH), the government agency in Washington that funds most bio-medical research at American universities, published in 1979 a set of rules that essentially have never been tested. These guidelines prohibit research unless approved by the agency's Ethics Advisory Board and the Director of the NIH, but the Advisory Board no longer exists according to one NIH official and besides almost no one has applied for a grant for such research.

The American Fertility Society (1984) with members from several medical disciplines has published a series of guidelines on embryo research. They permit researchers to "scientifically examine" human embryos up to fourteen days of age. The NIH, meanwhile, also sets a fourteen days limit but the experiments must involve only research on transfer of the embryo to the uterus.

In Japan there are nine centres carrying out research into *in vitro* fertilization. One of the leading researchers, Masakuni Suzuki (1984, p. 3) of Tohoku University, says that the Warnock Report will have a "big effect" in Japan although its main recommendations, he says, are already in effect as a series of guidelines. Tohoku University is where four of Japan's nine successful cases of test tube babies have been born. Suzuki says that Japan is six to seven years behind Britain in embryo research.

Pressure is mounting in Sweden to extend its current limit on human embryo experiments from fourteen to twenty-one days. The twenty-one day limit in Denmark permits Danish scientists to research on embryos that have developed the beginnings of neutral tissue. In Holland and France, committees are investigating *in vitro* fertilization and they will both report by the end of the year.

In Australia where research of frozen embryos is much more advanced than anywhere else, the recommendations of the Warnock Committee

Sit very comfortably with those of Australia's National Health and Medical Research Council. This is the view of Professor Richard Lovell who chaired the Council's Committee that looked into guidelines for *in vitro* research. Lovell says the Committee chose a seven day limit because it was a clear cut point in embryonic development before which the embryo could not conceivably be regarded as a person in most cases.

However, the National Health and Medical Research Council are later this year studying the possibility of using "brain birth" as the milestone that will decide the beginning of "life". Professor Carl Wood, leader of Australia's foremost *in vitro* fertilization team, says that the fourteen day limit of Warnock is an arbitrary choice and that it will have to be extended for future research. (*New Scientist* 26 July 1984.)

All this reflects the international debate that takes place around Warnock and the fourteen day cut off. Similar arguments appear in various British journals. For example, in Britain, the Council for Science and Society (1984) claimed that a six week limit on experiments is defensible as embryos are unlikely to feel pain before this limit. Whereas the famous Dr Edwards would place the cut-off point somewhere between day twelve and day thirty (Edwards 1984).

The Debate on BBC 2 TV

On the day of its publication, 18 July 1984, BBC 2 TV broadcast a special programme on the Warnock Report. The presenter, Fred Emery, was accompanied on the platform by Lady Mary Warnock and other members of her Committee. In the audience were many eminent doctors, scientists and theologians and people connected directly and indirectly with the Report, including Dr Edwards.

The programme, "Brass Tacks", devoted itself to discussing "Tomorrow's Babies: The Warnock Report". In the discussion, which centred mainly on embryo experimentation, Dr Edwards felt that the development of the neural tissue and sense would be crucial. He felt that the embryo could not feel pain before that time. Day twelve or thirteen is when the tiniest organs of neural tissue – that is the future brain tissue – begin to appear. By day thirty

> you have the development, just the beginning of the development of the fore-brain and the beginning of the development of the eye. So really very, very primitive minute forms at these stages of life, so I always say it should lie somewhere between day twelve and day thirty.

An American doctor, Garry Hodgen of the NIH, would place cut-off between day twenty and forty. However, Professor Marshall, who was one of the dissenting three on this matter in the Warnock Committee, reaffirmed his position in the same broadcast:

> I am not saying that embryos are persons at all. We make this very clear in the Report but the embryo has the potential to become a human person and, therefore, it seems to us, who sign the minority Report, to deliberately destroy something that has the potential to become a human person, even for good motives, was just not acceptable.

Mary Warnock and her Committee recommended, as I have already stated, a fourteen day limit and that beyond this limit the law should make experimentation a criminal offence, though Dr Edwards considered "criminal" a "terrible word to use". Mary Warnock went on to explain that the fourteen day limit

> was a balance between the very strongly held feelings that people have about protection that the human embryo should be afforded and the desire, that I think all of us share, that the research which is going to help the dimunition of genetic diseases should be allowed to go on.

Professor Ian Kennedy felt the Warnock Report could not

> make its own mind up ... because at one stage, you say it [the embryo] is deserving of some respect and on the other, they say, yes, it deserves some respect but you can experiment on it up to

fourteen days. Well, where is the respect being owed to it if you can use it an destroy it for fourteen days.

But this, of course, happens to all people in different areas of human living because all human life is devalued.

Mary Warnock replied:

> I don't think there is an absolute all or nothing case here. I mean our point was, and the majorities point, that you afford the embryo certain protection in law but not total and complete protection in law.

At this point, the Anglican theologian, Professor G. R. Dunstan, Department of Theology, University of Exeter, was asked to comment about the end justifying the means. In other words, would he agree that the beneficial ends of research justify embryo experimentation. He asserted that there were, in fact, two choices. First that absolute human status is given to the embryo and then all problems are removed. Or that the protection due to human life "grows *paripassu* with the embryo's own growth to maturity". Then there is the question of difficult decisions about the various weight of different considerations. He referred to the cut-off point of fourteen days recommended by Warnock, based on the primitive streak, and the cut-off point based on the capacity to feel pain which, he said, is about six weeks and then he added a third factor, namely "public sentiment" which is that "intuitive feeling" that people have about "playing about" with human life. Taking these three factors together and weighing them carefully, he (Dunstan) would opt to leave the cut-off point to a licensing authority, free to work as the circumstances and knowledge changed.

It was interesting to note that the most controversial question in Warnock, and the largest dissent in the Committee, centred on the question of experiments. The dissenters not only included Professor Marshall and others, but also Professor Anthony Dyson of the Social and Pastoral Theology Department, University of Manchester.

The Debate in The Times

On 23 July 1984, a letter appeared in *The Times* from Rev Dr. N. M. de S. Cameron, expressing astonishment that, in spite of their remit and the many paragraphs of the Report, Warnock failed completely to address the central question, i.e. the status of the embryo. Therefore, in his opinion, the members of the Committee circumvented the "principle question at issue in the debate". Before Parliament, he says, accepts the idea that embryos may be grown for experimentation, it must be convinced that the same ground

> could not also be used to designate, say, an abandoned, handicapped child with a limited life-span, or a demented and unwanted geriatric for the same purpose.

Dr Ian Morgan felt that the Report was using double standards in saying that the fourteenth day should be the cut-off point for experiments, after which the conceptus is covered by law, and the amended Abortion Act 1982 allows termination up to 168 days "the unborn foetus only have full legal rights after this time". He also felt that to recommend AID but, at the same time, to reject surrogacy, where a married couple could supply the embryo from fertilization of their own sperm and ova but inserted the embryo in a third party, was "contrary to logical thinking". (*The Times* 24 July.)

Another writer, accused an earlier (21 July) editorial in *The Times* of "finding surrogate motherhood more repugnant than killing a human embryo after experimentation ... Is prostitution, though repugnant, more repugnant than murder?" (27 July). A few days later, Dr de S. Cameron (31 July) returned to challenge a lawyer from the University of Aberdeen who had indicated that in Christian thinking there was another view about the beginning of human life, namely that the protection afforded to the embryo "varies with the stage of development". This thinking, Cameron denied.

The debate, of course, was not limited to professionals. Leo Abse, MP, wrote (7 August) to underline the merits of IVF and all of its consequences and stated that it was difficult to see why surrogacy should be prohibited in some exceptional circumstances. For example where the sister of a woman, with no uterus, offers to carry through pregnancy the child of her sister and brother-in-law.

Mr Abse added that to prevent embryo research is to hinder valuable work to alleviate fertility and remedy genetic defects. However, the new techniques should be subject to two limitations:

> Their development should not be distorted by commercial influence and they should be subject to strict regulation by a licensing authority of the kind recommended by Warnock.

Dr Snowden, Director of Population Studies, and Professor G. D. Mitchell, both of the University of Exeter, while broadly agreeing with Warnock on artificial insemination, were unhappy (*The Times* 9 August) about embryo experimentation, whether the embryos are "spare" or "deliberately created". This is to treat them as sub-human: "The community is deeply divided as indeed was the Warnock Committee about this issue". Therefore, there should be a moratorium on such experiments "while public debate takes place and suitable legislation is drafted".

It was surprising that a rejoinder was published from Dr de S. Cameron (8 August), in answer to the lawyer from the University of Aberdeen about the alternative viewpoint in Christian tradition:

> Such a tradition was really the outworking or contemporary ignorance of embryology: such that, for example, emphasis was laid upon quickening and upon the physical appearance of the latter foetus as that of a child.

At the same time, Mr Abse was taken to task by a fellow MP, Mr K. McNamara (11 August), for emphasizing the alleviation of infertility and curing handicaps at too high a cost. McNamara quotes Lejeune as demonstrating that work is being successfully done "without the use of human embryos.

The Committee ignored this evidence". He was dismayed that the Report was not more extensive in its recommendations of techniques to help the infertile, such as micro surgery to repair faulty tubes and other methods such as "low tubal transfer". To strive to overcome infertility and congenital handicaps is desirable "but not on the basis of the Warnock Committee's recommendation which subject some children to unforeseeable risks . . ." In the same issue, Professor Dunstan, referred to Dr de S. Cameron and those like him, who appeared "to discern in my article, a threat to firm convictions of their own". he asked them to read the article (Dunstan 1984, pp. 38–44) and then make a judgement. Furthermore, the article

> recalls and documents a succession of Christian theologians exegetes . . . from the fourth to the nineteenth century, who expressly denied that causing death of a human embryo [sic] before it was indisputably "formed" into the human likeness was to be reckoned and punished as homicide.

Another lawyer entered this debate in the person of John Finnis, a Reader in Law, Oxford University. Reference was once again made to Dunstan's article and Finnis (25 August) succinctly claimed that of the thirteen experts quoted in the article

> not one expressly denied that killing the newly conceived is homicide. Indeed despite the very misleading embryology of their era, no fewer than four (Basil, Tertullian, Raymond of Penafort and Sixtus V) expressly state that it is to be reckoned and punished as homicide. Pius IX agreed. Four more (Gregory XIV, Lapide, de Lugo and Alphonsus) state that it is to be reckoned homicide, always wrong, though subject to less severe penalties than other forms of homicide.

Another, St Augustine, in fundamental texts unmentioned by Professor Dunstan reckons it a form of visciousness or cruelty, tantamount to homicide and always wrong:

> The remaining three (Gregory of Nyssa, Innocent III and Aquinas) do not discuss the wrongfulness of such actions but, of course,

imply nothing against the constant teachings that they greviously offend against incipient human life or lives.

While this debate was in progress, Clifford Longley, the Religious Correspondent of *The Times*, insisted in one of his articles (30 July) that the Warnock Report was merely an essay in moral theology. He introduced a novel aspect to the debate on where human life begins. Again, while it is a religious question, nevertheless, moral theologians, he says, must return to the scientist for more information about the early embryo. But, he claims, one important fact has been missed so far:

> It is that early embryos are capable, like corpses, sperm and ova, but unlike developed foetuses, babies and adults, of deep freezing. A conceptus can be kept, in suitable conditions at the right temperature, for a long time, probably many years. Freezing halts the cell multiplication process which can be resumed long afterwards.

Longley asks, why can an embryo's life be arrested and not the others? An organism whose organic process can be discontinued does not possess life. Whereas life means continuous organic processes which once stopped cannot be restarted. There is a difference in kind here, he claims, which has not yet been fully understood by the conservatives.

Meanwhile, impatience was expressed by the ultrasound expert and Chairman of the Order of Christian Unity, Professor Ian McDonald, because of the possible expansion of abhorrent "experimentation, including cross-fertilization between species" before Parliament enacted some of the Warnock recommendations. He called for a moratorium and this was supported by *Life*. Some weeks after (29 November), the President of the Royal College of Obstetricians and Gynaecologists, wrote to refer to Downs Syndrome and other handicaps and called for more embryo research warning that those who deny this must "bear a heavy responsibility if the recommendations of the Warnock Committee on embryo research is banned." But the Bishop of Norwich asked (5 December) if this view represented the unanimous mind of the Royal College. He proceeded to quote Lejeune and then Lord Denning: "Is it [embryo] a thing? God forbid ..." He concluded by referring to the Christian conscience of the nation, to men and women of the broadest ethical and moral principles

> who are beginning to realize that to open the Pandora's Box of genetic engineering is to endanger the very basis of human and family life as we know it.

A Response from the Jews

In December 1984, the Chief Rabbi, Immanuel Jakobovitz, wrote an article in *The Times* (15 December) on the Warnock Report (to which we will refer later). He rejected many of its concepts which were out of line with the Judaeo-Christian tradition. He made a comparison between tampering with human life and the inner mysteries of nature, with splitting the atom. The latter resulted in the most universal threat to human nature in the annals of man. Jakobovitz approved of the "general theme" of Warnock but he was very critical of "some fundamental shortcomings". First by expressly dissociating the definition of couple from a legal husband-wife relationship, the Report failed to safeguard the family. He criticized its attempt to legalize false entry in official documents of AID and IVF children who are born to "parents who were in fact infertile". There is another imperative, he says, missing in the Report, namely the interests of the child:

> The practice of freezing, for use after the donor's death and thereby creating orphans, as well as the deception of children about their paternity by AID and fraudulent entry, and the conception of children by one mother to be borne by another, are all an indefensible violation of human rights.

One of the most objectionable statements in the Report, according to Jakobovitz, "is the considered refusal to limit access to treatment for infertility to legally married couples".

Rabbi Seymour Seigel had already noted (*Washington Post* 28 July 1978) in the United States that: "If nature played a trick as it has in this case, if we can outsmart nature, that is theologically permissible." But he added: "If conception cannot be accomplished in the usual way, then let it be done artificially as long as no third party is involved." (*United Synagogue Review* Fall 1978.)

Jakobovitz asserted that treatment of infertility outside marriage was an intolerable affront to the Judaeo-Christian heritage and a failure to safeguard the family. It would also cause incalculable harm to children in these situations. He felt that the falsification recommended by the Report is "abhorrent" and doubt would be thrown on the veracity of all birth certificates. However, Dr E. Jackson-Thomas castigated him (*The Times* 28 December) for presenting the morality and ethics of the debate in this context. He felt that Jesus, Himself, would be much more compassionate with infertile couples than the people of the Judaeo-Christian tradition.

The debate continued into the new year (1985). According to Clifford Longley (*The Times* 11 February) there was a strong reaction from the Liberal Jews to some of the Chief Rabbi's remarks. According to the Chairman of the Reform and Liberal Jews, Rabbi T. Bayfield, Jakobovitz was not representative of British Jews. Later, in the *Jewish Chronicle* (21 February), Rabbi Neuberger, stated that surrogacy

and all the issues raised by the Warnock Report were serious matters with complicated ethical and religious problems contained within them. There are no simple answers and many grey areas, we may not always agree.

Response of the Board for Social Responsibility of the Church of England

The Board was chaired by Bishop H. Montefiori of Birmingham. The Board welcomed the Report. In responding to it the Board would reflect on three factors, the intention of the agent, nature of the act and probable consequences (Board for Social Responsibility 1984).

It was unlikely that a consensus on matters of life and death, for which there is no precise precedent, would appear overnight within the Church of England. However, the Board (1984, p. 6) was conscious of the real need to help involuntary childlessness. But "a genuine desire to provide help ought not to override the need for rigorous and careful ethical thought and judgement".

Discussions of the Report took place under the headings discussed below.

THE BEGINNING OF HUMAN LIFE

The Board accepted the Report's recommendations as expressed in the Report, page 63.

AIH

The Report's recommendation was also accepted though the Board agreed that such a procedure separates procreation from the act of intercourse.

AID

The Board (1984, p. 6) considered page 22 of the Report, concluding:

> The majority of us agreed with the Report that those engaged in AID are, in their own view, involved in a positive affirmation of the family and hence AID may be regarded as an acceptable practice.

But the Board (1984, p. 19) felt that if AID is available the sale of semen should not be gradually phased out as the Report suggests: it should "stop forthwith". However, the Board did welcome the Report's recommendations that a child by AID should be recognized as legitimate and that, at the age of eighteen, the child should have access to information concerning the donor's ethnic origin and possibly some other basic information. The Board (1984, p. 11) also believed that there was an urgent need for research into children born from AID.

IVF

Once again, this technique involves separation of the unitive and procreative functions of marriage which the Board recognized. However, the Board accepted the proposals of the Report.

EGG AND EMBRYO DONATION

The Board supported egg donation. As to embryo donation, it is effected by fertilization *in vitro* by a donated ovum and sperm. Consequently, there are "four" parents. The semen donor, the ovum donor, the social father and social mother. Once again, there is a question of the separation of the acts of marriage and, in addition, there is the introduction of a third (fourth) element into the marriage by egg and embryo donation.

There was theological division in the Board (1984, p. 14) about embryo donation but it was agreed by others on the Board that egg, semen and embryo donation differ only in degree: "However, we are not able (by a small majority) to agree with the recommendation of the Report which favours embryo donation."

SURROGACY

Surrogacy, for mere expedience, was totally unacceptable. The recommendation to make surrogacy illegal in the Report was supported by the Board.

EXPERIMENTATION

The Board (1984, p. 17) contained a range of opinion on scientific research on human embryos but supported by a majority

the recommendation that research, under licence, be permitted on embryos up to fourteen days old and we support the dissenting note which would prevent the creation of embryos specifically for research purposes. We do not believe that there is either the consent or the control available to support the production of embryos for research.

The Board welcomed the recommendation that national licensing authorities be established to regulate research and to control infertility services. It regretted that the Report omitted to consider certain important considerations, such as who is to decide on research priorities and to what extent, and to whom resources are allocated to alleviate infertility. The Board recommends "that the Secretaries of State, to whom the Report is addressed, take steps to see that they are responsibly involved".

The Board supported all the Report's recommendations with the exception of embryo donation and the creation of embryos for research. The Board also believed that the recommendations of the Report should be strengthened in the following way:

1. Legal and financial provision to be made for statutory counselling services, not only during treatment for infertility, but also for couples who have had children by AID or IVF.
2. The sale of semen by donors should not be gradually phased out but should stop forthwith.
3. Research should be carried out on the special needs of children born through AID or IVF technology.

The Board also wished to include two further recommendations:

1. Provision should be made in the constitution of the Licensing Authorities for adequate representation by the Social Services, the legal profession and members of the churches, skilled in moral theology.
2. The Secretary of State concerned should take steps to see that questions concerning accountability of research bodies, in deciding priorities of research and the allocation of resources, are responsibly involved.

CONCLUSION

While the Board concluded that they accepted all the recommendations of the Report, with the exception of embryo donation and the creation of embryos specifically for research, nevertheless, they had one other disagreement, namely that whereas the Report recommended: "A gradual move towards a system where semen donors should be given only their expenses" the Board recommended that it should stop forthwith.

Response of the Church of England

There was grave dissatisfaction with the Report amongst members of the General Synod (*Guardian* 8 December 1984) and a questionnaire was sent to all members. The questionnaire was organised by nine members and supported by the Bishops of Leicester, Norwich and Salisbury. There were 237 replies to the questionnaire which came out overwhelmingly against AID – 84 per cent: 10 per cent disagreed and 6 per cent were uncertain. IVF was thought to be justified for married couples only. This was supported by 84 per cent: 10 per cent disagreed and 6 per cent were uncertain. On embryos, 71 per cent felt they should be regarded as human beings from conception and 81 per cent felt that testing and freezing embryos and their eventual destruction should be forbidden. *The Church Times* (4 January 1985) commented: "The deliberate creation of spare embryos for research was condemned by 90 per cent; 99 per cent opposed the purchase and sale of embryos."

Clearly the Board did not represent the views of those questioned. In fact, those questioned rejected the Board's recommendations that experiments under licence be permitted on embryos up to the fourteenth day. The vote against this was carried in the Synod on 14 February 1985 by 151 to 128 votes. Nevertheless, the General Synod met during the first week of July 1985. On 4 July they narrowly rejected criticism of the Warnock Report. Mr O. R. Johnston, of the Oxford Diocese and Research Director of the pro-life organisation Care Trust, unsuccessfully argued (*Guardian* 5 July) that the Synod should reject the use of third party sperm and ova in human procreation "as wrong in principle and contrary to Christian standards" but the proposals rejection was as close as 195 to 183 manifesting the divisions within the Church of England. The Synod supported as essential a suggestion in the Warnock Report for a national licensing authority to regulate research and control infertility. Again, while the Synod rejected all forms of embryo experimentation in February 1985, it failed to reaffirm this veto in July 1985.

The, then, Conservative Party Chairman, Mr John Gummer, said the Report contained too little about the status of children produced as the result of the new medical developments. Bishop Montefiori claimed that ethical matters could not be decided by a majority vote. The Church had to admit it was divided.

The fact that those questioned were overwhelmingly against the Warnock Report and the findings of the Board can be explained by the fact that less than one half of the members of the Synod replied. So really it was only a partial response. It was not altogether surprising then that the Synod vote on 4 July was more favourable to the Warnock Report. Presumably those that replied to the questionnaire would be the same members that were interest in a pro-life stance and were sufficiently committed to reply. However, when the Synod met at the beginning of July, most of the 550 members would have been present and this would allow for the middle ground and other stances to be represented. Moreover, the vote would also depend on who was actually present when the vote was taken.

In June 1985, a Working Party of the Board published another discussion document for the General Synod entitled *Personal Origins* (Board for Social Responsibility 1985). It was also to be sent to the dioceses for debate, discussion and response. The fact that four members of the Working Party were members of the Board connects this second document with the official report for the Board for Social Responsibility. However, there are essential differences. For example, the official response of the Board favoured limited experimentation under licence up to 14 days, whereas the logic of *Personal Origins* seems to argue for no experimentation at all or that experimentation should be allowed to continue up to 21 to 14 days when the nervous structure of the "body leading to consciousness is being laid down".

The official response of the Board accepted the Warnock proposals by a majority for AID, IVF and egg donation, whereas *Personal Origins* was divided on all three issues (Board for Social Responsibility 1985).

Having consulted the Chairman of the Board for Social Responsibility of the Church of England, it is fair to say that the General Synod changed its mind between the period of the emerging debate about experimentation, 14 February 1985, and the voting on the amendment, 4 July 1985. Hence the General Synod failed to reaffirm its veto on all forms of experimentation and therefore altered its view.

What is quite clear, therefore, is that the Church of England is very divided on these matters and mirrors the division and conflict in Britain as a whole.

The Catholic Response

CARDINAL HUME

On 19 July 1984, Cardinal Hume published a statement on the Warnock Report which, he said, dealt with some basic questions of life and death (Hume 1984). It was crucial that the findings of this Committee, he said, should be subjected to the most rigorous analysis and debate. He claimed that AID, egg donation and semen donation from persons other than husband and wife were unacceptable morally. Recommendations relating to experimentation on embryos conflict with basic principles of Catholic morality. Such practices were more likely to erode family unity than strengthen it. The proposals by the Report to preserve anonymity in these cases, he said, and that such offspring be registered as children of husband and wife adds up to a "mistaken kindness". The public good is "not well served by the systematic falsification of public records for generations to come". The right of the child to have full information about his true heritage should prevail. Nor could the Cardinal accept the proposals on embryo experimentation for the first fourteen days because "from the time of conception there comes into existence a new life and a process of continuous growth begins". He quotes the statement of the Catholic Bishops' Conference of England and Wales (1980): "Each new life is the life not of a potential human being but of a human being with potential."

At the same time Cardinal Hume (1984) agrees

> that there is considerable merit in the Committee's recommendation that statutory authority be set up with real power to regulate and monitor all future services and research in the field of human infertility through legal and ethical safeguards.

He would expect the Churches to be invited to nominate representatives to this body.

THE BISHOPS' JOINT COMMITTEE ON BIOETHICAL ISSUES

This response was issued on 11 December 1984 on behalf of the Catholic Bishops' Conference of England and Wales (1984) and was delivered to the, then, Secretary of State for Social Services (Mr Fowler). The Joint Committee was chaired by Archbishop Winning of Glasgow and comprised of fourteen members who were doctors, lawyers, philosophers, theologians and bishops. Their response contains 54 paragraphs and makes detailed comment on the Report. They welcomed the Secretary of State's invitation to comment and they hoped that the Government

> will be encouraged to act and act soon on the Inquiry's recognition that the embryo of the human species needs the protection of criminal law.

Yet the Inquiry's formal recommendations "afford quite inadequate protection to the human embryo".

Before commenting on Warnock's recommendations, the Joint Committee wished to point to a basic defect which rendered the Report unsafe: "In many respects an unsafe guide for Governments and Parliament". That defect consisted in a compromise of human rights. According to Warnock, the moral question which the Inquiry is addressing involved "not only a calculation of consequences but also sentiments with regard to the nature of the proposed activities themselves". For the Joint Committee, this really was not good enough because a

> principled concern for human rights involves attending not only to a calculation of consequences and to strong sentiments, but also to the rights which each of its members has by virtue of being a human individual.

A just policy demands a legislative framework which will prevent other individuals or groups from exploiting or suppressing the human individual in pursuit of their own calculations or consequences, or their strong sentiments. If moral judgement is reduced to a matter of consequences and sentiments, it makes the recognition of human dignity "a mere matter of sentiment and long-term convenience". The facts, therefore, of human embryonic life, are not allowed their full significance. Consideration of the benefits arising from research "is made to override the early embryo's claim of respect (a respect which should exclude intentional damaging or killing)." On the other hand, according to the response, there is

> the need to allay public anxiety that is considered to require erecting a barrier somewhere, since the very existence of morality in a society depends, according to the Report, on some such containment.

In particular, the Bishops' response mentioned the following:

The Warnock Report totally failed to mention the main points made to it on behalf of the Catholic Bishops.
A. 1.   The human embryo is not a "potential human being" but a human being with potential. [para 13]
2.   Every child has a right, as a matter of justice, to be the true child of a married couple. [para 13]
3.   The "producer-product" mentality involved in IVF is a

reason why separating human generation from marital intercourse is morally flawed. [paras 15–16]

B. IVF and artificial insemination may be legally permitted by the State but only under licence of a new statutory authority as Warnock recommended. [para 18]
But it should not be permitted at all if (as seems to be the case with current practice) the IVF team proposes to engage in some intentional destruction of developing human embryos, or if it involves research which subjects any embryo to risk or destruction. Unauthorized generation or handling of a human embryo should be criminal. [paras 26, 33, 46]

C. The Joint Committee stress that their view that non-destructive IVF practices, within marriage, could be legally permitted in a pluralistic society is not based on approval of IVF or artificial insemination. These practices, in all forms, are open to serious moral and social objections. [paras 18 and 26]

D. Artificial insemination by donor (AID) should not be available on a publicly approved basis or supported by public funds. There should be hard and fast rules to prevent AID for single women or homosexual couples. [paras 18–19, 22–25]

E. Freezing human embryos is an unacceptable practice and should not be licensed or permitted. [paras. 20, 26, 31 and 32]

F. Catholics and many other Christians will in effect be excluded from the proposed statutory authority if its functions include the licensing of freezing or destructive experimentation and similar practices. [para 21]

G. Fertility techniques using donated sperm and/or egg(s) should be rejected. [para 28 and 29]

H. The Warnock Report's recommendation that destructive experimentation be permitted for 14 days after conception is utterly unacceptable. The recommendation that after 14 days embryos used for research should be destroyed is shameful. The reasoning in this part of the Warnock Report contains serious errors, both moral and factual. [paras 34, 36, 38, 47]

I. The practice of generating "spare" embryos is unacceptable. All multiple fertilization is at least questionable. [para 39]

J. All trans-species fertilization is unacceptable. Generation of human embryos in animals should also be banned. [paras 40, 48, 49]

K. Sale and purchase of embryos is abhorrent. [paras 42, 50]

L. The Warnock Inquiry's recommendation about surrogacy should be accepted. But the Inquiry's reasoning about this is weak. [paras 51, 52]

M. The most urgent need is for specific legislation to give the protection of the criminal law to the human embryo, who is threatened in many ways by current practice. [paras 46 and 54]

Later, the Bishops reflected again on the question of IVF at their Low Week meeting. They did not wish to come to a conclusion about the morality of the theoretical "simple" or "straightforward" case in which one ovum of the wife is fertilized by the husband's sperm and then replaced. In other words, they left it an open question where morality was concerned (*The Tablet* 20 April 1985).

The Methodist Response

The Division for Social Responsibility of the Methodist Church (1983) was given the responsibility of submitting evidence to the Warnock Inquiry. The Division reminded the Warnock Committee that the Secretary of the Methodist Conference, Dr K. G. Greet, had already directed the attention of the Inquiry to *Choices in Childlessness*, the Report of the Working Party under the auspices of the Free Church Federal Council and the British Council of Churches. The members of the Division wished to associate themselves with *Choices in Childlessness* particularly as two of their group were also members of that Working Party.

The Division for Social Responsibility also drew attention to two basic concerns. First is a reverence for human life as man is a creation of God, made in the Divine Image, a point already made in the Methodist statement on abortion (1976). The second point the Division wished to emphasize was the concern for family life and stability.

Turning to some of the issues directly within the scope of the Warnock Inquiry, the Division wished to share the hesitations expressed in *Choices in Childlessness*. For many Christians, AID does raise serious moral issues, especially for those who hold that the unitive and procreative processes in intercourse ought not to be separated. While other Christians may not hold that view of the marital relationship, the Division was disturbed by the adulterous implications of AID. However, the Division did also believe that other Christians see no difference between AID and adoption.

IVF

In principle this method is therapeutic and does not raise any serious ethical or moral problems but the Report does not state that it should be limited to the husband and wife and thereby exclude a third party, although this is probably implied because it refers to AIH in the same paragraph. (Warnock Report 1984, pp. 29ff; also p. 10.)

Surrogate motherhood and womb leasing was rejected by the Division for Social Responsibility whose members made the following points.

They welcomed the Warnock Committee's Report and on two major points. Reverence for human life, affirming the Christian belief that man is a creature of God, made in the Divine Image. The foetus is undoubtedly part of the continuing human existence "but the Christian will wish to study further the extent to which the foetus is a person".

They welcomed the Committee's recognition of reverence for all human life and that the embryo of the human species should be afforded some protection in law, but they were divided in their judgement, like the Warnock Committee, on the recommendation

> that some research on human *in vitro* embryos should be permitted under licence. The majority are prepared to support the recommendation but a minority agrees with the Expression of Dissent on pages 90 and 91 [of the Warnock Report].

The division of opinion, the response noted, was also found in the response of the Board for Social Responsibility of the Church of England.

The second concentration was on family life and its stability. They recognized the positive contribution that IVF has made to childless couples.

> We support the Committee's recommendation that "legislation be introduced to render criminal the creation of the operation in the United Kingdom of Agencies whose purposes include the recruitment of women for surrogate pregnancy".

This is in harmony with the decision of the Methodist Conference in July 1983. They urged that Recommendation 19 of the Warnock Report be strengthened to include a reference for counsellors to have appropriate training and experience. As for AID, they strongly supported the statement to maintain the absolute anonymity of the donor and assumed that this includes the anonymity of the recipient as far as the donor is concerned: "If this assumption is not correct, then it needs to be included in the Recommendations at an appropriate point."

As to storage and disposal of embryos "we urge that Recommendation 30 be amended to include consultation with the couples concerned since this is referred to in Para. 10.8." They referred to the Recommendations of Warnock, 31, 32 and 33 and recommended that the words "disposal"and "dispose" be replaced by "destruction" and "destroy".

In brief, the Division for Social Responsibility generally supported the findings of the Warnock Committee. In 1985 the *Methodist Church Press* (3 July) released a statement:

> The Methodist Conference in Birmingham today, 3 July, passed a resolution supporting the Warnock Committee's Recommendation that "legislation be introduced to render criminal the creation of the operation in the United Kingdom of Agencies whose purposes include the recruitment of women for surrogate pregnancy".
>
> The decision, based on a Report from the Church's Division for Social Responsibility, reiterates the Church's concern for family life. It recognizes the positive contribution that IVF has made to the life of many childless couples, but also states that not every scientific possibility necessarily enhances family life.

Response of the Board for Social Responsibility of the Church of Scotland

The Board (1985, p. 13) stressed at the outset its deep concern over the failure on the part of the Warnock Committee to consider moral questions relating to the status of human life "from which indeed ethical questions concerning the treatment of human tissue arise". They considered it "invidious to elevate the interests of knowledge and technique over consideration of the subject matter", even though the cause was worthy, namely the relief of infertility.

The Board felt the Committee confined itself to the practical implications of scientific advance while no consideration was given to the morality of the acts.

It was clearly stated by the Board (1985, p. 31) that the human embryo is a human being from the first moment of fertilization, and it has the right to be protected and treated as such. Indeed there was serious ambiguity about an argument from the premise that the embryo is "potentially human", for the potentiality concerned is not that of becoming something else but of becoming what it essentially is.

The Report itself was seen as irrelevant in that it failed to confront the moral issues arising from science and society in these matters. The elevation of the requirements of infertility above concern for the welfare of human embryos was an Utilitarian perspective and treats newly created life as a means to an end. Indeed, according to the Board, Utilitarian criteria dominated the Report and the result was that the embryo's inherent rights and claims at all stages of its existence were discounted in favour of the ends, i.e. "the public good". This, of course, was to neglect the position indicated by the World Medical Association in its Declaration of Helsinki in 1964 and 1975:

> In research on man, the interests of science and society should never take precedence over considerations related to the wellbeing of the subject.

The Board reaffirmed its belief in marriage as the relationship in which human sexuality may be fulfilled. Methods of overcoming childlessness should, therefore, be directed only to helping married couples.

As to AIH, there was no objection to fertilization between

husband and wife through AIH when there is difficulty in the normal way, but it objected strongly to AID because it could not support the unwarranted intrusion of a third party.

When it came to the registration of AID children, the Board saw serious legal anomalies. But it was not clear on how to overcome the anonymity of the donor in regard to the right of the child to know its origins. It freely admitted that changing the law so as to permit the husband to be the registered father does not remove the implicit deceit which is currently present in registration.

As to IVF, it has no moral objection to the technique when used within marriage, but if super-ovulation is used, the embryo should be transferred to the mother's uterus, otherwise questions immediately arise concerning the deliberate creation of new life without hope of its potential being realized.

It was the Board's view that egg donation and embryo donation raise similar moral problems in regard to marriage as AID, and therefore, rejected these procedures. It also rejected the production of spare embryos or research on embryos within any time period. The Board would here call a halt on all experimentation and therefore lent its support to Expression of Dissent "B" in the Warnock Report. It would support immediately a moratorium on "all experimental works which are not part of treatment designed to improve the life prognosis and benefit to each and every individual human embryo so exposed".

As to storage of embryos, it should be undertaken only to facilitate conception. But then the Board (1985, p. 15) makes the curious statement:

> Embryos should be destroyed if the couples indicate that they have no wish for additional children. Embryos should be destroyed when the marriage relationship ends for any reason or where there is no agreement between the couple for their use.

This seems to contradict what the Board has already said about the status of the human embryo. If it is a human being, then how can it be destroyed?

As to surrogacy, the Board wished to assert that it is demeaning to both mother and child and that it should be made illegal.

The Response of the Baptist Church

The Baptist Church made its submissions and responses like the others (Baptist Union 1985). It considered the Report clear and well-written and felt Parliament should legislate to provide further controls in the area of human fertilization techniques and embryology. It regretted that the Report devoted so little space in examining the moral principles which lie behind the proposals. While granting the need for medical treatment when available for infertility, it raises the question of priorities and costs within health care and within the budget of the NHS.

It is of interest that the Baptist submission and response are practically identical with the Church of Scotland and the Catholic Church, with one or two modifications. The Baptists do not accept AID, IVF where a third person is involved, surrogacy, embryo experimentation and trans-species fertliza-tion. Respect was due to the embryo as a potential person and that claim outweighted all other considerations. It will be remembered that this was the view supported by the Expression of Dissent "B". As to spare embryos, it also agreed with the Expression of Dissent "B", that they should be allowed to die without being the subject of experimentation. This Church refers to the principle of "the lesser of two evils", and applies this principle to the life of the embryo. It can be allowed to die "in a way that we would not find tolerable in the case of persons, but because it is a potential person, we must still feel a sense of tragedy ..."

In discussing AID, the Baptist Church manifests its concern about the child who is deprived of the right to know the identity of its parents which "is built into the process". It is not satisfied with the Report's suggestion that the child should simply have the right to know the donor's ethnic origin and genetic health.

Finally, because of the exclusiveness of the principle of "one flesh" in Christian marriage, the Baptist Church, while allowing AIH, would reject AID and IVF when not confined to both parties within the marriage.

Analysis of the Churches and Religious Bodies

All the mainline Churches and religious bodies rejected surrogacy.

As to the other issues, there is a striking resemblance between the response of the Jews, Catholics, Baptists and Church of Scotland, whereas the Methodists and Church of England had very interesting similarities. The former group rejected AID as an intrusion into the marriage covenant. The Jewish, Catholic and Baptist Churches are very much alike in their concern about the child's right to know his origins. The Church of England does not spell out its concern about this point and anonymity, but rather indicates there is an "implicit deceit" involved in Warnock's recommendations that the husband should be registered as the father of the child and legalized accordingly.

The Jews, Catholics, Baptists and Church of Scotland would only accept IVF within legalized marriage. They also agree that no embryo should be brought into being purely for research, but the Catholic position rejects, as well, the creation of spare embryos unless they are intended for implantation:

> IVF being limited to procedures carried out with the settled intention of transferring in each and every case to the mother's womb, unimpaired and at all times and manner most appropriate in the interests of that embryo's future unimpaired development.

Whereas the Baptist position would refer to the lesser of two evils – the spare embryo can be allowed to die. The Church of Scotland is less clear in this regard and it does not explicitly deal with this problem, except to say that it would lend its support to Expression of Dissent "B", which, of course, condones allowing spare embryos to die if they are not implanted. The situation is further complicated when the same Church speaks of "destruction" of spare embryos.

The Church of England was divided on the main issues and reflected the decisions and conflicts in society as a whole. The Methodist Church, while manifesting a division of opinion, generally supported Warnock. One possible reason for these differences is the different traditions of the churches in spite of their Biblical background. In the case of abortion, for example, Protestant thinking allows for a variety of opinion and a readiness to admit exceptions for different indications. (McDonagh 1972, p. 134; Gill 1975; Gill 1977, pp. 52ff; Potts 1977, p. 7; Williams 1979, p. 10; Batchelow 1982, pp. 41ff). Indeed there are sound reasons put forward by some writers indicating that theology and society interact and that sometimes theology is deeply influenced by public opinion and social conditions, as in the shift from pacifism in the early Church to the justification of war in certain circumstances. A shift in public opinion is indicated in the West towards more liberalized abortion legislation. This is evident, for example, in the Church of England, and indeed other non-Roman Catholic Churches in the West, from a situation at the beginning of the century in which its official response to abortion would have differed but little from that of the Roman Catholic Church. Nevertheless, in 1965, it produced a report supporting limited abortion reform (Gill 1977, pp. 52–5). As the existing legislation prohibiting abortion changed throughout Europe and the United States, other examples of *ex post facto* theological justification and discernible shifts can be found in many non-Roman Catholic Churches. For example, in 1986, the Church of Scotland abandoned its strong anti-abortion stand (*Guardian* 21 May). It is, therefore, difficult to avoid the conclusion that there are discernible social determinants in the response to abortion. This is not to deny that, in some instances, religious affiliation may remain an important variable, shaping peoples' attitudes to abortion, but it does not follow that these attitudes will determine their actual decision and behaviour where abortion is concerned. This also seems to be demonstrated by the number of girls that come from Ireland and Spain to England annually to obtain an abortion, which is morally unacceptable to their Catholic belief – a point also demonstrated in the South American situation and in Italy where, in the case of the latter, it is reported (*The Universe* 19 October 1984) that there are 405 abortions for every 1,000 live births.

The Response of Life

In its submissions (*Life* 1983) to Warnock, the main concern of this organization was what the Inquiry said "about *in vitro* fertilization and the treatment of embryos produced thereby". *Life* appreciated the complexity of the issues and accepted that infertility could be distressful. Therefore, it was only right that human suffering should be relieved by every legitimate means: "Nevertheless we reject the Committee's central proposals."

In particular, the objection is to the recommendations that *in vitro* fertility treatment should be generally available, regardless of whose eggs and whose sperm are used. *Life* could not accept the approval of such practices as selecting "the best" embryos for transfer to the mother and throwing away or freezing the "spares". Nor could it accept the recommendation that human embryos should be used for research, testing drugs or any other experimentation of that kind.

The Report proposes the creation of second-class human beings who are "worthy of only some protection in law". This is as discriminatory as the Abortion Act 1967. *Life* claims that the Report is "an intellectually shallow and shoddy piece of work" and it "fudges major issues of moral principle".

A fundamental weakness of the Report, according to *Life* (1984), is an inadequate understanding of fertilization. It fails to take into account the "blueprint" of new human life with all its complexity "thus though it is true that human ova and sperm and embryos are alive, they are not all alive in the same way".

Throughout, the Report speaks of "infertility treatment" but always refer only to artificial fertilization techniques. No account is taken of the new methods like micro surgery. This ignores, according to *Life*, to list a "fundamental" argument against AID and IVF that both are a form of "making" children and thus morally unacceptable. Children are not things to be "produced in the lab".

In authentic parenthood, the child is a partner in the common life expressed in the procreative act of married union. To say, as the Report does, that there is a body of opinion which holds that it is wrong to interfere with nature or what is perceived to be the Will of God, is a hopeless understatement of the case.

It is absurd, *Life* claims, to go straight to deciding, how anything or anyone should be treated before you have found out "what and who it is that you are treating" and this is a basic error because the Report does precisely this regarding the embryo. Moreover "potential" and "opportunity" are confounded. What has been dismissed as a collection of cells, in fact, does have the potential for development but will not have the opportunity to develop if it is not transferred to a "human uterine environment, i.e. not implanted".

We are left to presume, *Life* adds, that the embryo is a "sort of human being".

The Report offers no argument but merely follows the more generally held position. *Life* also believed that the Report placed itself in an intellectually indefensible position by saying that once fertilization has occurred, there is no particular point in the process more important than another and there is "no single identifiable stage" which can have any scientific justification as the choice for a cut-off point. Yet, and in spite of this opinion, it chooses the fourteenth day as the cut-off point. It does so only to allay public anxiety and here *Life* refers to paragraph 11.19 of the Report. In my opinion this is hardly the complete picture because the Report did say that the fourteenth day was appropriate because then the primitive streak would have occurred and the conceptus would have stabilized with the beginning of the *individual* development. All the same, *Life* continues to assert that the Report's description is contradictory because the primitive streak "neither begins or ends anything". In fact it is just the biologically "identifiable stage of development".

Again it must be remembered that the Report held initially that fertilization was the only stage that could claim to be significant in the process. The primitive streak is jut one of the "myriad" events which take place in the astonishingly complicated first few weeks of human life. The primitive streak can happen as early as day one. The fourteenth day was simply the last time it *could* happen.

POTENTIAL LIFE

Life criticizes the Report because it lists as an argument against embryo research that every embryo "has a potential for life".

This is an understatement. The fact is, says *Life*, that the embryo is not merely a potential human being but already an actual one. Therefore, on this reasoning, research on embryos violates human dignity and human rights.

SURROGACY

Life is interested by the fact that in the middle of saying "yes", to almost everything, the Report suddenly becomes very outspoken about surrogate motherhood. The Report seems to have no objection in principle to the idea of a woman carrying a child for another, whether the egg is her own, the commissioning mother's or donated by someone else.

Yet the Report, according to *Life*, suddenly announces that surrogacy, for convenience alone "is totally and ethically unacceptable". *Life* challenges the Report as to why this should be. The objection of the Report seems to be connected with the danger of adults being exploited but there is no consideration given to the intrinsic nature of the act itself or the effect surrogacy could have on "parent-child" relations. In fact, the Report seems to be distracted by exploitation and the mention of money: "If money changes hands, there will surely be something wrong."

Hence the Report does deal seriously with surrogacy itself. It is strange, according to *Life*, that the Report is so uncompromising on this one occasion when on most other issues, it has been permissive, uncertain and confused.

Response of the Medical Research Council

In general, the Medical Research Council (MRC) endorsed the Report. In formulating its response, the MRC (1985) "had been aware of the need to strike a balance between the concerns of the public at large, on the one hand, and the benefits of research, and the protection of the scientists and clinicians engaged in it, on the other".

The MRC welcomed the opportunity to emphasize the reasons for carrying on research and its "potential benefits". It lists the benefits into three classes:

1. Treatment of infertility.
2. Prevention of congenital diseases.
3. The development of a more effective contraceptive.

It admitted the success rate of IVF "is still very low..."

Although noting the division of opinion in the Warnock Report on creating embryos for research, the MRC concluded, however, that it was necessary and believed that it was essential to carry out work on embryos because of what the MRC believed would be the better understanding of how disorders develop and the metabolism and nutritional requirement of the human embryo "thus to answer to some questions relating to human problems, it is essential to carry out work on human embryos".

The MRC felt the Warnock Report had left some important issues unresolved and advised that this should be rectified before legislation. This applies particularly to the definition of "research".

Another defect was that the embryo is not defined. Then the MRC makes the curious remark "that it would welcome confirmation of their understanding that this refers to a viable conceptus developed from a fertilized egg and not tissue or cell cultures of human origin ..."

This is not easily understood in view of the MRC's unqualified desire to create embryos specifically for research, which brings us to that point which will not go away, namely if, by the MRC's own words, "a viable conceptus" is different from tissue or cell cultures of human origin, how can one justify deliberately creating them for experimentation?

Nor does the MRC feel that the fourteen day limit for embryo experimentation was a useful one. They suggested, because of variation in embryonic development, there are advantages in specifying the limit "in terms of stage of development rather than days after fertilization".

Finally, in the light of a pilot study on the feasibility of follow-up studies of children conceived by IVF, the MRC will shortly be proposing a more extensive study programme.

It is extraodinary that the MRC, containing so many medical experts, could produce a document of this kind. No reference is made whatever to the equally eminent experts in the medical field, who hold contrary views in this very complicated subject of embryo experimentation and research, and who believe explicitly that embryo experimentation is quite unnecessary. However, the recommendation for follow-up studies on IVF children is sound and sensible.

The Powell Bill

Mr Enoch Powell's private members' bill was entitled the Unborn Children (Protection Bill). It had its first reading on 6 December 1984 and, on 15 February 1985, was presented before the two Houses of Parliament for its second reading. It was designed to prohibit creation of embryos for purposes of experimentation. The Bill would make it a crime for anyone to produce an embryo *in vitro*, unless it were done for the sole purpose of enabling a particular woman to bear a child. It makes it an offence to have in possession an embryo except with the authority of the Secretary of State, which is to be given expressly for the above purpose and no other. In other words, the Bill would allow IVF solely for infertility treatment. It forbids the production of human embryos specifically for research for experimentation and it forbids the use of "spare" embryos for research which is independent of the infertility treatment for which they would be produced.

Consequently, it would not restrict existing techniques of infertility treatment nor would it require that abnormal embryos be returned to the womb.

After winning a majority of 238 to 66 at the second reading, it passed through its Committee stage at a speed which exceeded all expectation. This was partly due to Mr Powell's skill – he noticed a vacancy in another standing committee's agenda and was able to transfer his bill to it, thereby "leap-frogging" the queue of previous private members' bills which were awaiting the Committee stage. In the meantime, the BBC TV programme "Panorama" was shown on 15 April which was followed by an article in *The Listener* (18 April). Both claimed that the Bill would "stop dead" further embryo research to prevent congenital handicaps – a point (as we have seen in Chapter II) which is rejected by the scientists. Not surprisingly, this was challenged later in *The Listener* (9 May).

Needless to say, the Bill had relentless opposition both inside and outside the Committee Room. At the Report stage, the Speaker allowed a vote on the first group of amendments but the opponents claimed that sufficient debating time had not been given. This led to a fracas in the House and the Speaker's chair was broken. The vote was 152 for the first group of amendments and that, of course, was carried by 152 to 82. However, in spite of the opposition, some Members of Parliament tabled an Early Day Motion asking the Government to allow extra time to enable the Bill to reach the statute book.

It can be said that the Powell Bill certainly addressed itself to the most controversial matter in the Warnock Report. It was based on the clear moral position that human beings are never to be treated by another instrumentally; their life is to be respected and protected for their own sake and that life, it claims, begins at conception. It would argue from the position that manipulation of human embryos is licit only if directed to the continued life of the true development of the embryo. Powell, therefore, would contend that to do otherwise is a betrayal of humanity.

However, it should be said here that in the particular situation of Britain, it would be curious to translate these concepts into public law, which already contains provisions running in a counter-direction – an aspect which was developed by a leader in *The Times* (7 June):

> The scruples here displayed about the treatment of an embryo are in painful contrast with the treatment the Abortion Law permits of the maturer foetus. What is more, consistency would extend these scruples to the prohibition of two widely accepted forms of so-called contraception, the intra-uterine coil and the post-coital pill, which operate to prevent implantation of fertilized ova (embryos) in the womb.

So the Bill would be presenting a challenge to law and practice. Its supporters point to the medical experts, who claim that there is little, if any, value in embryo research. Such knowledge could be obtained from experiments which exclude the human embryo. However, the opponents of the Bill claim the opposite.

In spite of the fact that the Bill was talked out, which is a common fate of private members' bills, and sent to the back of the queue where it looked as good as dead, it came to life again with the help of Mr Bowden, MP, who had been fortunate in the ballot for the other class of private members' business. He was awarded top slot for the motion of his choice. He brought Mr Powell's bill back before the House for its remaining stages which would allow the sitting to go through the Friday night, Saturday and Sunday if it took that long. However, according to *The Times* leader, wits were pitted against it in the person of Mr Michael Foot and others, who deliberately prevented the motion from getting its timely vote by keeping up points of order and other procedural devices so as to deny the motion adequate time for debate – a procedure which could hardly be described as moral. Dennis Skinner played a crucial part in preventing the debate on the motion and, consequently, it failed.

It was interesting to read an article by Mary Warnock (*The Times* 30 May 1985) condemning moral absolutism, and also letters in the *Guardian* (7 June) from Professor Stuart

Campbell of Kings College and in *The Times* (30 May) from Dr J. M. McLean of the University of Manchester, both stressing clearly the opposing viewpoints regarding embryo experimentation. In answer to Warnock, Cardinal Hume wrote a defence of moral absolutes in *The Times* (6 June).

The Government, in the meantime, has been reiterating its intention to introduce, at some future date, comprehensive legislation on artificial human fertility based on the Warnock Report. Yet it was curious to find Lady Warnock, herself, expressing opinions without that impartiality she manifested while the Committee was sitting. It would not be surprising then if some members of that Committee regarded that article as a stepping-stone outside her correct role. In the face of this it should be remembered that only nine of the Report's sixteen members approved of the creation of embryos for research. What is undeniable is that the swell of opinion in the House of Commons behind the Powell Bill has its counterpart in the country at large. There is no ground, then, for believing that such matters of life and death are better left to the experts than to the people.

On 3 July, the Christian Socialist Movement (CSM) released a copy of a letter to Kenneth Clarke, the Minister of State (Health), advising that a resolution was passed by its Executive Committee at its meeting in London, 29 June 1985 stating

> that CSM opposes the Enoch Powell Embryo Research Bill which has been hastily drafted without adequate public debate. Instead we propose a Government sponsored Bill which will allow research to continue to help prevent handicaps and promote fertility in infertile women. We deplore the pressure put on MPs by certain Christian bodies purporting to "speak for all Christians". My Committee would be interested to know whether the Government has in mind any legislation along these lines.

This letter was signed by the Secretary of the CSM.

The Marxist Factor

In an article published in *Marxism Today* (March 1985), the Marxists referred to what they consider another anomaly in the

Warnock Report, namely the acceptance of male donation in the form of AID and the rejection of female donation in the form of surrogacy. This, they claimed, had sexist overtones.

Conclusion

The questions that were really put to Mary Warnock were: How do you define a "full human being?"; and, secondly, "Does a human embryo fit that description?"

In fact, the questions were not really answered in her reply because she never faced the proper questions about man's humanity. We are human because God has made us in His image therefore man's religious and eschatological dimension cannot be omitted.

It can readily be agreed that religion should not be the total basis for legislation. All the same, one cannot ignore man's religious dimension – the very point where he differs from the rest of creation. To do otherwise would be another form of reductionism which reduces man to matter and neglects his spiritual and eschatological dimension which makes him an *Imago Dei*.

Nor does Warnock's argument, based on public feelings, rest easily with the attempt to discover a "common morality" or an "honourable compromise". It would be interesting to ascertain how she would extend the arguments of public feeling to the anxieties that have been demonstrated in the response to the Report, from the press debates, right across the two Houses of Parliament, not to mention the many signatories that support the Powell Bill. How, for example, would she allay the serious disquiet to which she witnessed, not only in the evidence submitted (Warnock Report 1984, para 5) to the Inquiry, but also the divisions on this question of experimentation, within the membership of her own Committee?

Perhaps it is not fanciful to suggest that this division reflected the deep concern in society itself which the Inquiry hoped to satisfy. Would it not have been fairer, therefore, if the Warnock Committee recommended to the Secretary of State a moratorium on all embryo experimentation pending thorough national and Parliamentary consideration of the question?

Warnock seeks "a common morality" as she terms it. It can be argued, of course, that legislation does not, nor is it intended to, merely reflect the mores of society. It should have an educative function, especially in the area of human rights, equality and social morality. This is not an easy task in a pluralistic society which produces its own dilemmas, not least, in finding compromises between individual viewpoints without jeopardizing the essential rights of minorities and individuals, or introducing disastrous consequences for the wellbeing of society itself.

As to the Churches and Christian bodies, there were interesting similarities between the Jews, Catholic Church, Baptists and Church of Scotland. The Church of England was divided on the main issues and reflected the differences in society. The Methodists generally supported Warnock.

PART II

A Comparison with the East: the USSR, Poland and East Germany

CHAPTER V

Life, Human Life and Marxist Thinking

(This, and the following, chapter is based largely on original Soviet sources and on correspondence and discussions with some Soviet academics and scientific experts in the leading institutes and acadamies in the USSR. The same applies in Chapters VII and VIII where, again, sources and individuals from the countries concerned have been consulted. Wherever possible translations and location of sources have been given in the Bibliography on their first appearance.)

Before examining the various approaches to bio-medical problems in Eastern-bloc countries regarding the reproduction revolution and embryo experimentation, it is useful to reflect on the Marxist approach to ethics as well as their concept of life and indeed human life in particular. It will be important to discover if the Marxist-Leninist attitude caters for an essential distinction between man and the rest of creation and, if so, the reasons for making that distinction.

In the USSR, officially at any rate, religion, mysticism and dualism, are not acceptable. Marxist-Leninism, a materialistic doctrine, is the standard of measurement. Yet many Soviet writers contend that man cannot be reduced to his biological and physical processes. To do so would be considered "reductionist" and "vulgarly materialistic" which ignores man's "social essence" (Graham 1980, p. 231; 1981, p. 151). It is stressed that Soviet dialectical materialism allows for "levels of being" with different principles governing the physical, biological and social levels. Nevertheless, it is difficult to find any definition of the social level or man's "social essence".

The Soviet philosopher, Ivan Frolov (1983, pp. 75–92), wrote that dialectical materialism allowed for the physio-chemical element in man which, at the same time, was not the full explanation. In a letter (August 1984) to me Professor Loren Graham states that:

> The whole question of the Soviet attitude towards a fertilized ovum touches closely on the Soviet debates on the relationship of the biological to the social on which there is a wide difference of opinion ...

Having reflected on some of Frolov's works (he writes in both Russian and English), it seemed to me that a new understanding was given to some of the Marxist thinking. I suggested to him in correspondence that in his writings there was no precise definition of man, humanity, progress and development. Furthermore, I indicated that his writings about concepts such as *personality* and man's *biological process* were ambiguous. In a word, I asked if there was a difference in kind rather than degree between man and the rest of creation. Frolov had quoted I. I. Schmalhusen as describing that "highly developed individuality is that form of it which is characterized by the highest activity" but nowhere is man's "highest activity" defined. This point I put to Frolov endeavouring to discern whether he would agree that "highest activity" was synonymous with intellectual and spiritual ability, which is attributed to man in some Western thinking. It could then be argued that this "highest activity" is the mind which interacts with the other human processes. In some Western thinking it has been stated that there is considerable evidence for mind–brain correlation as distinct from mind–brain identity. Our mental states are known by us directly while our brain states are known to us, on evidence (Hick 1976, p. 114). Here, then, there is a case of a faculty that can perceive the universal and the abstract which seems itself to be abstract and immaterial and which, I would argue, is different in kind, rather than degree, from the rest of man's composition. In my opinion, mind and brain are independent realities of basically different kinds, each of which, nevertheless, can causally affect the other. Some thinkers in the

West, and many of the theologians down through the Middle Ages and even back to the Fathers, would argue that this reality which we call the mind and some describe as the soul is capable of surviving death. Hence Aquinas (*Summa Theologica*, Pars Prima, Q75 a6 and a102): "The human soul which we regard as an intellective principle must, of necessity, be incorruptible". Furthermore, the experience and insights of the major religions all contribute to the claim that man is eschatological, that is to say, that man is partly spirit with immortal longings, made in the image of God and destined for eternal life. He is related to the future and the events of the future are the decisive guiding principle of the present. Karl Rahner (1966, p. 135) observed:

> Indeed Christianity declares that with the Incarnation of the Eternal Word in Jesus Christ, the last stage has already begun, that the future has already been decided as to its final scene, and content, and that now it only requires that what is already and remains to be revealed. Christianity no longer knows any ultimately open salvation-history but decrees that – since the coming of Jesus Christ, who is today, yesterday and all eternity – the end of the ages is really already present and that we live, therefore, in the last stages, in the fullness of time.

Therefore, bio-medicine and particularly human genetics, which require more power and more choice, require more wisdom if they are to add up to more humanity and thereby give added strength to the dignity of man. It is my contention that anything less would be unworthy of man's true nature.

Yet one of the most tantalizing problems about Soviet writing, and indeed all Marxist writing, is its ambiguity in the use of words. In his writings on immortality, Frolov describes it as "the creative activity" that remains after death – presumably of the individual. I suggested to him that if there were no survival after death, it would be difficult to claim that there was a fundamental difference between the biological processes and man's creative activity – all of which would cease at death. Unless then, we can claim that one's "social essence" is fundamentally different in kind from the rest of his processes, biological and otherwise, and that this "social essence" is capable of surviving death, it is hard to ascertain why Soviet thinkers can sustain their objection against reductionism which they say is "vulgarly materialistic". On the other hand, if the individual does survive in his creative activity, which is a reality in its own rights, either in his conscious-self, or in his person, or in his risen life, or with the mind or soul as it is called in the West, then, at least, common ground with Soviet thinking has been discovered and while technology and human genetics of themselves cannot improve the human condition, both sides could, nevertheless, claim logically that, because of man's higher nature, science must be guided by constant analysis which entails an adequate view of man in his totality. This, however, would go beyond the Soviet rules, namely, that science must not be subjected to ethical or religious interpretations.

Soviet Concepts

The Soviet concept of life, and in particular human life, means that the situation of bio-medical questions in the USSR is itself complicated by ambiguity; as we have seen, there is difficulty in finding a clear and adequate definition of *homo sapiens*. It would follow from this that there is even greater difficulty in describing the moral status of the fertilized ovum. Graham makes the point that Soviet Marxists usually define a *person* as an individual who has, or is capable of having, social relations and in this there is a likeness to some schools of thought in the West (Graham 1980, p. 220). It would be unfair to suggest that only in the USSR is there ambiguity of expression. In fact, the debate on *in vitro* fertilization, the moment of death and human genetics is complicated by a lack of clarity which is indicated by the contrary statements that are connected with the debate itself. (cf. The Warnock Committee. It has been remarked by more than one commentator that it is curious for a society which is increasingly tolerant of abortion in advanced stages of pregnancy to get so involved in a debate which is at pains to distinguish nicely between the very early stages of human existence. cf. Also what has already been written on the nature of personhood in Chapter I.)

It is true that the approach to values and religion is officially non-existent in the USSR, but much of the Marxist thinking that prevails there is already dominating our thought through secularisation here in the West.

Consequently, it is difficult, in this thinking, to perceive why some forms of human genetics are said to reduce man to the animal level. If humanity does not differ essentially from the animal species, how can it be reduced and why concern oneself with social mores, the sanctity of the family, or even the uniqueness of man? Marxism by definition is totally materialistic and some would say there is no room for an essential distinction between the herd, the flock and the human community. Nevertheless, the Marxist could reply that this would not be a fair comment as they do take into account language and history. Yet the senior geneticist and member of the USSR's Academy of Science, N. P. Dubinin (1968, p. 68) believed in the qualitative gap between man and the other animals:

> In research on human genetics the main task is to realize that the human race during its development excludes itself from the evolution of other animals ... Now social factors only, class struggle, industrial, cultural and scientific progress determine human evolution, anthropogenesis is completed and ended by the appearance of consciousness. Now social factors are primary and biological factors secondary.

Again, Frolov maintains that man is the most unique and amazing being "the most striking creation of nature and history". Philistinism, he says, becomes notoriously widespread when man's "spiritual" needs are neglected. He proceeds to claim that genetic engineering which ignores the significance of man's "social" factors, minimizes man and caters merely for the biological (Frolov 1976, pp. 14–16).

Dr Zhores Medvedev (1979, p. 225) rightly suggested that Dubinin was recognizing the human race as a "qualitatively different, new and final stage of animal evolution". However, Dubinin develops these ideas and the fact that he made this distinction is probably the reason why he objected to some forms of human genetics, claiming that they reduced humans to the level of animals. However, it would appear that Dubinin's view did not receive much support and it is interesting to read that Medvedev (1979, p. 226) states that Frolov organized a "round table discussion" sponsored by the Advisory Research Council on the problems of philosophy of nature at the Presidium of the Academy of Sciences. The discussion was published in the Soviet magazine *Voprosy filosfii* (1972).

Later, Dubinin attacked the prominent American zoologist and population geneticist Ernst Mayr. Dubinin believed that Mayr's views on human life, because of his stance and what he had written, could lead to racialism. Mayr did not ignore the social aspects of human personality

> but he considered all characteristics and qualities of individuals to be the result of the interaction of genotype and environmental and social influences. (Medvedev 1979, p. 228.)

From all this it would appear to me that Dubinin, at least, seemed to identify man's social element with consciousness-intellectual/spiritual activity which makes man *homo sapiens*. This thinking is similar to Frolov and Vygotsky and is very clearly evident in later work published by Dubinin (1977, pp. 106–9) when he says:

> It is obvious that consciousness – the supreme form of reflection of objective reality is characteristic of only man – developed through the process of peoples' social and productive activity and thus may have been indissolubly connected with the origin of language.

After the distinction between living and non-living matter, Dubinin claims that consciousness came next and although "brains are present in animals as well, they do not possess consciousness". Like Frolov, Dubinin uses words such as "personality", "intellect" and "spiritual" and classes them as proper to man alone. These factors can only be explained by man's social status, who is qualitatively different from the animals. Indeed Medvedev (1979, p. 229) comments on Dubinin's writing: "The ideas about the intellectual (or spiritual) aspects of human life became rather mystical." In any case, this is probably the reason why Dubinin, who feared human genetics, did much to restrict research in that field. Work in this area, he says, should certainly be controlled. However, he does not say what kind of control should be used (Dubinin and Gorodetskii 1978, pp. 67–74).

It is worth saying something here about the prominent Soviet bio-chemist who also underlines the social element in man and who deals with different levels of being. Professor A. I. Oparin (1968) seems to assume that living matter evolved from non-living matter, and human beings with their social element, emerged from lower forms of life. He does not give a satisfactory explanation as to how this could happen. There is a lack of precision in his description. Indeed he is quite adamant that the origin of human life can only be correctly understood in the context of dialectical materialism. There is nothing, of course, in his philosophy that requires an essential distinction between living and non-living matter. For him, this can be left an open question. However, in my opinion, matter is contingent and has not a sufficient explanation within itself for its existence whether it be viewed in time or eternity – a point that had been studied by the scholastics as well as Aquinas himself (*Summa Theologica*, Pars Prima, Q46 a1 and 2. To me it seems more reasonable to claim that whether one supports the "big bang" or "steady state" theory of creation, the Universe is dependent for its existence on a causality outside itself, namely the Will of God. Nevertheless, Thomas Aquinas held that it cannot be demonstrated by reason, that the world had a beginning. He quotes Augustine and indicates that a thing may have no beginning or end in time and yet be created. Hick (1983, p. 109) clearly outlines the question of eternity of matter when he states that "the religious notion of creation is neither confirmed nor in conflict with theories and discoveries in scientific cosmology."

As with living and non-living matter, Oparin gives no explanation as to the coming of *homo sapiens*. To say that man is distinct because of his social element leaves the situation unexplained and fails to clarify what it is in man that explains his humanity. Yet he underlines that he is not a mechanistic theorist who reduces all phenomena to "physical and chemical processes", nor is he an "idealist", he says, requiring a spiritual origin for creation. Yet it would seem that any Marxist is hard put to explain the origin and purpose of life. Nor is it clear how *homo sapiens* is not totally matter if he does not contain some transcendental factor which defines his humanity. As scientists (like Fred Hoyle) influenced by the accumulated knowledge of the working of the Universe would claim, the whole process seems to demand a supreme intelligence or deity. In other words, they seem to support the traditional classical arguments for the existence of God, namely that life does not start by a random process nor does it originate of itself from non-living matter and by chance, rather it demands a divine causality which acts through secondary causes and through which both matter and spirit receive their entity (Hoyle 1983, pp. 163–249). The Universe demands an explanation outside of itself. Even from this point of view, religion cannot be excluded from the treatment of man and the formation of law regarding him. To do so would introduce another form of reductionism by which man is reduced to physical atoms and mortality with no high purpose here and no destiny in the hereafter.

Although some Marxists disclaim a mechanistic approach, their reasoning does not differ fundamentally. The problem, of course, of the mechanistic theory is an old one. As far back as 1925 there was a strong current of opinion promoted mainly by Deborin, who held it would be impossible to reduce phenomena of a higher order like consciousness to inorganic matter. Therefore, he confronted the mechanistic approach with dialectical materialism; we will return to this later but here it is sufficient to say that Stalin opposed both theories in 1931 (that is the mechanistic theory and Deborin's approach) because he felt that both were not in line with true Marxism and Deborinism had leftish deviations. However, dialectical materialism did hold qualitative differences between inorganic matter, life and consciousness. Quantitative changes could become qualitative changes but nobody established how life could come from inorganic matter (Wetter 1954, p. 362). Again, nobody clearly indicates how consciousness emerges from matter itself. Critical justification for these leaps are entirely absent. There is no explanation as to how philosophical ideas (truth, relation, error, cause) or moral ideas (good, evil, right, wrong, honesty, justice) came from material processes unless it is admitted that there exists somewhere within the human individual a principle which is essentially different. Further light can be thrown on the question if we remember the distinction developed by the philosopher, Michael Polanyi, between tacit knowledge shared with the animal kingdom and explicit knowledge expressed in language and symbolic patterns such as mathematics, of which only humans are capable, which is close to the thinking of Teilhard de Chardin (1959, pp. 164ff) that the magic moment was when the capacity for reflection was born and in man the Universe became conscious of itself. This is also a religious event because part of this reflection was the consciousness of being in touch with some power beyond itself. Indeed this religious interpretation of man indicates that point at which man is distinct from the rest of creation. It is, of course, as we have seen, conceded by some Marxists that consciousness is qualitatively different from mere matter but no explanation is given as to how this could be.

Again, the use of "consciousness" indicates man's capacity for relationship with God and man which is more than the economic, the class struggle and the Marxist conception of history. Surprisingly, at times, some Marxists seem to say the same things that are found in religious writings. As we have indicated, words like "spiritual", "reflection", "conscience" and "immortal" are used and reference is made to man's uniqueness (Schaff 1970, pp. 94–102). That is to say their anthropology is similar at times to Christian thinking, except that eschatology would always be excluded and any reference to God would be unacceptable. However, when one compares Marxism with Western Secularism and Utilitarianism, there is, in practice, little difference except that Marxism is atheistic whereas Western Secularism would tend to be agnostic (Trotsky *et al* 1973, pp. 68ff). This point is illustrated very clearly in Frolov's writing, especially in one of his latest works (Frolov 1982, p. 268), and Szawarski (1983, p. 116) expressly writes that Marxist ethics is a form of Utilitarianism. This holds, he would say, at least in practice, though in theory many Marxists would disagree.

Marxist Ethics

Any attempt to provide an adequate summary of Marxist ethics is nearly an impossible enterprise. Should an ethics be sought in Marxism if one sees Marxism as a social science? Again it can be asked whether Marxism as a science excludes a bias towards any ethical standpoint. Or again because Marxism is exclusively committed to "class egoism" on behalf of the proletariat, some believe that it is rooted in a "prudential" not a moral standpoint. There is nothing like unanimity amongst Marxists as to the nature of Marxist ethics. There is much controversy. But whatever way it occurs, such debates tend to circle round the problem of defining "man", "society" and "progress". These controversies about the meaning of Marxist ethics are also rooted in conflicting interpretations of Marxism. Does the mature Marx have a view about the good of humanity as a whole? Grier (1978, p. xv) suggests that he does when, in his early writings, Marx criticizes "political emancipation" as falling short of "human emancipation".

That Marxism cannot be understood to have ethical norms was supported by intellectuals like Karl Kautsky. He, in turn, was influenced by Darwin in believing that the origin of morals can be traced to the animal kingdom. Therefore, moral duties must be subjected to evolutionary change. This thinking would demystify moral imperatives. Are animals moral and does human conduct transcend the merely natural? This recalls Marx's reflection about "human essence" and provides some insight into Marx's concept of the individual (Schaff 1970, p. 75). Man, he says, can be distinguished from animals

by consciousness, by religion, or by anything else you like. They, themselves, begin to distinguish themselves from animals as soon as they begin to produce their means of subsistence, a step which is conditioned by their physical organization.

So Marx did not deny that man is distinct from animals. In *Das Kapital*, published in 1867, he makes the famous comparison between the bee and the architect

> the bee makes a better honeycomb than the most talented architect could, but the architect is superior to the bee in that he *plans* what he wants to build before beginning his work.

Put in psychological terms, the activity of the bee is instinctive whereas that of the architect is conscious, so according to Marx (1933), a man is a tool-making animal. *Homo sapiens*, therefore, is characterized by his conscious productive activity, which is *de facto* a definition of Western Secularism!

It is of interest also to note that some thinkers were unattracted by Darwinian ethics. They preferred to think in terms of the influence of "historical materialism" without admitting that Marxism contained any ethical laws.

Some claim that Marxism does require an ethics but has not got one and any appeals to the material self-interest of the proletariat were inadequate. Others, of course, say that a Marxist ethic has still to be constructed (Stojanovic 1973, pp. 137–52; Grier 1978, p. xiii).

Stojanovic, according to Grier, believed that in the history of Marxism there have been two interpretations of Marx – ethical and a-ethical. In Stojanovic's opinion, the explanation of this fact lies in Marx's own ambiguity. Another view is the one which I favour, that the very nature of Marxism gives rise to the belief that the wellbeing of the proletariat is a measure of all its concern. Being a materialistic philosophy, it can be argued that it is not interested in the good of "all humanity" as such. The interest of the proletariat is furthered by social revolution and this is its moral commitment; i.e. "a revolutionary morality". However, this might be challenged by the Leninist thinking that the interests of the proletariat override the interests of particular works stratum or particular parts of the movement.

It can then be argued that the interests of the proletariat cannot be inconsistent with the good of "all humanity". The fact, of course, is that the wellbeing of "all humanity" has never been attempted by Marxism. Even today its record regarding the Third World is even worse than the Capitalist West.

Hodges (1974, p. 155) advocated a revolutionary Communism vehemently committed to the abolition of exploitation of the poor and oppressed. No ethical theory is necessary in Marxism, he would claim; hatred of the exploiters is sufficient. Hence there are controversies about the nature of Marxist ethics which, in turn, are linked to the different views of Marxism. In a very clear and concise article on ethical standards in Marxist thinking, Hollenweger (1973, p. 292) aptly summarizes:

> The ethical issues of the thinking of Karl Marx are best explained on the basis of his understanding of man. The central question for Marx is not what is a good man? But rather what is a true man? And the answer to this is quite clear: true man is emancipated man, freed from the bonds of religion, of society and of state ... Strictly speaking, the history of man begins only at the point where he begins to shape his own history by determining the forces which are responsible for his morality ...

What we can say, in any case, is that Marxism is a secular philosophy – a modernized pelagianism in a societal context in that Marxism totally rejects the divine and the divine creation. History is the creation of man. Man, therefore, is the creator. Marxism admits that man is a conscious being which involves self-reflection but, whereas for believers this indicates spiritual and personal immortality, in that the self-reflecting faculty is not co-extensive with matter, for Marxists it means no more than the fact that man is a "species being".

As has been indicated already, within Marxist materialism, two groups are distinguished, namely the "vulgar" materialists and the dialetical materialists. The former are referred to as mechanistic because it is argued against them that man cannot be reduced to his physical processes as this would be an inadequate concept of man and would omit his "social" aspect.

However, there have been very different opinions about dialectical materialism. The problem of its role in Marxist philosophy, and hence the relation of Marx to Hegel, was a central issue of the philosophical disputes of the 1920s. As I have related, Deborin and his followers were staunch advocates of dialectical materialism. Yet Deborin's interpretation of it was rejected at the October 1930 Conference of the Presidium of the Communist Academy (Jarovsky 1961, p. 259). It is suggested that Deborin's work was insufficiently critical towards Hegelian idealism (Bogdanov 1978).

Deborin also held that no genuine Marxist account of ethics could contain universal obligatory norms of conduct (Grier 1978, p. 81). To support his view, he cites Engels. Moral duty is nothing more than the "social instinct" and "social feeling". This theory was attacked by other philosophers because Deborin also identified human morality with that of apes – he had stated that "social feeling" was in some degree present in animals which "live in herds". While Deborin did oppose a purely mechanistic materialism, he, at the same time, denied the spiritual and eschatological aspects of man, claiming there was no such reality as eternal truths. It would seem that Deborin, in relying on a general "moral feeling" in his critique, was not very different from the Warnock argument (mentioned in Chapter IV).

Some have seen this last episode as an argument over the relationship between simple universal norms of morality and class morality (Grier 1978, p. 81). But others disagree with this interpretation. However, the attitude of the Soviet regime in 1930 surrounding the Deborin affair, was seen as indicative of a collapse in the necessary conditions for independent thinking. So the question remained – whether peoples' moral consciousness was formed entirely by social conditions and socially improved patterns of individual upbringing, or whether some universal moral law dwelled in "psychic substances" within each individual and was placed there by evolutionary mechanism originating in some ancestral forms of collective herd existence (Grier 1978, p. 83).

Siskin (1973, pp. 14–26) rejects any claim that within class society there exists along with class morality an "all human morality" which is distinct from class morality but enters into "dialectical interaction" with it. He argues that however eternal the ideas of "justice", "good" and other abstracts are thought to be, the content of these concepts has "very substantially changed from people to people and from class to class". In any case, he proceeds to say "all human morality" would become possible when society is transformed into a single all-human association. It is interesting and indeed curious that, once again, there are shades in one respect of religious thinking, namely there is implied the idea of a global society with respect for the universal brotherhood of man, even though the Fatherhood of God is not contemplated. Indeed the brotherhood of man replaces the Fatherhood of God and is the ultimate reality for the Marxist. The most, however, that would be said about this morality is that it is humanistic and "this world" orientated.

Three Polish Philosophers

Since Poland is one of the Eastern European countries with which we are concerned, it is interesting in regard to man, his nature and his duties to look at the thinking of three Polish philosophers, Adam Schaff, Marek Fritzhand and Zbigniew Szawarski.

SCHAFF

Adam Schaff (1970, p. 245) is a materialist and a Marxist and expressly declares he has no belief in anything beyond this life.

He is also a dialectical materialist and believes that good social conditions are the product of man. He sees man as the creator of himself, in command of matter and life: "To Marx's vision of progress, we can now add many more elements, particularly in the field of health and eugenics ..."

But Schaff adds that the possibilities now looming will not become a reality by fate. They will depend on social conditions and these, in turn, on human struggle and action. However, if there are no other standards than man's material or earthly wellbeing, if there are no principles higher and independent of man, no ethic except the Communist world view, no eschatological dimension, it is difficult to see how an approach to the great questions like death or the bio-medical questions can be other than secularist or materialist, with no reference to the *Imago Dei* or man's intrinsic value which contains the transcendental. According to the Marxist views outlined here, the individual is part of nature and society and that determines his status. For Schaff, the Marxist theory of man is man-centred, rather than God-centred anthropology. Like the plants and animals, and in spite of appeals to consciousness and other qualities, he is essentially dust. Attempts to distinguish the social from the biological by some exponents and rescue man from vulgar materialism has, in my opinion, little meaning in reality. Therefore, in this context, discussions about the dignity of humanity and the moral status of the human embryo will have little significance as man is not essentially different from other realities and there would be no reason to treat man differently say from the animal. Schaff, like some Marxists, tries to avoid this conclusion by insisting on the "social" essence of man. That is to say man has a *social* involvement "enmeshed in concrete human relations" as Schaff would say. As we noted, of course, Marx himself declared that man was different from the animals by his "conscious" productive behaviour. But, once again, we are brought back to this word "conscious". Schaff makes a gallant effort to see more in man by emphasizing his individuality and personality. He describes man as a "complex physico-spiritual unity". Personality is not some independent or autonomous spiritual being but is a social product functioning of social relations between concrete individuals. So human personality is not something that is given, it is something that is made – "It is a process."

However, he does admit that personhood is unique and not repeatable. Here he finds common ground with many thinkers in Western society who hold that personality is an achievement rather than an endowment. But like so many secularists, the hereafter or the eschatological have no meaning, even though once again Schaff uses terms such as "spiritual", "immortal" and "person". Once again, it is a question of a problem of the use of language.

FRITZHAND

Marek Fritzhand is also a Polish Marxist philosopher and asks whether Marx's writings contain sufficient evidence to show that he professed a certain system of ethics. According to Fritzhand (1961, pp. 9–28), ethical questions do occupy a prominent place in Marx's earlier works. In his opinion, Marx did have an ethical system which is organically connected with the whole of Marx's theory.

In Fritzhand's opinion, the point of departure of Marx's ethical doctrine is the conviction that man is the supreme value – the axiologically final points of reference: "Man is concrete, real ... and that means every man." There are, therefore, two fundamental principles. The principle of self-realization and the principle of socialization. According to the former, everybody has the right to develop all his abilities and personality. The latter principle, that of socialization, complements the former. It requires that our neighbours are treated not only as a means but, above all, as ends. But it is only in the establishment of Communism that man will be enabled to live in accordance with these principles. This thinking is supported by Stojanovic (1973, p. 155), which two-fold principle, he sees as components of de-alienation and the fundamental value commitments of Marxist work (Grier 1978, p. xiii).

As a result of this analysis, a picture of Marx's ideal for man emerges. It is a man whose attention is concentrated not on the beyond or tomorrow but on the actual life on this earth. He is a human, *social* man, bonded to his fellow within the human community. But it is not possible under a system of ownership of the means of production.

At the same time, Marx's ideal of man, according to Fritzhand, is "total", "personal" and "self-active". He develops as an indivisible whole and his life is determined not by some alien inhuman forces but as a result of his personal characteristics, tendencies and efforts. He is self-active and, therefore, free. He controls not only the forces of nature but also the social forces which he, himself, produces. Marx, according to Fritzhand, upheld human values and among these are moral values – not a morality opposed to man, i.e. alienated morality, but a true human morality which looks to man's need, happiness and perfection. In the period of transition to Communism, another concept is involved, namely the class struggle and proletarian revolution against the inhuman capitalist system. This principle is specifically associated with the principles of "self-realization" and "socialization" and Fritzhand argues this is an ethical system – a claim loyally supported by Stojanovic. Does this imply that the end justifies the means? Some Marxists, like Trotsky, would answer affirmatively but Fritzhand disagrees. As to the question of ends and means, there are different opinions (I will reflect on this question towards the end of this chapter).

Finally, Fritzhand believes that the central ethical ideas developed in the early works of young Marx are found in the later phase of his activity. He claims against Popper that the ethics of Marx is not a "historicist theory of morality" but an ethics of real humanism.

Hence, both Schaff and Fritzhand follow the Marxist–Leninist philosophy of stressing a "this world" view and completely denying any reality outside of it. Man's apex is his social aspect and there are no other standards apart from the Marxist philosophy. Standards are based on man's social essence which is linked to his social relations but, according to their thinking, his greatest dimension, namely his relationship with God, is denied. For them, as for other Marxist thinkers, man's relationship with his fellows is bonded together humanistically in a true social involvement and actualised by following the tenets of Marxism. The approach to morality is, like the secularists, based on consequences, and as we will see in the celebrated debate between Trotsky and Dewey, there is little difference in their utilitarian thinking.

SZAWARSKI

Zbigniew Szawarski believes that there is no unified Marxist philosophy and no solutions to questions like the body–mind

problem. It is almost impossible, he says, to produce a generally accepted definition of terms like "social element",
"essence of man" and so on. Some see them as self-evident,
others see them as simply theoretical. Moreover, just as there
are different schools of Marxism, so also Polish Marxism
differs from Soviet Marxism. The former is anthropocentric
and humanistic, whereas Soviet Marxism is much less so.
However, there are some universal agreements by all schools
of Marxism. The human soul, spirit or person is not immortal.
Human kind is mortal. But many are ready to accept that man
is *non-omnis moriar*. Not all dies – that which persists is the
natural result of one social activity so, in a sense, the individual
can overcome his own death by leaving for his successors
natural traces of his being in this world. Here Szawarski's
thinking is very similar to that of Frolov (1983). So what is
really left after death is "just a memory".

Since the human being, according to Szawarski, is the creator of ideas, he can create spiritual values. As to the body–mind
problem, he claims that the traditional approach of Marxism is
something like emergent materialism. Nevertheless it is, in his
view, quite possible to support reductive materialism – a view
which is popular amongst some Western Marxists (Neilson
1971, p. 351). However, as has been demonstrated, many
Soviet Marxists will class this approach as "vulgar" when
pressed as to what it is in man that makes him more than
matter. Szawarski replies that the highest activity in man is
"thinking" and many Marxists would claim that "thinking" is
a function which is directly explained and produced by physical processes. He freely admits that ambiguity enables one to
propose both forms of materialism, namely, that emergent and
reductive are possible answers.

When it is suggested that there is no half-way point between
matter and spirit, Szawarski replies that there is no simple
answer. Nor does he indicate immediately what is human as
distinct from animal in *homo sapiens*. All schools of Marxism,
according to his thinking, would support evolution and see the
human being as the highest point in it. As to how *homo sapiens*
is specifically different, he points to his 1978 article and his

attempt at solving the problem (Szawarski 1978, p. 16). Szawarski freely admits that he does not find any satisfactory
Marxist solution to these questions and he refers readers to the
express words of Marx himself:

> Man is directly a natural being. As a natural being, and as a living
> natural being, he is on the one hand, endowed with the natural
> powers of life – he is an active natural being . . .

So man is totally matter but some would like to add that his
highest point is his "social essence". Szawarski describes this as
humanistic thinking. And while man's highest faculty can be
called "spiritual", it dies with matter. So having examined
these three Polish philosophers in the light of their Soviet
colleagues, it can be said that Soviet and Polish Marxism, like
secularism, is an ideology of closure which limits human questioning and concern to this world. It is also as Szawarski would
say, like a pot "with plenty of holes" where words are given a
Marxist meaning, i.e. immortality, spiritual, self-consciousness. So, on the one hand, Marxist thinking upholds that man is
no more than matter, some believing that he can be reduced to
chemical and physical processes, yet, on the other hand, in the
history of Marxist thinking there is an attempt to rescue man
from mere matter by appealing to his "social essence". But the
latter, like the rest of man also ends, as Shakespeare would say
in "dusty death". Therefore, it too is earth bound and in that
sense materialistic.

Utilitarianism and Marxist Leninism

Marxist discussions, the problems posed, and the attempts at
solutions are similar, as I have indicated, to the Social Utilitarianism which began in the eighteenth century. Both systems
are concerned with the social order and its preservation against
individualism or self-interest. Hence the "greatest happiness of
the greatest number" is a standard that has a reality for the
Marxist. For the Utilitarian this principle was held to be the

only rational guide, both to private morals and public policy. Some contemporary Marxists adopt similar arguments, transferring the locus of value from the individual to the community. The "social" interest as distinct from the interest of individuals serves as the ultimate criterion of right and wrong.

On the question of the primacy of the individual as distinct from society, the latter is always preferred. This position would be in sharp contrast to the thinkers of the French Revolution who emphasized the rights of the individual. Some Marxists and in particular Soviet theorists, adopt similar arguments to the Social Utilitarians seeing the individual as essentially a "social" being.

At numerous points in their expositions of aspects of Marxist ethical theory, Soviet authors refer to the "science of history" which provided the main foundation for their claims about the nature of value and moral norms. The universe is neither good nor evil because the universe has no goals; it is history that exhibits the properties of good or evil (Grier 1978, p. 159). However, there is one great point of contrast between the Soviet ethical theory and the Social Utilitarianism of the Enlightenment. The agent for change and the formation of humanity according to the latter is the State, whereas the former believe it is history and in this process the Communist party is to be guided by the Marxist–Leninist knowledge of history. The science of history is supposed to provide the foundation of Marxist morality and is the only true indicator of value. It demonstrates, according to many Soviet thinkers, which social interests, values or moral norms are progressive (Grier 1978, p. 159). The problem here is that this presupposes some prior set of value-judgements as to what constitutes historical progress and so the claim that historical progress is the genuine indicator of moral value is logically inadmissable. Again, if these values are historically produced demonstrating what is of value, then we, as people, never choose or decide, we just learn. But Marxists do not behave in this fashion, they strive to make the means fit the ends. Another difficulty in regard to the "historical-progress-assumption" is its implications of determinism which eliminates evaluation and the place of man in the Cosmos. Indeed it seems to contradict Marx's own words:

> Nature herself has determined the sphere of activity in which the animal should move and it peacefully moves within that sphere, without attempting to go beyond it, without even an inkling of any other. To man too the Deity gave a general aim, that of enobling mankind and himself, but he left it to man to seek the means by which this aim can be achieved; he left it to him to choose the point in society most suited to him, from which he can best uplift himself and society. (Marx and Engels 1975, p. 26.)

For the secularists who are also materialists, Utilitarianism forms a convenient moral approach. As I have mentioned, Marxism is atheistic, secularism here in the West is often agnostic. Arguably Marxism and Utilitarianism are the two most popular approaches to ethics. Both are nineteenth-century creations; both were innovating systems conceived to advocate change and both are "umbrella" terms in the sense that both Marxism and Utilitarianism accommodate widely divergent views. For example one can find Christians who are also Utilitarians or Marxists. Not all secularists are agnostic. Some would believe in God but restrict religion to a very personal or private part of their lives and thinking, so that religion becomes for them a very private affair while morality and choices become more secular. However, all these factors pale when compared with the main point of contact between Marxism and Utilitarianism, namely the consequential framework in which both are cast, so that the morality of all action is judged by its consequences. In Marxism, of course, there is no simple slogan like "the greatest happiness of the greatest number" and this can be partly explained by the inevitability of the "historical process". For ethics becomes a matter of endorsing this "process" in terms of the abolition of capitalism, or ownership of the means of production, or the victory of the proletariat which are inevitable and any results or consequences of one's actions that serve the advancement of the historical process are justified and in this way the end justifies the means (Brown 1983, p. 4).

At this point it is appropriate to refer to the debate between L. Trotsky and J. Dewey on ends and means (Trotsky *et al* 1973). Trotsky believed that the end justified the means on condition that the "revolutionary proletariat" was advanced. Deceit and violence, if they are placed in the service of a justified end, should be employed without hesitation. Here Trotsky by the exclusion of some "means" is being pragmatic rather than moral. For Trotsky there is no such thing as *per se* morality – no ideal of eternal morality. Morals are relative to the social class. Dewey, the Utilitarian, like Trotsky, believes that the end justifies the means. Indeed it is the only rule of action. Consequences were the only justification for the means. However, for Trotsky, the end that always justified was the abolition of "social oppression". Dewey agreed that this was a worthy objective but disagreed that the "working class" should be the agency to accomplish it. According to Dewey, all people of goodwill should be engaged for that purpose. The dispute was, therefore, one of method – there was little difference about their general consequentialist thrust. Again, it should be noted that many East European philosophers would not consider Trotsky as a genuine representative of Marxism.

Another Marxist, this time from Western society, Kai Neilson (1971, p. 522) asserts that his thinking is also akin to J. S. Mill "while being no means identical to Utilitarianism" and another Marxist writer in the West asks: "What can justify means except ends?" (Ash 1964, p. 161). Indeed Szawarski (1983, p. 106) makes the interesting comment:

> Marxist ethics is similar in its practical solutions to Utilitarianism. It seems that it is the practical type of Utilitarianistic ethics. A follower of Marxist ethics will have no doubt that one should always choose the lesser evil.

(This, according to Szawarski in private correspondence with me, was the only section of his 1978 article that the authorities wanted to delete!)

And so it is that both philosophies, Marxism and Utilitarianism, have a consequentialist framework and both believe that, in their terms, the end always justifies the means. Or, to put it in the words of Szawarski, the Marxist ethics will have no doubt that the lesser of two evils should be chosen. This, of course, is alien to St Paul's thinking (Romans 3:8 and 6:1) and indeed to much of Christian reality where it is claimed that one cannot do evil that good may come. In fact, there is a detailed discussion in modern times on the implications of this principle (Ramsey and McCormick 1978). Some would say that the principle of the "lesser of two evils" applies only in the case of two alternatives, either of which is bound to happen if the other does not. The classic example is the ectopic pregnancy. Failure to act will cause the death of mother and child. Again it is indicated that self-defence and indirect killing are areas of choosing the lesser of two evils – or doing evil to achieve good. The distinction, however, between this position and that of the Marxist–Utilitarian stance is to be found in that the former takes the intention and consequences together. That is to say that "doing evil that good may come" is unacceptable when the evil is *intentional* and follows *directly*, as in the case of bombing civilian targets, or in the use of the H-Bomb. It does not apply to *indirect* and *tolerated* evil where no other action is reasonably possible. In a word, then, Marxism and Utilitarianism are cast in a consequential framework. Marxists use the same kind of arguments as Utilitarians though not always expressed in Utilitarian vocabulary. Indeed Schaff (1963) and Allen (1976) claim that Marx was, himself, a Utilitarian, even though he did not claim to be such. Hence I would suggest there is no relevant difference in practice between Marxism and Western secularism, particularly in Utilitarian thinking. In theory, of course, one can argue otherwise – Marx (1933, pp. 672–74), himself, did criticize Bentham. But, in fact, both Marxism and Utilitarianism are inadequate philosophies where there is no place for the dignity of man, and where there is no allowance made between what is *intended* and what is merely foreseen in moral action. If killing hundreds of innocent people, directly and intentionally, in blanket bombing, shortens the war, and saves millions of others, it is only part of the equation in that the good consequences, by a head count, are greater than those who have been directly killed. But this is not the whole of the equation because it takes no account of what has happened to the rights of the innocent people who have been intentionally killed. Both theories fail at those crucial junctures where human living and human liberties matter enormously. This inability to account for the special importance of human rights and justice is an indication of the bankruptcy of both philosophies which fail to cater properly for the whole of human reality. More importantly, I believe, these theories do not take into account the greatest fact of human reality, namely, that man is made in God's Image and is – "on the way" – to fulfilment with his Creator. The Kingdom of God, its values, the promise of eternal life, all these realities which are essential ingredients in the meaning and direction of human life, are excluded from the soulless calculations of Marxism and Utilitarianism. They deal with a part of man, namely his physical component, while his highest faculties, powers and vocations and aspirations are totally excluded. All the same, Marxists, in fairness, do argue that their philosophy does provide a theory of human dignity. Indeed Marx, himself, claimed that Communism is humanism *in praxi*. But what sort of humanism it is, gives rise to another question. In any case, in the Christian view, it will always neglect the transcendental in man.

I claim, therefore, that it is impossible to understand human life in its beginning, transmission and end, except in the context of a journey or pilgrimage with a beginning and end. Consequently, human actions cannot be evaluated in isolation from the ultimate purpose and direction of human life. The dignity of the human being can only be seen in the *whole* of human reality and interrelated with the other pilgrims, who are members of a redeemed community, and also on a journey. It is this sense of purpose and direction in human wholeness that are completely lacking in judgements which are based on Utilitarianism and Marxism.

From this analysis of the Marxist–Leninist philosophy, one would be surprised to find any real difference in approach from the Western secularist regarding human life in its beginning and transmission in the USSR, Eastern European socialist countries and Western society. Both philosophies are materialistic. Both are unconcerned with the transcendental nature of man. Whereas in the past, and certainly in Christian thinking, as in most other religions, people as individuals were seen to have an equal intrinsic worth. This was based on man's rational-spiritual nature which is discontinuous with all other forms of life. It also takes account of man's eschatological destiny. Certainly as far as the Christian is concerned, people have a unique value because they stand in an all-encompassing relationship with God and because of his Grace, have a relationship with each other as members of a redeemed people. This relationship must also include all lesser ones. In other words, God knows us and loves us not apart from such mundane matters as economic and social relationship and our psychological history, but in, with and through them. The world in all its complex and partial relationship is part of that totality with which God is concerned. Every person has, therefore, an intrinsic worth and much of our aesthetic and moral values are derived from this thinking. The intrinsic worth of an animal, if it is recognized at all, is given a finite value in the sense that it is less than human and more than that of a flower, but for the Christian, at any rate, the intrinsic worth of the human is held to be of sacred value because he is made in the Image of God and called to the eternal kingdom. This attitude to human life should form a correct basis for an approach to bio-medical problems, especially at the beginning of human life. In Western secularianism and Utilitarianism, as well as in Marxism, there is an inadequate basis because both philosophies do not cater for man's relationship with God and his total humanity. Therefore, they are not capable of fulfilling the most important role, namely of protecting those people who do not want these new techniques such as IVF, AID and surrogacy, and preventing the likely and unimaginable consequences some of these techniques can bring about.

CHAPTER VI

The Soviet Factor

Advances in bio-medicine have resulted in many new issues and problems and in this chapter I hope to reflect on the Soviet attitude to some of them.

Although the issues are the same as in the West, with their various complications, nevertheless, social and political factors in Eastern-bloc countries play a most important part in shaping the whole debate or controversy. Again, religious belief has to be taken into account. Sometimes its role is surprisingly ambiguous but, nevertheless, it has an influence on the lives of ordinary people. At times it is curious that religious belief has not played a greater role (in places like Poland for example) in the abortion issue; yet in other places it would seem to have a considerable influence – as in the Muslim populations of the USSR. In short, social, political and religious attitudes are not passive absorbers of the impact of science and technology.

Hence, while the problems of bio-medicine and bio-medical ethics in the Eastern bloc are similar in some ways to those in the West, they also display characteristics resulting from the specific culture of that nation or area. With these thoughts in mind, I will explore the question of human genetics in general in the USSR and then reflect on specific biological questions at the beginning of human life. Moreover, since the treatment of anything must depend, in the last resort, on what it is, an attempt was made in the last chapter to understand the Marxist–Leninist view of "life" and human life in particular, which will help us to see more clearly the Soviet approach to questions at the beginning and transmission of human life.

Human Genetics

(I am indebted to Professor Loren Graham of the Institute of Technology, Massachusetts, who is a leading authority in the West on the Soviet approach to ethical issues of modern bio-medical research. Due to his correspondence with me and his many contributions, one can give a summary of the background to the question of human genetics in the USSR. The debate on human genetics and its complications is very much in progress in the USSR among philosophers and scientists and it contains both political and intellectual elements.)

Professor Graham divides the Soviet literature on genetic engineering into two phases. The dividing point is 1975 when the Asilomar Conference took place in the United States to discuss the control of recombinant DNA research. It received international publicity. Graham calls the period up to 1975 the "Speculative Period" and the second phase since 1975 the "Practical Period". The first period was concerned with theoretical issues and philosophical questions. The second was concerned with more practical issues about certain research and its control, while the ethical questions were not without importance and still remained in the immediate background.

The discussions in the USSR were really initiated by the President of the Academy of Science who requested that more attention should be given to human genetics. Much of the thinking and writing on the subject appeared in Soviet publications like *Voprosy filosofii* and subjects such as cloning were indeed mentioned. This, in turn, involved more discussions on how the subject of human genetics was related to Marxism. A. A. Neifakh, a doctor of biological sciences, defended genetic engineering and its application to mankind. He stressed that cloning offered some desirable progress for the wellbeing of the human race. The better combination of genes found in people of high quality could be preserved and he emphasized that it was a question of "improving rather than changing genetic constitutions". Neifakh was aware that eugenics was condemned in the USSR for more than thirty years and, consequently, he was careful to indicate that what he was saying was *not* applying to eugenics which concerned change – it merely applies to improvement. Neifakh defends nucleus transplant by arguing it is not eugenics which poses problems of changing and improving the genetic nature of mankind as a whole. In the case of nucleus transplant, he says, nothing is changed but only retained! Thinkers differed in their approach and Academician Dubinin criticized Neifakh for his views because he attempted to treat humans as animals. It is of interest to study Dubinin's reason which stems from the meaning of man and it is tantalizing to find that, while he contends that human phenomena cannot be reduced to physical and chemical explanations, he does not clarify what really makes man unique, though he does refer to the origin of consciousness. Here again clarity in definition is lacking. He states that the social element of man is the determining factor in education and formation and he seems to come very close to Christian thinking about the sanctity of human life. He was also deeply concerned about the effect of human genetic engineering on the family. For some, this kind of reasoning seems curious in the light of his Marxism.

However, the debate and research continues although many scientists realized it was a sensitive issue, especially because of the Lysenko Affair which had hinged on the political control of biology (Medvedev 1979). Scientists realized that molecular biology could easily raise questions once more of social ethics and political control. In spite of this, the debate was sustained regarding the relationship of science and ethics. The discussions involved topics much broader than genetic engineering, such as how far new possibilities and questions should be handled, which might not be covered by existing law. Questions about the moment of death and the meaning of personhood and AID, which were vigorously discussed in the West in medicine and philosophy, were now coming to the fore in the USSR.

As I have hinted already, the concerns of leading American and Soviet biologists were different in the early and middle 1970s. The American concern was the possibility of pathogenic organisms being accidentally produced by recombinant DNA research and then being allowed to escape from the laboratories. The concern of the Soviet scientists was the danger that the debates on the recombinant DNA would cause reimposition of political control over biology like the Lysenko period. When the Asilomar Conference took place in 1975, Soviet scientists attended and the attitudes of these delegates were very much determined by that thinking. Engelhardt and Academician Baev had the Lysenko Affair very much in mind when they were at pains to point out that the dangers of recombinant DNA research were not in the experiments themselves but rather in the misuse of the research. In other words, the problem was not with science but with the scientists and though this would not happen in the Socialist countries of the USSR, it was rather a danger for the capitalist countries (Graham 1980, pp. 222–23). Baev remarks that in capitalist countries, scientists have a tendency to blame science for abuses for which the social order of those countries is responsible. He argues that a negative approach to scientific development is particularly widespread in capitalist countries, where people try to explain the problems of science by blaming science, technology, individuals, or other local and chance factors rather than the basic contradictions underlying capitalist society. Scientists cannot operate independently of the society in which they live. Society, after all, and indeed social conditions not to mention the interest of states, classes and parties, determine in the end, the fate of science, scientific discoveries and of scientists themselves. This, Baev says, does not deny the importance of scientific development nor does it deny the personality of the scientists or the moral criteria. They exist alongside and act with social factors. They must be taken into account when considering particular situations. The scientist, he says, must warn society of the consequences of experiments and be able to predict them. This is the minimum required of the scientist. Baev (1976, pp. 8–18) adds that:

We in the USSR do not fear the future, nor are we afraid that some sort of powerful and blind forces could direct research in genetic engineering along evil paths, contrary to the peoples' intentions and wishes. We are sure goodwill and reason will triumph here. The gloomy predictions and almost panic which one reads in specialist and general publications in the capitalist world seem exaggerated but, at the same time, comprehensible. These attitudes are supported by developments in capitalist reality; the growth of violence and terrorism ... All this gives rise to feelings of uncertainty and the fear that someone may use scientific discovery for evil ends and bring mankind harm rather than good.

Baev reminds us that knowledge in itself cannot be a source of evil. After all, he says, Pliny the Elder wrote that iron can be made to make ploughs or weapons. The danger of using genetic engineering, for example, for biological weapons, is not greater than using any other science. He mentions that Pope John Paul II spoke against genetic engineering in UNESCO (Paris) in 1980 but did not specify the danger. The campaign, Baev claims, against genetic engineering in 1981 was largely in the United States.

The same point was made earlier by another writer, S. T. Alikhanin (1976, pp. 150–73), who wrote:

> In spite of our opinion, there is no sense in talking about the ethics of gene engineering. We should rather speak of the ethics of gene engineers and the ethics of gene engineers should be the same as every honourable person.

Not all could accept this reason as it could be argued that genetic engineering in itself is at least highly dangerous. In any case, according to these thinkers, there was nothing to fear. One must not blame nature for what man himself is responsible. The new science was just another technology which could be used for good or evil. Nor were they keen on review boards to evaluate research and certainly not review boards consisting of non-scientists as in the United States. Nevertheless, Soviet philosophers and others in the USSR were beginning to be aware of the deep controversial issues of genetic engineering. Indeed there was a need for Soviet philosophers and scientists, wrote the philosopher, R. S. Karpinskaia (1978, pp. 95–106), to dialogue much more about the ethical issues and to subject experimentation to a humanitarian as well as a scientific viewpoint. Graham (1980, p. 225) indicates that Karpinskaia's assertion that philosophical interpretation is an integral part of scientific research, is a telling point. In other words, what is being stressed is that there must be a closer relationship between Soviet Marxist philosophers and Soviet scientists. This bears out what Professor Frolov (1976, p. 17) wrote:

> It becomes clearer and clearer that science cannot develop in a "social vacuum" in isolation from its world outlook, socio-philosophy and ethical bases ... Scientific ethics are firmly established as a vitally necessary condition for all the effective functioning of scientific knowledge directed towards humanism.

Or, as Jurgen Moltmann (1979, p. 131) believes, if science and ethics are separated, ethics always appear too late on the scene. All the same, whatever academics may think, the Soviet regime does not appear to see ethics as an independent method of evaluation as in the West. In my opinion, the world-view of Marxism–Leninism is the only guide. In other words, the guideline must be the Communist morality and any ethical conclusion must support it. Consequently, if genetics are in harmony with Marxist–Leninist thinking, there is no need for any further evaluation and certainly there is no place for religion.

Frolov disagrees with Baev that genetic engineering is just one more technology. Frolov is probably one of the outstanding philosophers in the USSR and he believes that we can certainly speak of a new stage in the development of science. In other words, human genetic engineering is a completely new breakthrough but he would not agree with Dubinin that it should never be used nor does he agree that it should be simply restricted to the prevention and reduction of disease. He says that it could be used by reactionary forces in the West but it was nevertheless more than a scientific question and should involve a philosophical interpretation (Frolov 1976, p. 17). So while Baev was concluding that Soviet biologists could proceed as usual, Frolov was arguing that the new eugenics need a new approach. He criticized Dubinin as being simplistic in claiming that genetic engineering should never be used to mould man's future. Frolov claimed that Marxism is based on a realistic vision of the history of civilization in which moral standards evolve in step with the development of material culture. Therefore, the possibility of the conscious and widespread application of genetic engineering in the future (even in ways that seem morally offensive now) cannot be excluded. On the other hand, maintained Frolov, it would be a great mistake to make such an effort now. For the time being all eugenic ideas must be sharply rejected. The reasons, he said, are two-fold: "The science of genetics is still too incomplete and, even more important, power in the world is too unequally distributed."

In 1982 Frolov wrote that there are grounds for believing that the task of genetic engineering will not arise for

> a very long period of time since mankind can develop successfully through its present genetic foundations. When mankind actively confronts the problem, it will find worthy forms for solving it. (Frolov 1982, p. 2.)

Moreover, when this situation does arise, man's "social essence" must be recognized as well as his biological nature.

The problem with Frolov's stance is that it does not meet the immediate questions that are rapidly arising in the whole matter of human genetic engineering, such as cloning, and what in addition must be done about the host of questions that are springing up in the area of IVF.

In the United States and Britain, and to a certain extent Australia, the question of review boards was very much in the fore. There is deep concern in most places as to who should decide what is permissible in genetic engineering. After the Lysenko Affair, Soviet Marxists worked out a new approach between science and philosophy: "Leave science to the scientists." But with the advent of the debates on genetic engineering, it became less clear that the post-Lysenko attitude about separate spheres for science and philosophy could be maintained (Graham 1980, p. 235). In the United States, advisory boards and committees have been set up to monitor genetic engineering and have been recommended for Britain. Australia has got its own methods of monitoring (Mahoney 1984a, pp. 285–91). Some of these boards include clergy, moral philosophers and lay people. But the Soviet scientists would be uneasy about any suggestion of an open meeting. Baev and Engelhardt felt there was no need for special evaluation from review boards with non-scientists. Indeed to include lay people would be introducing an emotional element:

> Without adequate competence, it is difficult to overcome emotional reactions and to think through peacefully a complicated subject like the role of science in philosophy.

A SOVIET REVIEW OF SOME WESTERN THINKING

A. D. Kerimova, a research assistant at the All-Union Scientific Research Institute in the USSR, reviews articles and books about different aspects of genetic engineering that first appeared in the United States. In one such review, published in 1980, she provides a comprehensive and quite good indication of a Soviet view on Western genetic thinking. She observes that there is no unity of opinion in the ethical and philosophical literature, even about the cardinal aspects of genetic engineering. However, she says, these discussions are comparatively recent and final decisions cannot be expected:

> Nevertheless, the ethical basis of science, the scientists' moral achievements require thorough discussion on a whole range of related problems, not only by the representatives of individual branches of scientific knowledge, but also by the general public in all countries of the world. (Kerimova 1980, pp. 165–71.)

Kerimova concludes that international agreements on ethical criteria about the implications and aims of scientific activity in general, and genetic engineering in particular, are only possible on this basis. The development of such an approach, she claims, can be made on the basis of Marxist–Leninist thinking.

She seems to imply here that science and genetic engineering in particular, should have sufficient direction and guidance within itself provided it is based on Marxist beliefs but, as she adds, at the same time, the prevention of an anti-human use of science does require thorough discussion by the general public in all countries. It would be interesting to hear Baev's opinion on this attitude because he would claim that capitalist thinking would merely pollute the thinking in the USSR.

AID and Surrogacy

Artificial insemination in animals has probably been done ever since classic antiquity. The method was scientifically described in the 1780s by the Italian, Spallanzani. In the early 1900s insemination treatment of sheep, cattle and horses was developed by the Institute of Fertilization Physiology in Moscow.

Artificial insemination in humans was first used in the USSR, according to the Kharkov experts Grishchenko and Parashuk, in 1952 in Kharkov. Eight women were treated and three conceived (Grishchenko and Parashuk 1984, p. 3). According to this report, the Department of Clinical Obstetrics and Gynaecology in Kharkov Medical Institute is working on AID. These experts note approvingly the article in the Bulgarian legal code on the family which was introduced regarding AID on 22 May 1968 and states that: "Paternity may not be disputed if the mother has been artificially inseminated with the agreement of her spouse." At present, similar to other places, it appears that the USSR has to catch up legally with the various questions that are arising in the bio-medical area.

In an article that appeared in a Soviet periodical, the author, M. N. Maleina, a graduate student at the All-Union Correspondence Law Institute, clearly states that many of the problems arising from artificial insemination by donor (heteronomous insemination) need urgent legislation as they are not sufficiently covered under the Article of the Principles of Legislation in the USSR and the Union Republics on Marriage and the Family. This point is also indicated by Grishchenko and Parashuk. Maleina confirms that the USSR is engaged in genetic engineering. He also confirms the fact that there are children in Russia who are the result of AID which leads on to the discussion about the rights of the child to know its origins although this question has not been legislatively resolved. He admits the danger of a collision of interest of spouses, donors and children. He also reveals that not all doctors and lawyers in the USSR agree with AID (because infertility is not a disease). There is need for regulation of the conditions under which AID is performed and indeed a clear definition of the status of the child that is artificially conceived. There is also need to expand the principles of legislation on heath care. Under Article II of the Principles of Legislation in the USSR and the Union Republics on Marriage and the Family, all questions pertaining to family life are jointly resolved by the spouses: "On the basis of mutual consent and the interest of family life as a whole." (Maleina 1984, pp. 48–57.)

It would appear, then, that artificial insemination should require the consent of both spouses. The question, Maleina says, may arise whether a woman, capable of natural child-birth, has an absolute right to artificial insemination. At the present time the question must be answered in the negative. Again, lack of restriction on artificial insemination could, to a certain degree, downgrade the social significance of the family, of maternity and paternity. The position taken in the USSR is that artificial insemination is admissable in the event of persist-ent infertility, illness of the spouse, or danger to the health of mother or child. The author makes an interesting comment by claiming that 20 to 25 per cent of all cases of artificial insemina-tion by a donor (heteronomous insemination) culminate in abortion, deformities, tubal pregnancy or premature birth and, therefore, the medical, psychological and other aspects of the procedure should be discussed in detail with the physician. Maleina is also deeply aware of the conflicts of interest that result regarding the child's claim to know his origins; the interest of the spouses, the donor, and the child in this area must be legislatively resolved. Finally, implantation of the artificially impregnated ovum of the wife into another woman's body is discussed. He grants that an opinion has been expressed that the spouses should be deemed to be the child's parents only if the woman who carried the child rejected him or her, and assuming the spouses adopted the child, since it is scarcely legitimate to regard the woman who carried the child as an incubator with no biological bond to the child. A biological *bond* does develop between the surrogate mother and the child she bears, but this is distinct from a biological *kinship* which is established by the genetic material rather than by the bearer. Here again the implantation from an outside source can result in dramatic collision of interests. The legislation on the family, he believes, must be expanded to meet these questions.

Another Russian writer, D. M. Chetchot, reminds us that AID for animals was used in the USSR as long ago as the beginning of this century and, since 1981, under the permission of the Ministry of Health, AID for humans is carried out in clinics in Moscow, Leningrad and Kharkow.

> It is interesting to consider the use of the given method mainly as a means of strengthening and stabilizing marriage and only after that as a way of stimulating the birth rate. (Chetchot 1984, p. 202)

Chetchot, like Maleina, seems to think that legislation is needed. He believes that the law should stipulate that AID should be voluntary and restricted to married couples. It should be performed only in state registered clinics. The law should also decide the responsibilities the married couple should have in regard to the AID child and prevent the husband from questioning his fatherhood. The law should prevent a donor from bringing a case to establish his paternity. It should also guarantee absolute secrecy of the AID procedure. This recommendation, forbidding the semen donor to establish paternity, was also contained in the Warnock Report. Unlike the Report, however, Chetchot would restrict AID to married couples, whereas Warnock would not. As the Warnock Report (1984, p. 10) says:

> We are not prepared to recommend that access to treatment should be based exclusively on the legal status of marriage ... The Report

takes the term "couple" to mean a heterosexual couple living together in stable relationship, whether married or not.

Chetchot's recommendations of restricting AID to marriage is also implied in Maleina's article but whereas the identity of the donor should be left to the wishes of the couple, according to Maleina (though he later seems to change his opinion and opt for absolute anonymity), Warnock and Chetchot both recommend anonymity. But what can be said, without qualification, is that Chetchot and Maleina were at pains to underline the importance of marriage and the family – they give no reasons.

Meanwhile, G. I. Litvinova (1981, pp. 117ff) adds that legalizing AID will contribute to the decrease in the number of one child, and childless, families and increase the birth rate which is "one of the aims of the demographic policy of the Soviet State". He favours anonymity of the donor and discusses the "paternity" of the husband in AID. As to surrogacy, he feels that the dangers of its abuse, as in the case of women hiring others to avoid the discomforts of pregnancy, are an insufficient reason "for refusal to implement an important medical discovery". He also considers that the woman who carries the child and gives birth to it is the real mother rather than the woman who is genetically related to it.

IVF

Dr A. I. Nikitin, of the Institution of Obstetrics and Gynae-cology, Leningrad Academy of Medical Sciences, reviews foreign work on *in vitro* fertilization. He refers to discussions in the West and to moral issues without providing any analysis of them. He, nevertheless, believes that they are largely problems arising out of the socio-economic conditions existing in capitalist countries. In discussing and solving the moral and ethical issues arising from human embryo transplants, the first priority must be given to the medical aspects of the problem, namely the task of preserving the nation's health. No attempt is made to give a moral analysis. (Nikitin 1982, pp. 94ff.)

However, Dr A. P. Dyban, of the Institute of Experimental Medicines in Moscow, when interviewed on the subject of bio-medical problems at the beginning of human life was very much aware of the difficulties that can arise from genetics, whether in the USSR or elsewhere. He too referred to problems of AID according as it is more widely practised. The interviewer asked him about IVF in particular and Dyban (1978, p. 13) immediately stressed that he saw no moral flaw in the technique itself to help parents (literally married couples or spouses).

Graham (1980, p. 231) adds that Dyban did not rule out "the possibility of the eventual use of IVF even for third parties" but as the text says "for the time being we should use the method only to help parents".

Another point of interest, according to Dyban, was the fact that IVF's morality could only be measured by its social conse-quences. IVF research is being carried out in Leningrad by Pimenova *et al* (1983, pp. 10ff) at the Institute of Obstetrics and Gynaecology. They are among the leading Soviet researchers, together with M. A. Petrov-Maslakov, A. I. Nikitin and M. P. Nikolaichuk of the same Institute. Indeed the popular health magazine *Zdorove* reported in 1986 that the first Soviet baby had been born as a result of IVF. The work was carried out by the Ministry of Health, at the Research Institute on Mother and Child Health under the direction, according to *Zdorove*, of Dr B. V. Leonov. It was also reported that scientists were working with another woman who was ten weeks pregnant as a result of IVF. The whole article was written in terms of helping the childless and without any hint of any ethical concerns.

Speaking of artificial insemination· by donor (AID), the interviewer did make reference to the possibility of sperm donation from a third party in regard to IVF. In this case, the father of the child would not be the husband of the woman. Indeed one can go further, says the interviewer, and visualize that the ovum which is fertilized could be transplanted to a completely different recipient who would also give birth to that same child. Dyban agreed with the interviewer that very great ethical problems are present and refers to the fact that in the United States, AID is becoming more widely practised. A danger could arise, says Dyban, from the desire of a mother to find out who is the father of the child. This might encourage bribery, personal detectives, attempts to penetrate secret safes in order to uncover the secret. He asks who would consider herself the mother of the child? The woman from whom the ovum was taken or the one who bore the foetus. If the desire to find out about the father of the child becomes irresistible for the mother, what indeed can be said about the craving of the child itself? Meanwhile, A. A. Neifakh (Institute of the Biology of Evolution of the USSR Academy of Science) asks if a

> woman has the right to carry a child which is genetically not hers, even if she agrees to this voluntarily? Of course this will essentially be her child, she has carried it and gives birth to it, she will bring it up as a mother but genetically it will not be hers. Can this be permitted? In practice, we have already permitted this for a long time. We know about artificial insemination, which is now applied not infrequently, and we know about adopted children. A woman takes an adopted child with an unknown genotype, brings it up as hers, and has the right to consider it her own. (Cited in Liseev and Sharov 1970, p. 108.)

Dr Dyban's attitude to IVF is considered by some as being morally sound in itself. This is rather different from some views in the West where some consider the technique to be unnatural or morally flawed. For example, Professor Singer of Australia quotes opinion polls on IVF in the United States, 1978, by Harris and Gallup in which 1,500 people were interviewed. Harris interviewed women only, while Gallup interviewed both men and women. The polls were taken after the much publicized birth of Louise Brown and the Gallup Poll showed that 93 per cent of their samples had heard or read about the birth. The polls indicated clear majority approval of IVF as a means of helping couples, but the Gallup Poll put the question in the following manner:

> Some people oppose this type of operation because they feel it is not natural. Other people favour it because it helps a husband and

wife to have a child they could not otherwise have. Which point of view comes closest to your own?

Replies received were divided as: 60 per cent said they were in favour; 27 per cent opposed the operation; 13 per cent had no opinion. Of those who disapproved, the reason most of them gave was that it was *unnatural* (Singer and Wells 1984, p. 33).

However, there are theologians and churches in Western society who fault IVF for other reasons. Amongst these are Professor Kass of the United States, Professor Ramsey, the Methodist Theologian at Princeton, Corkery of Maynooth and many submissions to the Warnock Inquiry. First it is rejected on the grounds that IVF is morally flawed because it separates the unitive and the procreative aspects of marriage, and, secondly, because in practice IVF always entails the creation of spare embryos which are discarded.

The Catholic Bishops' Conference of England and Wales Joint Committee on Bioethical Issues, in their submission to Warnock, expressed concern about the severing of procreation from sexual intercourse. Here a very detailed argument is put forward against IVF as such. They claim that the result of the IVF technique is a product, an object which will be subject to "quality control, utilization and discard". Theologians like McCormick, Ramsey, Corkery and others felt that the twofold nature of sexuality (i.e. the procreative and the unitive) should not be ruptured. They argued that it would depersonalize the process of human procreation. Indeed Ramsey (1977, p. 33) proposes his understanding on the basis of the biological or fleshly aspect being an essential part of human procreation and parenthood. He uses Ephesians V to support his argument. An ethic that in principle sunders two goods – regarding procreation as an aspect of biological nature to be subjected merely to the requirements of technical control, while saying the unitive purpose is the free, human, personal end of the matter – pays disrespect to the nature of human parenthood. Professor Kass (1972, pp. 18–56) reminds us that human procreation is an activity of an embodied man and woman. Professor R. McCormick (1972, pp. 531–52) at first supported the claim that IVF does de-biologize marriage and the family and puts forward some telling arguments for his position. However, he subsequently (McCormick 1981, p. 326) revised his position when he wrote:

> There seems to be no argument that shows with clarity and certainty that husband–wife *in vitro* procedures using their own sperm and ovum are necessarily and inherently wrong . . .

Professor Joseph Fletcher (1971, p. 779) will have none of this. To him, the setting up of an antimony between "natural and biological reproduction and 'artificial reproduction' is absurd".

On the other hand Pius XII (Acta Apostolicae Sedis 1949) would also object to this technique because of the way sperm is obtained. According to him obtaining human semen by masturbation is directly and precisely aimed at the complete exercise of man's natural faculty of generating and this complete exercise outside marital intercourse involves a direct and improper use of the faculty. Pius believes it is precisely in this improper use of the faculty that the intrinsic infringement of the moral law consists. Therefore, IVF, according to this teaching, would not be morally acceptable because of the means of producing the semen. The Pope also refers to the unity of the procreative action:

> It is never permitted to separate these different aspects to the point of positively excluding either the procreative intention or the conjugal relation.

Some years earlier he made explicit reference to artificial insemination:

> To reduce the shared life of a married couple and the act of marriage to a mere organic activity for transmitting seed would be like turning the domestic home, the sanctuary of the family, into nothing more than a biological laboratory . . .

In its natural structure, the marriage act is a personal action, a simultaneous and immediate cooperation on the part of husband and wife, which by the very nature of the participants, and the character of the act, is the expression of that mutual self-giving which, as the scripture says, brings about the union "in one flesh". In other words, the procreation of a new human being results from a union not just of bodies but of persons.

According to this, it would seem that a human being should only be generated from mutual loving intercourse. But, Fr Mahoney (1984, pp. 14–17) asks, is this the only possible vehicle of creative married love? What about the infertile couple who desire to express their union and their love by having a child? Can this not be realised in the IVF technique? The basic argument against masturbation is that it frustrates the purpose of the faculty of human procreation. However, Mahoney argues that in the instance of the infertile husband and wife, the opposite could be the case for the purpose of masturbation here *is in order to procreate*. It is difficult, he says, to argue that it is a solitary introspective expression of sexuality because in the situation of husband and wife desiring to have a child by IVF the opposite intention prevails, namely there is a procreative action which is part of the series that leads to the full expression of love in the procreation of their own child within their marriage.

As to the USSR, it can be assumed that there are people who would consider IVF "unnatural" or "a violation of religion" but Soviet Marxism does not provide support for these positions and thus their objection would not reach the Soviet press as legitimate viewpoints. At any rate, we can conclude that, like Frolov, Dr Dyban is cautious, especially about human cloning and hopes that nature continues to make it technically impossible. On the other hand, IVF is a reality and has vastly increased the potentialities for human manipulation. One can obtain in a test tube the earliest stages of the human embryo. By producing DNA, or cells cultured in a laboratory in this early stage of the embryo, the possibility exists for introducing genetic change in the cells of the body, including the sex cells. Then the changes would be passed to subsequent generations.

The Soviet biologist, A. A. Neifakh referred to the possible improvement of man by genetic engineering. Indeed what he described was similar in procedure to IVF. He was obviously excited by the possibilities offered by cloning.

Cloning

Dyban was also asked if cloning was permissible. He refers to moralising on this matter in Western society but he concludes that another aspect arises, namely its impact on the human race. Would it lead to degeneration or the development of human kind? He raises other questions about the morality of cloning, such as how would parentage be determined? What would be the reactions of the individual if he discovered he was the product of cloning and what circumstances would permit the use of cloning?

It is interesting to note that Dubinin claims that if cloning is successful a set of standardized geniuses will be produced, contradicting the idea of a genius making a unique contribution to art or science. Further scientific progress is seen to be through the work of collectives of talented individuals rather than that of isolated geniuses. Enormous progress will be made, he says, as people develop their talents under Communism, and standardized geniuses will be unnecessary.

But cloning geniuses, says Dubinin, would split people into a race of geniuses and others, leading to a new form of racism. Some foreign biologists talk of "sub-human" between man and monkey, or a race of people developed specially for a particular occupation. A number of foreign scientists see the possibility of a new form of racism as a threat to mankind, with eugenists perhaps turning mankind into an experimental herd. There is no threat if genetics remains in the right hands (preferably socialist). Genetic engineering can be useful applied to animals and crops, and to human beings if limited to curing illnesses or making transplants possible.

Returning to Dyban, he feels we are not ready for cloning where human beings are concerned and it is a fortunate prohibition of nature that cloning is not yet a reality. Hence the title of the interview published in *Literaturnaya Gazeta* in 1978.

Abortion

One of the most hotly debated bio-medical and prenatal problems in the USSR is the issue of abortion. This debate has continued since the beginning of Christendom. Even an examination of the Jewish traditions in prehistoric times reveals indications of it. The debate has accelerated in recent years. On 22 January 1973, the United States Supreme Court handed down its historic decision on abortion (Roe v Wade, Doe v Bolton). The reactions were swift and oftentimes predictable.

Nevertheless, the question of abortion had been flaring up in Western society immediately preceding the decision of the Supreme Court. In Britain the Abortion Act of 1967 had already caused an agonizing discussion on the moral status of the unborn and *Theological Studies* (March 1970) devoted a whole issue to clarification of the various aspects in the argument. In country after country in Western society, passionate controversy took place. Catholic hierarchies in England and Wales, Ireland, the United States, France, Italy, Holland and Germany, Poland and Scandinavia all made a contribution in pastoral letters delivered according to the nature of the societies or countries in which they lived. The American bishops could fall back on a shared Anglo-Saxon legal tradition and the Judaeo-Christian ethic. To avoid the appearance of sectarianism, they appealed to the United States Constitution and United Nations Declaration. The Scandinavian hierarchy, on the other hand, recognized that they faced a totally different situation. The abortion laws vary considerably from one country to another and the Scandinavian bishops were not in a hurry to oppose them completely. It is the right not to have an abortion that they had to defend. The Polish hierarchy had something in common with the Scandinavians. They chose to address the different groups individually, but their pastoral letter, both in content and in tone, was unlike the others mentioned as it contained a highly emotive appeal. The other countries in the East European bloc were taking steps to increase their birth rate. Poland's birth rate, said the hierarchy, is on the decline. They argued for a change of public opinion. Educators should teach the value of bringing life into the world; jurists should defend the right of the family; town-planners should provide suitable accommodation for bringing life into the world, which is itself a social service. The best form of investment, they claim, is manpower.

The Soviet situation differs considerably and is only comprehensible in the context of the USSR and its social, political and religious history. There are similarities between the USSR and Poland (as we shall see later), but in other ways they are very different.

Of the earlier accounts of this problem in the USSR, especially up to the 1960s, M. G. Field (1956, pp. 421–27), Lawrence Lader (1966, pp. 120ff) and H. Kent Geiger (1968, *passim*) have provided most useful information. A good summary of their information is included in a work by Daniel Callahan (1972, pp. 220ff).

In 1955 the law was "liberated". It was believed at that time in the USSR that the prohibition of abortion could neither increase the birth rate nor eliminate illegal abortions (Geiger 1968, p. 106). K. H. Mehlan (1966, p. 212) has given further reasons for the change. He lists amongst others the absence of effective contraceptives, and a desire to bring all women under closer supervision. But Klinger (1965, p. 90) has pointed out that the 1955 liberalisation law was not intended to be permanent. Yet abortion has increased and Mehlan reports "nearly three of four pregnancies are terminated by abortion". Mehlan also reports greater numbers proportionately in urbanized areas than in rural areas. Callahan (1972, p. 224) makes the extraordinary statement that the Soviet population over the last 50 years has declined by more than half and, he says, that during all these years, the USSR was experiencing a rapidly expanding industrialization and a great increase in the number of women at work. He fails, of course, to include a most important point that the USSR lost about twenty million people in the Second World War. He adds that it is a constant factor everywhere that in industrialized countries, the greater the industrialization, the greater the fall in birth rate; the greater the number of working women, the greater the decline in the birth rate. The USSR is no exception. One other interesting factor quoted by Callahan (1972) and reported by Mehlan (1966) is that the abortion rate for working women is three times greater than for housewives. Other reasons given are housing shortage, particularly in the cities and Lader (1966, p. 123) adds that Soviet women marry late – abortion is a common practice amongst university women students determined on finishing their course or education.

As we have seen, the present abortion law in the USSR dates only from 1955 and there seems to exist, as Helen Desfosses (1981, *passim*) points out, an abortion tradition. She claims that there is a predisposition by Soviet women to accept abortion as a means of birth control and that it is as intense as the attraction of the pill for American women. Indeed the prominent Soviet demographer, Urlanis, makes the telling point that in Central Asia, almost no one uses contraception (David 1970, p. 53). It seems that contraception is seen as unreliable and, therefore, only a small percentage of birth control is carried out by it. Nevertheless, the abortion pattern does vary from region to region and seems to be correlated with urbanization, education level, womens' involvement in work and growing material and cultural standards. However, abortion still continues to be the major method of birth control. It is estimated by some Western writers (Lapidus 1978, p. 299) that some eight million abortions are performed annually, amounting to double the number of live births in some areas. So it is that the incidence of abortion has increased substantially since legislation in 1955 which, as I have said, was a statement repealing the previous restrictive law. To put this Western estimate in context, there were 4,600,000 births in 1975 and 4,850,000 in 1980. The birth rate in 1982 was 18.9 per thousand population in the USSR but falls to 14.6 in Latvia and 14.8 in the Ukrainian republic, compared with 35 per thousand in the predominantly Muslim Uzbek SSSR and 38.2 in Tadzhikistan. Here it is clear that the Muslim birth rate is double that of the non-Muslim parts. Thus while the high fertility rates in these nations are, in some respects, a welcome compensation for the low rates prevailing elsewhere, they create additional and delicate problems of their own. Again, Barbara Holland points out that abortion is less common in the traditionally Muslim areas where it is discouraged by social custom (Holland 1979, p. 94).

I discussed this point with the Director of the Society for Central Asian Studies in Oxford, Dr Enders Wimbush, and he asserted that many children is part of the cultural heritage of Muslims in the USSR. The large family is an extremely important social unit. Furthermore, Muslim society is rural and there are few impediments of the kind we identify in modern society to producing more children. Hence, Wimbush says, housing is not a critical problem:

> In most parts of Central Asia and the Muslim Caucasus, the people are self-sufficient in food and necessities. Hence there is little pressure for women to go to work ... Birth control, as a whole, is of the most primitive sort.

But Wimbush adds one more fascinating reason for the large Muslim family. He claims that there was a conscious attempt by Muslims to outgrow the Russians who dominate their society: "I can assure you that this justification for large families is widely held and systematically employed."

Evidence is scarce regarding abortion amongst Muslims and Barbara Holland would claim that abortion is common amongst Muslims but less widespread in comparison with Russian women. She quotes from a detailed survey which was made about Kazakh and Russian women in the City of Alma-Ata. Nevertheless, Enders Wimbush would doubt this assertion. He states:

> I do not believe it ever was common amongst Muslim women and nothing leads me to believe that it will become so, rather quite the opposite for all the reasons I noted earlier ... But what is clear is that the Soviet leadership would like abortion to become more common amongst Soviet Muslims as a means of impeding the high birth rates.

He further states that the preference of Muslim women for large families will operate in the future. He sees no reason why this trend should weaken. And so it is that with respect to the non-Muslim areas of the USSR, the declining birth rate causes intense discussions on population policy. It has implications, according to Soviet reassessments, for economic growth, political and military power and ethnic balance in the years ahead.

The restriction of abortions is the most obvious method of increasing the birth rate since abortion forms at least 75 per cent of birth control methods in the USSR today. However, this course of action has not been adopted and there have been no major attempts to promote other birth control methods. Reasons for abortion are listed as economic conditions, unsatisfactory housing, shortage of day-care centres, the mother–worker conflict and the desire to regulate the number of children. The existing Soviet law, of course, gives women the right to choose. In spite of the factors just mentioned, the authorities seem determined to pursue a pro-natalist propaganda campaign. Some sociologists discuss ways of evoking child-bearing as a patriotic duty, while others believe child-bearing is a private affair. Meanwhile, great emphasis is placed on the idea that the single child family is harmful to a collectivist society. Nevertheless, in spite of the Soviet regime's policy towards pro-natalism, abortion remains incredibly high and the birth rate has not increased. Most authorities in the USSR have pursued the mother–worker theme as the best vehicle for self-expression for Soviet women. Some claim that three children is just the number at which the interest of society, on the one hand, and parents' interests on the other converge. However, there is a sharp controversy about this combination of the mother–worker situation; meanwhile the advocates of the government policy direct attention to *changing* peoples' attitudes to reproductive behaviour rather than *coerce* the behaviour itself.

In conclusion, it is important to underline that, unlike the moralising in Western society, no reference is made to the moral status of the unborn child. Abortion is not normally permissible after the twelfth week except on medical grounds, nor is it permissible within twelve months of a previous abortion, although in very special cases it may be allowed, but these limits are fixed on the basis of a woman's health and not because of any foetal rights. Here is an interesting difference between attitudes in the USSR and in Western society where the moral status of the unborn child has been very much under discussion and is a most controversial point. In short, foetal rights never enter Soviet consideration (Holland 1980, p. 60). Abortion, therefore, is not classed as morally unacceptable nor is there any ethical debate about it. The law fixes the start of independent life at the time the baby's head emerges during birth. Dr Michael Ryan, of the University of Swansea, mentions an article in a particular USSR journal entitled "Induced Abortion – Is it murder by the skilled?" His observation is that the article shows no interest in the ethical issues of abortion in the USSR, even though the title implies an ethical position (Ryan 1981).

EVALUATION

The Soviet regime faces a dilemma in this regard. It cannot be involved in boosting the birth rate in non-Muslim areas without doing likewise in the Muslim regions where the birth rate is already very high. Nor can there be selective population reduction in Muslim areas as this would appear discriminatory and would probably incur disfavour outside the USSR, especially in places like the Middle East. The Soviet population policy is marked by the tension between conflicting priorities such as the commitment to female independence and equality in regard to special rights and responsibilities of motherhood, and on the other hand, the need for population increase. Again, there is tension between the emphasis on the right of the individual couples where reproduction is concerned, as against the well-being of the community and national needs. A few social scientists have pointed out the advantages of lower birth rate and some have argued that smaller families mean a better quality of upbringing. However, the Soviet leadership is cautious in its approach to the limited options on population. The

one option that provides a partial solution is a massive technological transfer from the West, this reducing the need for more
hands. While, therefore, the Soviet regime has sound motives
for increasing its birth rate, there are apparent contradictions
and hesitations in its policy which reflect real dilemmas. There
is also a conflict of views about the future role of women in
Soviet society. They are needed as mothers but they are also
needed as workers and herein is the conflict.

Soviet society contains a number of religious collectivities
which, because of their historical background, have not the
same attitudes as in a pluralist Western society (Lane 1978, pp.
218ff). They are rather isolated and out of touch with similar
organizations both within and outside their own country.
They are not in touch with any modernizing and ecumenical
ideas. The official ideology in the USSR stresses "this world
orientation" and claims to give meaning to individual life by
linking it to the collective endeavour for the building of a full
Communist society. It is difficult to determine to what degree
Communist ideology has succeeded in replacing religion as a
fitting alternative world-view and to what extent religious
non-affiliation is merely prompted by fear of State reprisals.
Nevertheless, Medvedev (1979, pp. 204ff) makes the point that
Marxism is still very much believed in the USSR:

> Some intellectuals may become disillusioned by "classical" Marx-
> ism and may start to look for alternative ideologies, sometimes
> even religious, but such trends are not common. The major part of
> the Soviet intellectual community still frankly remains within the
> framework of Marxist ideology ...

Not all would agree with Medvedev here. If he is correct, these
are the very people who will be involved in decision-making
regarding human genetics and other important bio-medical
questions.

Up to now, unlike the great philosophers and major religions, Marxism has very little to say about the individual or
person. For instance, there is the problem of self, the body–
mind question, the epistemological problem of cognition,

matters concerning moral sense, consciousness, the existence or not of the soul, death and personal survival. *A fortiori* it would have very little interest in the ethics of genetics, IVF, abortion and other bio-medical questions in so far as they pertain to the individual person. Marxism's main interest would be how far they effect the human race in a Marxist context. There would be religious groupings or collectivities within the USSR that would have definite views on some of these questions, as in Western society. At least some of the Christian communities would be cases in point though the birth rate of some of the latter is surprisingly low.

And so one can say that there are some convergencies between Western capitalist society and Soviet society in the way that secularisation has preceded ethical questions. Both are materialistic and both have very little interest in the fundamental and ultimate questions already mentioned. However, there are essential differences based on the differing political ideology and cultures of both societies. In the USSR, the official ideology stresses "this world orientation" whereas in the West, secularisation is merely indifferent. In the USSR there is an atheistic and non-religious posture. In the West, however, a pluralistic society exists and the State is tolerant. Groups, some churches and sects in both societies, feel deeply about the ethical aspects of genetics, AID and surrogacy, IVF, cloning and abortion. But one has to suggest that the result of both societies in regard to these fundamental questions will be the same, since the Marxist–Leninist philosophy is not fundamentally different from secularisation in regard to the origin, nature and destiny of man.

Conclusion

It is difficult to avoid the conclusion that in the USSR there is no interest as such in the individual person. Because of the official view on human life, it would seem that the ethics of genetics and abortion are determined totally by Marxist–Leninist thinking. This would explain why unborn life has no moral status. It would also suggest a reason for the absence of discussion about the morality of abortion. Genetics, AID, IVF and cloning are assessed according as they advance or hinder human progress in the Marxist context. For some, at any rate, the fertilized ovum would then be seen as biological material and a fitting subject for experimentation when the ends of science are advanced. This was neatly highlighted in a letter to me from Dr Zhores Medvedev, to whose writings we have already referred:

> As a biologist I would certainly not consider fertilized ova, spare zygotes "a new being" – for me these cells are not much different to many human cell cultures which are used by biologists all over the world for different processes, from keeping human viruses alive, to studying the ageing in culture in cancer as a form of transformation ... However, I never considered this problem from a moral or ethical point of view.

At first sight, then, the diagnosis seems quite clear but, in fact, some of our findings are out of character with the expected thinking. The Director of the Institute of Obstetrics and Gynaecology in Leningrad, Professor Alipov, in correspondence with me, states quite clearly that his research centre would never allow the human organism to be used as a biological model, nor would experiments on human embryos be permitted. This practice is much more in line with the Expression of Dissent "B" in the Warnock Report in which it recommends that experimentation on the human embryo should not be permitted (Warnock Report 1984, pp. 90–4). This dissent was based on the belief that the embryo was at least a potential human being. The attitude of Alipov's institute is also in line with those people who would go further and contend that the embryo is a human person from the beginning of conception or, as others would say, it is more than a potential being; it is a human being with potential. The concern of the Institute of Obstetrics and Gynaecology for the embryo, and the respect it shows to the human organism, does not fit easily into a materialistic philosophy like Marxist–Leninism, nor does this attitude reflect the liberal attitude to abortion that exists in the USSR. What is also of interest is the parallel thinking in Britain where much agonizing debate about the moral status of the embryo, in the very early stages of its existence, is in marked contrast with the liberal attitude to abortion since 1967.

Another curious factor arises in this area. The scientists from the All-Union Research Centre for Maternal and Child Health Care of the USSR Ministry of Health, do not maintain that the fertilized ovum is a human being. These scientists, headed by the Correspondent Member of the USSR Academy of Medical Sciences, Professor E. Vikhlayeva, believe that experimentation on spare embryos is acceptable. Therefore, the view expressed by the Department of International Relations of the USSR Academy of Medical Sciences, Moscow is clean contrary to the views expressed by the Director of the Institute of Obstetrics and Gynaecology, Leningrad. Again, the practice itself of IVF in the USSR is implicitly confirmed by the information from Leningrad and Moscow. As I have already said, this point is also substantiated by the work of Pimenova *et al* in the data provided by the research team at the same Institute of Obstetrics and Gynaecology, Leningrad, and also by the work at the research centre led by Leonov.

It also seems clear that human embryo experimentation is monitored not by regional or other local monitoring bodies but directly by the Council of the USSR Ministry of Health. Moreover, there is no process similar to the Warnock Inquiry. It is also odd that Dr V. V. Smyslov, Chief of the Department of International Relations of the USSR Academy of Medical Sciences, claims that the philosophical and ethical aspects of problems of experimentation are not widely discussed in the press "as they are clear to Soviet scientists". Judging by the information from Leningrad and Moscow, this is not the case.

Soviet geneticists have successfully implanted embryonic human brain tissue into rabbits, making the animals respond more promptly to light and smells (*The Times* 26 November 1985). Biologists from the Academy of Sciences had cut a tiny hole in the rabbits' brains under anaesthetic and, using a thin pipe, injected them with brain tissue from human embryos. It was also claimed that it would be possible to perform brain tissue implantations to correct mental and neurological defects in humans. It is alleged the brain tissue used in the operations, which were performed at the Academy's Institute of General Genetics, came from human embryos which "failed to develop". But it is not at all clear what is meant by the words which could include "discarded" embryos, "non viable" embryos, "unsuitable" embryos, or even embryos specifically created for this purpose.

In the meantime, the Parliamentary Assembly of the Council of Europe (1985) continued with allegations that human embryos were being used for cosmetic purposes. And the *New Scientist* (10 October 1985) reported Horst Haase, a West German Social Democratic Party MP, as alleging that 500 human embryos were seized by Californian police. These were intended for cosmetic purposes, while French customs officers seized a consignment imported from Romania. All these techniques contain a serious threat to the human embryo in the future in the areas of science, commerce and industry.

And, therefore, all the problems which face Western research in regard to bio-medical questions at the beginning of human life are also prevalent in the USSR. They clearly reflect the general feeling that now that science, as a whole, has the potential to control almost all aspects of human life, more rigid rules in some form or other must be developed against unlimited scientific freedoms. But pressures that can be applied in Western society are different from those pertaining in the USSR. Science in the USSR is less free to ignore government attitudes as it is financed exclusively by the State budget and the State industrial systems. Moreover, lack of freedom of the press prevents the general public from knowing the real situation within scientific establishments, and hence from organizing movements against some negative features of scientific research, such as animal experimentation, forms of genetics and environment. Whereas in the West, a major part of the research budget depends on grants, private contributions and attitudes of the general public. Furthermore, in the West, information has more or less free access, especially through the mass media, whereas in the USSR, one institute or region, as has been demonstrated, is often not aware of what is happening in another. Therefore, it would seem that research in the USSR, although a matter of public concern, is more independent of public opinion than in the West. Consequently, it will be much less accountable to the public community (Medvedev 1979, p. 206).

CHAPTER VII

The Polish Factor

(I am grateful to members of the Universities of Krakow, Lublin and Warsaw, and also other Polish academics, who have been so helpful in discussing these issues with me and sometimes becoming involved in lengthy correspondence to clarify their points of view. Dr W. B. Skrzydlewski, who is a lawyer and philosopher and lectures at the Dominican College, Krakow, and also Professor Slipko, Ethics Department, Krakow University, went into great detail describing the Polish situation, as too did Professor Szawarski, Faculty of Philosophy, University of Warsaw, who has sent numerous letters and articles on this subject. In this chapter, I have followed the usual procedure of concentrating first on the new reproductive techniques and, later on, the question of the unborn.)

The Polish Commonwealth effectively ceased to exist in 1795 after successive partitions shared between Austria, Prussia and Russia. Poland was declared a republic in 1918 and invaded by the USSR and Germany in 1939. Having been "liberated" by the USSR, it became a Communist republic in 1952 though it remains a largely Catholic country, with a population of about 36,500,000.

The recent technological revolution in the area of human embryology and fertilization is, in the main, not a reality in Poland at the moment although AID is practised in certain places and much discussion about these issues is taking place amongst lawyers, philosophers, doctors and moralists. As we have seen, after nearly twenty years of restricted laws, in 1955 the USSR introduced considerable "liberalization" regarding abortion and this seemed the pattern for other Eastern European countries. Poland introduced a permissive system in 1956 as did Bulgaria and Hungary; Yugoslavia followed in 1960. The exception was the German Democratic Republic (East Germany). It, together with Albania, did not follow the trend of its Eastern European neighbours. It is not altogether clear why this should have been the case (discussed in the next chapter). Meanwhile, the other Eastern European countries followed a general move towards "liberalization". According to Andràs Klinger (1967, p. 89) the reasons behind the movement were freedom of choice on the part of women and protection of the health of women. No doubt other factors had a part to play but these were the key issues. Callahan (1972, p. 220) claims that the lack of effective contraceptives was also significant. In the Eastern European context, Poland is of special interest. It is an intensely Catholic country, even though it has been under a harsh Communist government where there were severe conflicts between the Church and State. Furthermore, the Catholics and the Marxists approach the question of life, its beginning and transmission, from fundamentally different aspects because they have different anthropologies. The Catholic theology is grounded on belief in man's divine image, creation, redemption and eternal destiny, whereas the Marxist position is, as we have seen, totally materialistic. Yet, in spite of the fact that the majority of the people have a Catholic commitment, there is at times a large gap between theory and practice, or belief and commitment. This applies particularly to the question of abortion and, to a certain extent, attitudes to the new reproductive techniques.

Genetics and the New Reproductive Techniques

As far as can be ascertained, the first official attitude of Polish medical experts on genetics and reproduction techniques was published in the well-known Polish weekly *Polityka*. The information is largely about AID and IVF techniques and their future possible use in Poland. Professor M. Troczyniska, Head of the Midwifery and Gynaecological Clinic at the Warsaw

Institute for the Mother and Child, has serious reservations from the moral standpoint and professional honesty. She feels that there is no need for "manipulating and engineering" nature and that far more important problems exist which should demand our attention. Furthermore, in Poland, she says, facilities for this kind of work simply do not exist and she adds that it is a technique with a high risk of failure "placing women in a state of anxiety and stress for many weeks". So, she asks: "Does IVF make any sense?"

Professor Z. Sternadel, Head of the Antenatal and Gynaecological Institute in Warsaw, states that infertility is the problem of the few. People talk of success but no one mentions the high failure rate which is as high as 95 per cent. Additionally, he asks, where are the financial resources to be found to fund this technique? Nevertheless, he would not exclude it from the medical future of Poland. On the other hand, Professor Lucian Wisniewski, Chairman of the Genetics Institute at the Centre for Child Health, does not think IVF would raise legal problems. It will be seen as normal medical treatment and there are medical centres in Poland ready to start the treatment of IVF – people are waiting for help. It is true, he says, that IVF by a donor is not covered by law but it would be "lacking in humility to formulate rules for something that is not yet practised".

Other specialists are also enthusiastic about this new method and it seems just a matter of time before it is operative in Poland. Dr P. Czerski asserts that from custom, practice and a moral point of view, he does not see any reason why AID, and in the future the implantation of a "foreign fertilized egg" should not be treated as adoption, albeit early adoption:

> From a psychological point of view, it can be expected that these mothers are likely to be more closely tied emotionally to their children than in later adoptions.

Professor Miroslaw Nestorowicz, of the University Mikolaj Kopern ik in Torun, also highlights the problem in Poland by indicating that about 1 per cent of marriages are infertile or have limited fertility. Of these about one-third could be helped by IVF and a further one-third by AID. However, in the case of IVF involving a third party, he lists the well-known problems, especially the question of the maternity of the child – is it the woman who supplies the egg or the one who bears the child? The problem is not solvable in the present state of the law. The ancient Roman law *Mater semper certa est* is being challenged. Certainly help can be got from the present legislation; for example, in Poland, Articles 62 and 85 of the Code for Family and Guardianship establish paternity no matter how fertility occurs between husband and wife, even without the consent of the husband. Again from the present Polish law, it cannot be argued that a donor has duties of paternity because the article requires that the donor cohabits with the child's mother to establish these responsibilities. On the other hand, Nestorowicz does admit that while some new legislation is needed in these new fertility techniques, the present law does give some guidance. Nestorowicz is certainly well acquainted with the various forms of reproductive techniques in the West and the problems, legal and otherwise that accompany them. Indeed, besides considering surrogate motherhood, he examines the question of liability and compensation in the case of damage as well as future experimental techniques such as cloning, nucleus transplantation, parthenogenesis and claims the need for the intervention of the law in research described as the "new biology" or human genetics. While one need not ban research altogether, one should define its limits. Nestorowicz (1985) quotes Professor A. Esera of Freiburg University, who aptly stated:

> The time has long passed in many disciplines in which it is judged that one can have unlimited freedom to do basic research whilst giving the responsibilities for its technical application exclusively to politicians. This is particularly relevant to atomic and genetic research, as here even basic research can change the natural conditions and create a source of threat.

The implementation of Esera's observation is desirable and is permanently arising in various considerations in this book.

Discussion about genetic engineering exists very much in

Poland but not with the same frequency and vehemence as in Western society. In 1975 the Marxist journal *Czlowiek Swiato-poglad* published several articles about genetic projects. These studies concentrated on the biological aspects but indicated certain dangers involved without passing any moral judgements. More recently, Fr Lucjan Bolter, a Polish priest, translated an article on biology and morality by the writer Hans Jonas (1984, pp. 51ff) which was published in America. It appeared later in Polish. The author points out that the whole biosphere has now to be considered, as one man's action can effect the whole world. Man, as a primary force on this planet, no longer has the right to think only of himself. Ethics must, therefore, concern itself with mankind and all forms of life in our environment. Man must become the protector of all creation and must look to the consequences of technology. We have to consider what is good or bad for humanity. Even that which is good here and now, may prove in the long term very bad. In this new technology, especially that of bioethics, greater responsibility is demanded, otherwise man is in danger of destroying himself. Positive genetics, he says, is morally evil. Above all, man the creature, should not play the Creator.

It seems that the first Polish philosopher to give attention to the question of the new eugenics was the Marxist Professor Marek Fritzhand (1982). He condemned positive genetic engineering and approved of negative engineering with a few exceptions. Some six years before, in 1976, Fr D. Kornas had written about eugenic experiments and gave moral comments in the popular theological journal *Chrzescijanin w swiceie* Later, in 1984, Kornas also put forward a dissertation on medical experiments on the human organism in the light of theological reflections. As well as Kornas, other academics such as Professor S. Olejnik and S. Rosik of Lublin University have written about particular biomedical questions. In 1983 in the Faculty of Philosophy, University of Lublin, a symposium was held on bioethics in which Professors E. Bone and S. Olejnik, Fr Furger J. Bogusz and W. Luipin took part. In 1984–85 Professor T. Slipko, SJ gave outline lectures in the Philosophy Department of Warsaw Catholic Academy.

Professor Slipko wrote that the moral status of the embryo is perceived in different ways in Poland and, although Poland is a Catholic country, pluralism pervades, as in other places. Some people, he says, see the embryo as a simple living cell, equivalent to other cells. Giving the Catholic approach he, himself, suggests that two questions should be distinct, i.e. the moral status of the embryo if it is ensouled from conception and, on the other hand, the status of the embryo if animation is delayed. If the former, he says, then respect due to it is the same as that given to any member of the human race. If the latter opinion is true, and animation is delayed, nevertheless, the embryo is the developing being participating in human dignity and with an inviolable life. So that in both cases, the zygote has a moral dimension and "for that reason is essentially different from other biological entities". Here Slipko's argument is in total agreement with official Catholic teaching as expressed through Vatican II: "... from the moment of conception, life must be guarded with greatest care, while abortion and infanticide are unspeakable crimes". In expressing his doubts about the time of animation, he is very much in line with the Statement in 1974 of the Sacred Congregation for the Doctrine of the Faith (1974, p. 734). This Congregation declared explicitly that it did not rest its condemnation of abortion on the time of ensoulment "for the matter cannot be established". The declaration advances two arguments against abortion. First, in the experience of certain knowledge, it risks killing an ensouled foetus. The second line of argument stresses the inviolability of human life irrespective of whether the soul is present.

As to embryo experimentation, Slipko feels it is morally unacceptable whether it is a question of spare embryos after IVF or manipulation of an ensouled foetus, for this is a case of using people as a means to an end. Even though the ends are good, he says, it does not justify evil means. When speaking of the "simple case" of IVF between husband and wife, he says, some Polish philosophers consider all artificial fecundity and insemination immoral because they depersonalize the marriage act by introducing technical intervention. This belief is also held by some moralists in the West. However, Slipko, himself, holds a different viewpoint. He contends that when IVF and artificial insemination are used by a husband and wife, then these techniques *in se* do not appear morally unacceptable because the technical element "enhances the moral good of the marital union".

However, in practice, difficulties arise in another area. There is the problem of masturbation and Slipko sees no way of escaping it. Once again, he quotes the principle that the end does not justify means that are bad in themselves. Slipko also refers to Dr Iglesias's article in *The Tablet*, where Iglesias (1984a) deals with the IVF technique and suggests that there is no such thing as the "ideal case" because in practice there is no team working on IVF which openly adheres to the principle of respect for every human life: "The aim is successful pregnancy and the progress of science; newly conceived human beings are regarded as expendable for these purposes." She points out that the aim of existing clinical teams is to achieve a pregnancy with the most economical and least troublesome means, even if countless newly conceived human beings must be sacrificed in the process. To achieve that aim, the present practice of induced super-ovulation is employed. A comment is added by Mahoney who argues against her position on the grounds that every conception and pregnancy is fraught with risk for the child and that, in any case, if there is an abnormal pregnancy, the principle of "allowing to die" can be invoked. Again, he adds, amongst other reasons, that conception does not necessarily result immediately and instantaneously in an individual human person of "paramount value". Slipko rejects Mahoney's approach as a quibble based on a relativist viewpoint which worships "experimentation".

It is difficult to assess the attitude of the Polish people to AID and IVF when a third party is involved. Obviously such practices are against Catholic teaching, but Professor M. Kozakiewicz indicates that no survey has been conducted on genetic manipulation in Poland. But as far as Poland's Family Planning Association is concerned, even when the gametes are from an extra-marital donor, the procedure would be acceptable to them, except in rare cases of selfishness. Nestorowicz, however, writes that artificial insemination, while increasing everywhere in Poland, is at the same time causing legal, religious and moral controversy. Z. Radwanski and K. Krzekotowska express their approval with certain restrictions and Nestorowicz, agreeing with them, adds that it is essential to have control over the dissemination of the donor's sperm so as to prevent incest. It should be forbidden for married women who have not had their husband's consent and also for the unmarried. However, serious reservations were made by B. Walaszek. He believes that it creates dangers for the continued functioning of marriage and this can lead to the breakdown of marital intimacy and, in consequence, the break-up of the family. Indeed the parental instinct, he says, can, to a great degree, be satisfied by adoption. The fact that the donor is paid is even more objectionable and doctors should be forbidden by law from practising AID. There is, however, no direct legislation in Poland but Nestorowicz believes that the present legislation as contained in Article 85 in the Code for Family and Guardianship should be sufficient to cover the question of paternity and anonymity. In any case, one cannot "stop the development of social behaviour by law". It would, he says, be as ineffective as the laws in certain countries banning abortion. It would cause illegal and unprofessional operations and interfere in the sphere of personal liberty. Nevertheless, he agrees with Radwanski and Krzekotowska that certain restrictions are necessary, especially where the danger of incest is concerned. Meanwhile, in Poland the argument regarding the donor's anonymity and his responsibility continues. Slipko believes that his enquiries demonstrate that, in the main, people favour the absolute anonymity of the donor and he adds that AID is practised in public institutions and in clinics in places like Poznan and Warsaw.

From this research then, it can be seen that the new reproductive techniques, with all their complexities, are known to experts in Poland because of their perusal of the appropriate journals and text books. Furthermore, they are aware of the intense discussions and debates about these topics in the West. On the other hand, the ordinary people would have but vague knowledge of these matters because little information is divulged in the mass media.

Attitudes to Unborn Life

Before 1956 induced abortion was illegal in Poland, except when allowed by a court or recommended by a physician. Nevertheless, it was suggested that several hundred thousand abortions were performed illegally. Now with the change in the law, induced abortion is also allowed for broad social indications. Under the law, abortions were to be performed by specialized physicians in the State maternity hospitals or private outpatient clinics. Now ambulatory facilities, run by medical co-operatives, joined State and private practice. Abortions performed in hospitals are free of charge for those employed in the socialised sector, while abortions in co-operative or private ambulatory facilities involve a doctor's fee which can be substantial.

One of the extraordinary factors about abortions in Poland is that when measured against the total population, they are significantly high. This is demonstrated when compared with Britain, the USSR and the United States. One should however, point out immediately that there is a discrepancy in the United States figures. That is to say, the figures as reported in the United Nations *Demographic Year Book* (1982) are substantially different from those recorded in the *Statistical Abstract of the United States*. According to the *Demographic Year Book*, abortions do not exceed one million per annum until 1977, whereas in the *Statistical Abstract*, they exceed one million per annum by 1975. I reported this to the Reference Centre of the Embassy of the United States, London and emphasized that there was also a discrepancy of nearly 200,000 per annum. The Embassy could not account for this discrepancy and referred me to the sources of the *Statistical Abstract* where the numbers were based on a survey conducted by the Alan Guttmacher Institute, New York. It, however, transpired that the figures in the *Demographic Year Book* are based on official reports to health departments but the Alan Guttmacher figures are de-

rived from surveys on all abortion providers. Many of these do
not report to health departments. Nevertheless, allowing for
these discrepancies, the comparison is still a most interesting
one.

The second extraordinary factor about abortion in Poland is
the amount of discrepancies that occur in the annual abortion
rate as reported by different sources. Official figures are much
lower and it is indicated by numerous researchers that the total
varies from 130,000 to one million per annum. Professor
Okolski (1983) suggests some reasons. As well as a large
number of abortions which are not reported for various
reasons, such as financial gain and evasion of taxes, there is also
the fear that were the actual figures known, society would
become more concerned with the abortion issue and this could
mean a change in the abortion law. It would become a political
point. Even those abortions that are disclosed are incorporated
in statistical sources forming one highly aggregated category
under the heading – "Abortions performed in ambulatory
facilities". Because of the poor quality and lack of data, not
much can be deduced from official figures. Always the actual
official number shown per annum will be less when compared
with other sources and few conclusions can be drawn from
them, except that there seems to a continuous shift from
hospitals to co-operative and private clinics.

Speculations about the true magnitude of abortions have not
been consistent and, as I have indicated, vary considerably
with the sources. Although official statistics serve as a starting
point, further estimates can be usefully submitted. Okolski
suggests that the total number of induced abortions in Poland
can be estimated as high as 310,000 to 510,000 per annum.
Smolinski estimated that the total number of induced abortions annually is as high as 400,000 to 450,000. It will be noted
that this total is more than twice the official figure. In a letter to
me, Dr Skrzydlewski, OP, mentioned the figures 300,000
(circa) induced abortions for 1983 and 280,000 (circa) for 1980.
He feels that the 1983 figure is confirmed by the research
carried out by Fr Jan Wójtowicz, Head of Pastoral office,
Diocese of Przemyśl, who studied figures in that area and

extended his findings to the whole country, making adjustments for the biggest cities like Warsaw. If these figures are correct, then the abortion rate increased between 1980 and 1983. Again, the statement made on 18 June 1970 by the Polish bishops to the government on "Biological and Moral Threats" to the Polish nation mentions the number of abortions as one million per annum. A memorial dated 3 February 1981, prepared by the solidarity section of the Medical Academy of Sczczecin estimated the number at 700,000 to one million per annum in 1981. Other sources give 600,000 to 800,000 per annum. Two writers, W. Fijalkowski and J. Sobala-Bednarek, in a paper to the Third Session of the Polish Population Conference in Poznan, estimated 600,000 to 800,000 per annum. Meanwhile, the well-known government spokesman, Jerzy Urban, places the figure for 1983 at 131,000 and claims that this is 8,000 lower than 1982 and 2,000 lower than 1981! He justifies the abortion incidence as the lesser of two evils. He also expressed delight at the increase in the birth rate throughout the 1970s. However, even if one accepts Urban's figures, which by other standards are considerably reduced, they are, in fact, exceedingly high for a country like Poland.

In its civil law and in its general rules concerning "Personal Law" and the Law of Succession, Polish legislation considers the unborn a human person from the first moment of his/her life. For example, if the legal father dies after the child's conception – even in the same month – the child has the right of succession. Again, if someone attacked the expectant mother and damaged the unborn child, indemnity by law could be demanded for the child. Hence the law permitting abortion is an exception to the whole of Polish law regarding the unborn.

As we have seen (Chapter I) Szawarski has written on the moral status of the unborn. It will be remembered that he rejected abortion except in two cases, namely the gravest medical reasons, such as German measles, and over-population. These exceptions were based on the argument of the lesser of two evils which reminds us of the stance of Jerzy Urban. Szawarski's was also probably the first article of its kind to be published in Poland. However, he is severely criticized by a fellow countryman, Janusz Gula of Lublin University. Gula argues that Szawarski fails to distinguish between responsible parenthood and abortion. In other words, he says, limiting procreation can be classed as control, whereas abortion is simply destruction.

The Catholic Church has broadened its opposition to abortion in Poland through its very large pastoral activities. Premarital courses have been made obligatory since 1970. No one can be married in the Catholic Church in Poland without having undergone such a course. Thousands of Marriage Advisory Councils and Centres exist and information and personal advice is freely available. Perhaps the most distinctive feature of the Church's attitude to abortion was expressed in an interview with the Polish primate, Cardinal Joseph Glemp, printed in *Polityka* (31 July 1981):

> For the Church, the problem of induced abortion is precisely the problem of the human being set within religion, that is, in God. Moreover a legal act which allows the termination of life is a breach of moral norms from a humanitarian point of view, as it presumes that it is possible to force physicians to take an emerging life. Our insistence on the withdrawal of that act runs parallel to our work in shaping such a moral attitude in man that he considers the taking of life as a bad deed. The legal act deforms consciences in such a way that man tends to consider good what is in accordance with the law.

However, while the official Catholic position regarding abortion is well known and Polish Catholics would, in theory, accept this teaching, in practice, they seem to follow the argument of the lesser of two evils and this is really the Utilitarian approach. No matter how important their religious commitment may be, other factors cannot be excluded or easily controlled. People marry young and live with one or other set of parents-in-law for up to ten years or more. When eventually an apartment is available for them it usually consists of a bathroom, one bedroom, living room and kitchen. Therefore, for them it is imperative to restrict family sizes to one or two children. In this situation, abortion is seen as a realistic, though immoral, solution. Moreover, modern and effective contraceptives are not obtainable. Less effective methods frequently lead to unwanted pregnancies and ultimately abortion. It seems legitimate to argue that, in Poland, abortion is a fertility-regulated-method that substitutes for contraception. Added to this is the incidence of working women and "the woman's right to choose" syndrome. Yet disapproval of abortion is widespread in Poland. Indeed surveys indicate that two-thirds of married women of reproductive age disapprove. But the differences, as in the USSR, between different social groups are striking, so that the percentages of disapproval are higher in villages and smaller towns than in cities. Strangely, in the rural areas attitudes seem to be ambiguous and here there is a definite difference from the USSR. One naturally asks what is the cause of this ambiguity? J. Ziolowski (1974, pp. 445–88) indicates that this ambiguity of attitude demonstrates that Catholic women who obtain abortions do so with a guilty conscience. Coupled with this is the approval of abortion according to the different levels of education, a point that was noted in the last chapter on the USSR. There seems to be a correlation generally, but not universally, between attitudes to abortion and the level of education. This is possibly explained by the fact that education gives greater independence, more opportunity for employment outside the home and, therefore, more liberty.

EVALUATION

It has been seen that in Poland, as in the USSR and the West, the new reproductive techniques present the same complexities. Bio-technology is far in advance of the law. The social and moral problems are formidable. While some of the new methods are not yet a reality in Poland, it is just a matter of time before the country is faced with the same problems that accompany them.

As Poland is a predominantly Catholic country, where according to Catholic teaching induced abortion is morally unacceptable, there must be very serious reasons which motivate people to seek abortion. It is interesting that the figures given by the Church are much higher than those of the government – the Church would not have any vested interest in inflating the figures. On the contrary, high abortion rates would be an argument against the effectiveness of its teaching. The government, on the other hand, would certainly have an interest in keeping the figures low for a number of reasons to which we will return later. In the meantime, it should be said that while Poland is predominantly Catholic, uniformity of belief and practice cannot be assumed. Within the country there are Marxists, agnostics, secularists as well as Catholics. This indicates a significant heterodoxy. Even within the Catholic community itself one cannot assume homogeneity in belief. Frequently, as some experts note, the stresses of recent years, the eruption of Solidarity in 1980 and its subsequent suppression under Martial Law, have led to the resurgence in religion, seeing the Church and Christianity as alternatives to the influence of official ideology and the Communist Party. For some people, religion is as much, if not more, attributable to political commitment rather than personal belief. Professor A. Pospieszalski suggests that Sunday Church-going can be a way of expressing outrage and protest against hated secular authorities, rather than a conscious option for God (*The Tablet* 18 May 1985.)

The Church, furthermore, is a focal point not only for religion but for dissent – a sort of "independent culture". So, in the case of abortion, the burden of evidence would suggest that it is unwise to place too much weight on religious motivation when other factors have not been controlled. As in the USSR, there is an acute housing shortage as well as the mother–worker conflict and the woman's "right to choose". One writer points out that in a cold country where people "live in" most of the time, the housing problem is accelerated. In countries like Britain, people are out of the house much of the time but not so in Poland. Additionally there is the free access to abortion with complete anonymity. But probably the most important factor is the psychological one. Western people sometimes change their religion or confession in order to have more permissive ethics. Poles do not normally change their faith and so, in practice, experience a conflict between belief and moral practice. Put in another way, some try to solve their problem by changing the rules or abandoning them. But others try to meet these problems by retaining their beliefs but behaving differently. Skrzydlewski places this moral conflict in the form of a question:

> Are Polish attitudes and behaviour worse than those of Western people? What is better: to sin morally but to be faithful to the religious convictions or to change these convictions in order to have moral freedom? (Skrzydlewski 1984, p. 6.)

Sometimes this conflict is described as a disparity between the "objective attitude" regarding people in general, and the "subjective attitude" which concerns the particular person in the concrete situation. Ziolowski (1974) suggests that this is probably the motive for peoples' behaviour.

There are, of course, other reasons which might explain the high abortion rate in Poland. There is the impact of another ideology with powerful means at its disposal. Deceptive terminology is used to describe abortion as a "medical intervention" like extracting a tooth, rather than killing the unborn. Perhaps, even more confusing, is the point that Cardinal Glemp made in his statement I have quoted, namely, the fact that abortion is legally permissible, is sometimes seen and understood to give moral approbation to the operation. Last, but not least, is the fact that the medical profession acquires significant profits from such a practice.

Some experts emphasize that Poland has adopted a contraceptive pattern which involves the most inefficient methods. This is not unlike the attitudes prevalent in the USSR. When failure occurs, women resort to abortion. Indeed it can be added here that one reason why official figures are lower than other sources is that a high abortion rate indicates the failure of the government's policy in housing and other areas.

Conclusion

There are close similarities, as we have seen, between Poland and the USSR in the question of the beginning of human life and the new reproductive techniques for its transmission. In Poland, of course, while debate proceeds amongst academics, IVF is not yet a reality. Nevertheless, the same complexities and challenges are present in the literature regarding AID, surrogacy and IVF, particularly about the identity of parenthood and the anonymity surrounding the donor. At present AID is practised in places like Poznan and Warsaw. However, as Slipko states, the opinion of the ordinary people regarding the legal, social and moral complexities has not yet been tested.

Amongst the medical profession, scientists and other academics, different opinions, according to Szawarski and Slipko, circulate regarding the moral status of the embryo.

As to abortion, the fact that Poland is a Catholic country makes little impact on the rate of abortions per annum. On the contrary, and by any standards, the abortion rate is amongst the highest in the world. There is, therefore, a *de facto* convergence of permissive attitudes with those prevalent in the USSR and Western society. These attitudes, *in practice*, are Utilitarian though, *in theory*, many would see abortion as morally unacceptable. Moreover, the approach to abortion seems to follow similar educational and economic patterns as in the USSR, especially regarding urbanization, housing shortage, working women and the right to choose. Nevertheless, in Poland abortion is an ethical issue: in the USSR it is not.

CHAPTER VIII

The East German Factor

The German Democratic Republic was created in 1949 from the area of Germany occupied by the USSR after the Second World War. A Communist government was installed. The population is about 17 million, chiefly Protestant but with a Roman Catholic minority.

Genetics and the New Reproductive Techniques

In June 1985 an article in *The Times Higher Educational Supplement* by Barbara van Ow, "Eichmann slur on Genetics", indicated that there was concern amongst society in East Germany, which was echoed by writers and artists, about the possible consequences of bio-technological progress. Notable amongst these writers was Heinar Kipphardt who attacked modern genetic scientists as the "Eichmanns of today".

In this chapter I will try to examine once more the question of genetics, the new modern reproduction techniques, and the attitude to the unborn, especially as demonstrated in the incidence of abortion.

Meanwhile, the debate continues in East Germany regarding the social and ethical problems of the modern techniques. The discussions are largely confined at present to the academic *fora*; the State and Party leadership remains silent on the issue. As we shall see, some of the experts mentioned by Barbara van Ow, such as Professors Helmut Kyank, Wilken and Geissler, react to the warnings and statements by the writers and artists. The virologist, Geissler, deplores the fears amongst writers and artists which are multiplied by groundless arguments. He reluctantly accepts that there are fears and misgivings in wide sections of the population about the ethical misuse of science and technical progress. In the literary monthly *Sinn und Form*, Geissler stresses that the problems of the 1980s and 1990s can only be solved by "combining the advantages of socialism with the achievements of science". He lists some of the positive contributions of modern genetics such as synthesis of insulins, interferon, growth hormones and other active substances, prenatal diagnosis, increased agricultural yield and energy conservation, which are either ignored or described as utopian and unreal. Geissler does recognize, nevertheless, that scientific discoveries can be misused to man's detriment but he is rather naive in suggesting that large-scale misuse of genetic research need not be feared. He remarks, as if to alleviate all fears, that "some of the extraordinary views of genetic engineering are based on ignorance". He claims cloning is possible in the future by nuclear substitution. He contends that the clones would not be complete copies. However, this causes people to feel uneasy. In the conference organised by *Voprosy filosofii* and the Institute of Medical Genetics in 1973, he refers to Niefakh, the leading Soviet scientist. As we have already seen, Neifakh is interested in reproducing highly-talented people by cloning. Geissler believes that this is not a practical proposition and then, in order to set the records straight, he mentions Marx and Lenin in regard to variety in man. When socialists speak of equality, they mean social equality. This in no way refers to the physical and mental capacities of the individual. So Geissler does not support the idea of cloning and sees it as contrary to the Marxist–Leninist philosophy.

However, Barbara van Ow classes him as a "hawk" who is "pushing bio-technologies with almost missionary fervour" and this group, she would contend, is led by Geissler "who categorically discards any ethical doubts about modern genetic technology". I believe, having read Geissler, that this is a rather hard judgement on him though I doubt if many people's fears will be removed by his optimistic approach.

Professor Wilken, the Director of Rostock Gynaecological University Clinic, who accepts embryo experimentation as ethically unobjectionable, underlines that genetic engineering could be most important but ethics or moral reasoning must wait till later!, "when exact information is available" (Wilken, Fleiss and Sudik 1984, pp. 1473ff.).

AID

The AID technique is legally safeguarded in East Germany. Parents make a legally binding declaration to the Commissioner of Oaths that they recognize a child conceived by this treatment as their legitimate child with all the legal and social consequences, and that no action disputing paternity will be taken afterwards.

Surrogacy is not practised or advocated; rather adoption is recommended. Dr Böhmer, Senior Medical Consultant of the Inner Mission Hospital, Wittenberg, stresses the importance of the social parentage of the child. "It is certainly more important than genetic origin for the psychological and emotional development." He certainly underplays the importance of the genetic origin of the child. He proceeds to make an interesting point, namely, that in the last years of the Second World War, and in the post-war years

> very large numbers of children became orphaned or were separated from their parents through circumstances of fate. These children were then brought up by adoptive parents. Many of them found their genetic parents again, after many years, but did not develop any emotional relationship with them. This unintentional mass experiment in psychology ought to have demonstrated that stable social parents are more important for child development than knowledge of one's genetic origin from which, on its own, no consequences for individual psychological development have resulted. Here, therefore, we attach greater importance to the stability of the marriage and to psychological investigations into the management of this anti-natal adoptive treatment. (Böhmer 1981)

There is no doubt that this is an interesting observation and, while one accepts the importance of the social parentage factor, it does not in any way negative the equally important point of genetic origin and the child's knowledge of it. In reality these two factors are not mutually exclusive. Indeed, in Britain the Adoption Laws were changed by the Adoption Act of 1975 precisely to meet the question of genetic origin. Some recent work has been done on this point by Dr Triseliotis (1973) who studied a number of Scottish cases of adopted children in Scotland who had gone in search of their parents. Another recent piece of research on this question was conducted by Polly Toynbee, who states:

> I am now quite certain that the idea of the importance of blood ties and genes is common to most people, and they feel profoundly deracinated if brought up with no knowledge of their blood origins ... The current debate about surrogacy, *in vitro* fertilization and artificial insemination by donor should all centre around the needs of the children who are created by these methods. What the adopted children in this book say about our laws of identity shows how dangerous it is to confuse a child's origins. Adopted children are, at least, an accident and deciding how they should be brought up is not easy. But it seems to me that it would be a very alarming development to bring thousands of new children into the world on purpose, who would be destined to lose their biological parents. (Toynbee 1985, p. 196.)

The 1975 Act in Britain gave back to the adopted child an identity that was lost. It required they underwent a counselling session with a social worker to ensure a correct preparation, and this procedure naturally asked the question why in AID or other forms of reproduction should the child be deprived of knowing his parents. Or, as Iglesias (1984) said:

> Why should an action for which we are responsible – if it is a morally good action, or for example, an action voluntarily done as an act of generosity to communicate life – be always kept anonymous?

To base social relations between parents, and family relations, on grounds which are not open is to build a society with an insecure foundation.

In East Germany, on the basis of the experience of an interdisciplinary concillium consisting of representatives of gynaecology, genetics, psychology and forensic medicine, a proposition was elaborated for the regulation of AID to serve as a basis for discussion (Glander *et al* 1983). The legislation now valid was interpreted, in principle, in comprehensive works by Keune and Rothe (1985, pp. 1815–16). Some of the agreed viewpoints were:

1. Infertility.
2. Stable Relationship.
3. Equal rights of the AID child with the rest of the family's children.
4. Limitation of risks of incest.
5. The donor renounces all claims.
6. Payment to be in accordance with the orders of the Health Ministry.
7. Anonymity of donor.
8. AID is performed by a doctor in special institutions of the Health Service.

It should be mentioned that the well-known objections to AID are also discussed in East Germany. J. Zander wrote an article in the Munich medical weekly, *West German Journal*, "Medical Ethical Problems at the Start of Life" in which some of the objections are discussed. Nevertheless, AID is recognized as a method of treatment and juridically safeguarded under East Germany's laws.

IVF, ET and other Reproductive Techniques

In East Germany, IVF is practised not as a matter of routine but as a specialized treatment for infertility. There is no commerce in spare embryos and IVF and ET are free of charge. ET itself is seen as the earliest form of adoption. Indeed it is seen as the most favourable form. Professors Wilken, Fliess and Sudik, while supporting this position, add that it is not clear whether the agreement of the genetic mother is sufficient, or whether, in the case of embryo transfer, the agreement of the genetic father should also be obtained. They are unhappy too about surrogate motherhood because of existing legality and the strong bond that would be created between mother and child. They describe surrogate motherhood as "ethically problematic" and in conflict with the socialist humanist character image when an embryo is carried to term for payment "by women who are psychologically inferior and economically dependent". Yet it is of interest that they would not state categorically that the possibility of surrogacy is to be completely excluded and would always be described as immoral in socialist conditions:

> It will have to remain an open question whether surrogacy will be desirable, ethically defensible and feasible at least sometimes in the future and in exceptional conditions. (Wilken, Fleiss and Sudik 1984, pp. 1473ff.)

But this would require legislation and clarification. At present surrogacy is to be rejected.

Surplus Embryos

How are surplus embryos to be treated? Uwe Körner, a Marxist philosopher, and Hannelore Körner, a biologist, describe the various possible uses of embryo surplus – freezing, availability for adoption, destruction and experimentation. They argue that the question of one's approval of experimentation is a question about the value of embryonic human life:

> In our view, a prenatal life which has no potential chance of development has forfeited its value to potential human existence. They become valuable through human effort and activity. (Körner and Körner 1984, pp. 1067ff.)

However, they argue that embryo experimentation should be performed with the greatest of restraint and only when there is absolute necessity, and when the embryos are really classed as discarded. They add that, even when discarded, they should not be treated as merely tissue cultures or laboratory animals. This point was supported by Böhmer. It is also supported by

Wilken, Fliess and Sudik. Experiments are to be carried out for the purpose of gaining knowledge of infertility and making IVF and ET more effective. Recommendations for East Germany have been formulated by the interdisciplinary Working Party "Ethics and Medicine". It is underlined that experiments are to be carried out only on surplus embryos which differs from the Warnock stance because the latter recommended, by 9 to 7 votes, that the creation of embryos for experimentation was justified.

Wilken, Fliess and Sudik state quite clearly that AID, IVF and ET are ethically acceptable. They consider "the simple case of IVF" where gametes are taken from the partners in a marriage relationship. They believe there is far reaching agreement that the technique in itself is ethically sound and also that the debate regarding the genetic origin of the child is not applicable here. This immediately indicates that the question of identification of origins is also a vexed question. Not withstanding this, Wilken, Fliess and Sudik believe that, in the case of ovum and sperm donation, anonymity of the donor should be preserved and his/her consent must be respected. If this is so, they would claim, the procedure is ethically acceptable.

Embryo Experimentation

There is general agreement that experiments on the embryo are ethically justified if they are performed, as we have said, with a view to increasing scientific knowledge or improving medical treatment. This is similar to the Warnock approach. At the moment the Committee of Gynaecologists and Obstetricians is working and hoping to achieve a common position in East Germany. IVF is performed, but not as a routine practice, in a few university hospitals. Again, there is no official evaluation of these reproductive techniques amongst the Protestant churches. Professor Helga Horz discusses this question in relation to ET. Her principles are broadly sketched and fit the socialist framework which contends that man must not become the object of science. However, when I pressed her to elaborate on her thinking regarding ET she failed to respond.

Professor Helmut Kyank, of the Wiehelm Pieck University, deals with questions of ET and extra-corporeal fertilization and outlines the range of ethical and legal problems including surrogacy, payment, the concept of marriage and donors. He also grants that there are arguments about the discarding and destruction of embryos, though he, himself, compares this procedure with the loss of zygotes after natural fertilization in the early stages of pregnancy. But he also admits that embryo experimentation is highly disputed in East Germany, especially when the experimentation is for the purpose of studying development "or for the breeding of a bank of organs for transplant purposes, all of which are possible for IVF". (Kyank 1983, pp. 1–4.)

Some writers, namely Geissler, E. Horz and H. Horz, have written a paper which throws further light on East German thinking. They consider cross-fertilization of human sperm and hamster eggs as morally acceptable and feel this should not be tabooed:

> In our opinion there is not even cause to object to the, at first surprising, fact that, trans-species hybrids are being produced, that hamster eggs are being fertilized with human sperm. (Geissler, Horz and Horz 1980.)

The inter-disciplinary team "Ethics in Medicine" at the Academy of Further Medical Training of the GDR, medical scientists, social scientists and biologists discussed the problem of IVF. As a result certain recommendations were made. In short, the technique, they said, was in keeping with humanist principles of the socialist society and medical ethics. The "simple case" of IVF was considered unproblematic and spare embryos can be preserved by freezing for the period of child bearing life. Operations undertaken sheerly for ova-donation are not justifiable. Embryo donation is compared with adoption and is to be treated as in AID. However, the written agreement of both donors is necessary and they must renounce all further rights against the women recipients. The interdisciplinary team confirmed the rejection of surrogacy especially for commercial purposes. Women are more than child-bearers. No experiment should be carried out on embryos intended for ET.

So it is that the problems – social, legal and moral – of modern reproductive techniques are present. So far, the discussion is confined largely, although not exclusively, to the academic forum: the State which supports bio-technology has remained silent. Weibering (1981, p. 196) a theologian and Körner and Körner in their works, form the basis of most of the official statements of scientific groups in East Germany, and this applies to both the Marxist and the Protestant approaches which have been stated by Böhmer and others. There is no official attitude of the Protestant churches to these matters.

The Catholic Church follows the same approach as the official position which I have already stated. There is, of course, limited debate on whether the "simple case of IVF" is morally flawed and a few theologians debate the limits and moral implications of embryo experimentation, though the vast majority would reject it and follow the official position of the Catholic Church.

Attitudes to the beginning of Human Life: the Abortion Factor

East Germany presents a different picture from that of any of the other Eastern European countries. It did not follow the trend of its neighbours in the late 1950s and early 1960s towards liberalized abortion laws. At that time, its birth rate was the lowest in Europe and this might well be a possible explanation. Yet East Germany was the first country after the Second World War to introduce relatively liberal abortion laws. It was desired to reduce illegal abortion yet, in fact, as Mehlan reports, the illegal abortions did not decrease. On the contrary, there was an increase.

At the end of 1950 the law was tightened and only strictly medical and eugenic indications were acceptable for abortion.

Thereafter, the number of legal abortions became the lowest in Eastern Europe. More effort was placed on family assistance with the hope that this would reduce illegal abortions. The abortion rate was relatively low and static until changes were introduced in 1965 and the regulations were made more lenient which, in turn, led to an increase in the abortion rate although it is difficult to obtain any figures from 1963 to 1972.

On 9 March 1972, the law transferred the right to decide about abortion from the local boards to the pregnant woman herself. This was linked explicitly with financial assistance for families with children as well as an acceptance by the socialist State of increased responsibility for the constant improvement of health care for women. They also encouraged families to have more children. With the liberalization of the law, the abortion rate jumped to 577 (per thousand) as will be seen. It rose from 80 (per thousand) to this figure, making the rate in East Germany twice as high as Poland for the next few years. It should be said, of course, that the legislation emphasized that contraception was preferable to abortion. Indeed premature termination is considered as the last resort. Once the decision has been made, the medical service will do its part to ensure that the operation is carried out in the safest manner. Counselling should be provided regarding the dangers and consequences of abortion. This freedom of decision for women extends to the twelfth week. After that, only doctors can decide. Again, if less than six months has elapsed since the last abortion, then the use of the law would be counter-indicated except in the case of the threat of serious danger to the mother's life or where grave circumstances arise, or in the case of rape (Paragraph 121, Criminal Code) or coercion or sexual abuse (Paragraph 122, Criminal Code). According to Paragraph 113, Section 1, No. 2, of the Criminal Code, the taking of life, outside the law and before birth, is considered manslaughter: after birth it is treated as murder.

J. Rothe stresses the importance of dialectical materialism for a realistic assessment of the reproductive process. Thereby, he says, realistic ethical conclusions are made possible. However, apart from its usefulness when applied to constant movement, change and development, no further clarification is given.

Rothe then discusses in detail the many stages of the zygote's development and criticizes some of the terminology that has been currently used such as "destruction of the life of the human individual". He describes the embryonic development as a qualitative change which begins from conception. It can be classed as embryonic life which is not viable but, he says, it cannot be called "individual human life". Again (Rothe and Henning 1984, pp. 57–66), he stresses once more the qualitative changes of embryonic development and goes on to point out that this should not be identified with "individual human life" until all the necessary criteria exist. Kraatz and Körner (1984, pp. 67–79), however, feel that more needs to be said about this situation and that Rothe and Henning do not sufficiently define human life nor do they meet the question of why should we respect embryonic life in the first place. They claim that there are really two approaches. First, there is the case of those who believe that developing human life is a spiritual being from conception. In this situation any termination, at any time, is murder and this was the teaching of the West German Catholic Bishops at their Conference in 1972. The other school of thought believes there is no human life till after the twelfth week. Kraatz and Körner rejected the first school of thought but, at the same time, admitted quite candidly that the second school does not adequately meet the problem. Hence they come to a compromise whereby they grant that the embryo is at least a potential human being and abortion is, therefore, evil, though it is the lesser of two evils. Having said this, they proceed to argue that the present legislation cannot be easily changed because of the "woman's right to choose". In practice, they say, other methods should be emphasized rather than abortion.

The Attitude of the Churches

According to Denkschrift, in principle, abortion is not allowed except in the case of grave medical indications in the mother.

For this reason, abortion for non-medical indications is not carried out in hospitals of the Inner Mission, even when the law of the State allows the operation. In a letter (12 April 1985) to Karl Huth, Böhmer says, nevertheless, that:

> There are very good reasons for Christian hospitals having a different opinion on this question. It is just those women patients, who often are so overburdened with personal problems that they think they are unable to give birth to another child, who are pastoral problem cases that we will never reach if we close our doors on them.

Böhmer in another letter (9 January 1986) goes on to state that

> both the Protestant and Catholic Churches have made announcements speaking out against the termination of pregnancy which is not medically justified. In Church hospitals, abortions for which there is no medical indication, are not performed.

However, it must be added here that even where medical indications are present, the Catholic Church does not see direct abortion as morally acceptable.

PART III
Conclusion

Conclusion

The preceding chapters on the USSR, Poland and East Germany demonstrate that there are significant differences in the patterns of abortion. Yet certain trends and similarities are evident.

It can be seen that in East Germany the abortion rate was much lower than Poland until 1972. After that it rose from 80 (per thousand) to 577 (per thousand) making the rate twice as high as that in Poland for the next few years. However, it subsequently declined to 328 in 1978. High as the abortion rate is in Poland it is, therefore, significantly below that of East Germany and other East European countries which does say something about the socialist system. Indeed in Poland there is a sustained decrease. In East Germany, the rate is low till 1965 but with the relaxing of the law came a steady increase until 1972. After the change of the law in 1972 it peaked at 615 in 1973. Since then there is a steady decrease but, as David's and McIntyre's figures indicate, the rate is still very high and much higher than Poland. (David and McIntyre 1982.)

As to Poland, it shows the lowest legal abortion rate per thousand live births in Eastern Europe but it should be added immediately that the rate is much higher than most Western countries. It can also be noted that in Poland, various studies suggest that there is a substantial disapproval of abortion amongst the people. There are, of course, degrees of opposition – some want restricted abortion; others, complete abolition. Perhaps this, to some extent, is linked with the influence of religion and the new pre-marital programmes that are extensively organized by the Catholic Church in Poland. It could also be explained in that some people might be giving the answers expected from them in that kind of society.

There is a strong suggestion that the possibility of simple and readily accessible abortion leads to a dependence on it as a means of birth control. Behind the Eastern European abortion figures is a number of social and cultural factors; high and increasing levels of industrialization; an increasing rate of female participation in the workforce, combined with the belief in female equality and freedom; bad housing; increasing urbanization; changing patterns of sexual behaviour. While the three countries we have considered are under Communist governments, there is still a Christian influence, especially in Poland. Nevertheless, it is difficult to assess at present the power of this ethos. Certainly, the fact that a country has a Christian influence, as in Poland, provides no guarantee of low abortion rates. Indeed, as we have seen above, the greatest influences in the three countries are urbanization, industrialization and the general living conditions which tell us much about the Socialist–Communist policies.

As to the new reproductive techniques, the permissive attitude to abortion will, at first, suggest a similar approach to the human embryo in East Germany and the USSR, and eventually in Poland when IVF becomes a reality. But this would go beyond the evidence, as demonstrated by attitudes in Britain where abortion was legalized in 1967, but in spite of this factor, there was an agonizing controversy with the coming of IVF about the moral status of the human embryo. What was of special interest in the USSR was the approach of Professor Alipov of Leningrad. In the USSR, abortion is not an ethical question yet, surprisingly, he stated that the human embryo would never be used by his team for experimentation. When I expressed my surprise and asked him to reconcile this thinking with the attitudes to abortion, no reply was forthcoming. Perhaps it can be tentatively suggested that, while the abortion rate is much higher in East European countries than in most countries in the West, the attitudes to the new reproductive techniques are not significantly different, as we have seen, from the Utilitarian and Secular approach here in Western society.

IVF, remains then, a technique at present complicated and wasteful, and indeed not highly efficient. It is often alleged that those who express grave concern at the new technology of artificial reproduction are insensitive and it is argued that only by IVF can a cure for infertility be found. As I have demonstrated, both allegations are false. Even considered in its narrow application to suitably selected couples, IVF involves problems of discarded embryos, depersonalization and experimentation. But its extension and abuse outside this narrow field of application is even more disturbing. IVF has to be seen and assessed in the whole area of artificial reproduction – AID, egg donation, surrogacy, not to mention the associated techniques such as genetic manipulation, species cross-fertilization and cloning. The dangers inherent in DNA recombination, which were discussed at Asilomar and to which reference has already been made, and the risks involved in various forms of genetic engineering, constitute a genetic time-bomb which could have the gravest consequences for humanity. Furthermore, there is no unity of opinion amongst scientists, lawyers and philosophers regarding the cardinal issues – they simply do not know. Since the consequences cannot be predicted, and the outcome controlled, it is clear that the risks are far too great for the possible benefits. Indeed more caution and wisdom are necessary.

Again, while aware of the desire of some to have children, one has to face the question as to how one alleviates the pain of *some* without releasing on society a force that is destructive of *many*. Furthermore, the artificial reproduction techniques can be, and are being, extended outside marriage, even to single women with no male partner who are anxious to have a child but wish to avoid involvement with any member of the other sex, moral, emotional or legal (Peel 1986, p. 21).

To say that only by IVF is infertility cured is to ignore the facts surrounding this condiition. Much more emphasis should be placed on prevention rather than cure. Indeed to do otherwise may inhibit alternative research and development of treatments likely to elucidate the causes and prevent the condition rather than simply alleviate it.

Indeed many of the new reproductive techniques are geared to the rich Western world. Money and scarce resources are used for the benefit of the few to the neglect of the more demanding diseases in the international community, such as malaria, malnutrition, tuberculosis and river blindness. One has to ask, how can we balance the efforts in biology and medicine against efforts to eliminate poverty, pollution, discrimination and hunger? Are the priorities to be given to the rich and the few or to the many, and especially the poor? Society, it is suggested, should give more serious consideration to the direction in which medicine is moving so that the needs of the vast majority of people are more adequately addressed. Frequently, as in the case of the nuclear bomb, the energies of science and technology are misplaced and fail to serve human life and its quality in the world community.

Behind some of the thinking regarding the new reproductive techniques, is the belief that every human has an absolute right to have a child, which argues the principle of self-fulfilment to the exclusion of other moral considerations. And yet, on the contrary, one may be morally obliged to avoid a pregnancy if it can be foreseen that the result would be a severely abnormal child. There is concomitant with this thinking, seeing the child as a means not an end. Indeed the Houghton Committee in 1972, set up to consider adoption, stated that the interests of the child should always take precedence over the requirements of the couple. And the Louis Blom Cooper Report on the Jasmin Beckford Inquiry, upheld the same principle (*The Times* 3 December 1985) which has been stated in this book: "We must get the focus back on the child." That is to say, the child should not become a commodity for the gratification of the parents.

The question, therefore, must be faced: how is this principle to be applied in the case of children artificially conceived and deliberately deceived (as Warnock suggests) about their origins? Society is learning to appreciate the importance of biological roots, but the recommendations of Warnock encourage a biological rootlessness in society so that self-identity, both of future generations and future society, could be very much in question. The many children born by AID throughout the world will be denied knowledge of their genetic origins. I have suggested that the public good is not well served by systematic falsification of public records; the question of identity is indeed of paramount importance. The new possibility of separating genetic parenthood from social parenthood raises serious problems for society. Who is the parent of the child and who is liable if things go wrong? What if the genetic parents are determined to have a healthy child and refuse to accept a handicapped or retarded one, as in the case of Baby Doe in the United States? Who has rights and responsibilities regarding the child? Suppose the surrogate mother attempts to extract extra payment beyond the agreed fee and threatens to abort it? How is this to be resolved? In all these areas of genetic manipulation, the experts disagree. Once again, they simply do not know the answers. The risks outweigh the possible advantages. Indeed we have neither the wisdom nor the knowledge for such undertakings.

Furthermore, because of the reasons I have given, marriage in spite of its difficulties, continues to provide the most favourable circumstances for loving, begetting, transmitting and nurturing human life. In justice then, children have a claim to this protection because they have a right to be born in a context which tends to be best for promoting their individuality and identity. Therefore, marriage should be supported rather than weakened, but the new techniques fail to do just this.

As to embryo experimentation, whether one believes the zygote is a potential human being or a human being with potential, becoming what it already is, experimentation on human life is a backward step. It is true that all want to eliminate genetic diseases but not at any price – certainly not at the price of human exploitation. As we have seen, some medical scientists argue that embryo experimentation is quite unnecessary and that gamete research prior to fertilization is more important. Others suggest that embryo experimentation is not the most profitable and others that, at any rate, the rejection of embryo experimentation is implicit in the code of professional ethics relating to all human experiments and which, from time immemorial, has been endorsed by the medical profession and confirmed by the World Medical Association. The central principle is that the interests of the individual must prevail over the interests of science and society. Developing human life, which undeniably begins at fertilization, should be protected from all Faustian bargains which promise knowledge in return for sanctioning experimentation on our humankind. Furthermore, to get accustomed to using human life as a means to an end, as we have done in other areas, is itself corrupting and dehumanizing.

My findings suggest there is little, if any, difference between the Marxist approach in the East and Utilitarianism in the West. Despite the attempts at the refinement of these philosophies, both fail to give an account of large sections of ethics. Both philosophies have an inadequate view of man though Marxist consequentialism is more long term than Utilitarianism and seems less sensitive to the need of respecting the rights and interests of the individual in the present and immediate future. In the case of Utilitarianism, the criteria of what is good is replaced by what is useful. It is true that the useful and the good can lead to the same conclusion, but not necessarily so. The blurring of the distinction between them is to a considerable extent the product of our society and a result of the dominant culture in the world around us. So high a value is placed on technology, production and efficiency, that there is a tendency to measure the worth of what we do primarily in terms of practical results. But in medicine, as in other areas, this does less than justice to the wellbeing of the whole individual, his dignity and his eternal destiny. To deliberately terminate the life of a mentally handicapped child may be useful in the eyes of some, but from the point of view of human rights, it is inadmissable because the most basic good of any human being is human life itself. So in our attitudes to unborn life, the temptation is to replace what is right by what is useful and Utilitarian.

Marxism and Utilitarianism, as we have seen, are consequential philosophies and in both cases the individual, as such, is devalued.

It was not surprising then that the attitudes in the East European countries, which have been analysed in this book were not essentially different from the West. In both capitalist and Communist countries, the interest of the State takes priority over the interests of the individual. What is more, even where religious belief is present, as in Poland, it is generally not a predominant factor where important choices have to be made. In some instances, at least, religious affiliation, while remaining an important variable in determining peoples' attitudes to the unborn, does not seem to determine what happens in practice. Many reasons have been suggested to explain this situation. There are, as we have seen, striking similarities between the attitudes in Poland, the USSR and East Germany. There is too the strong indication that readily accessible abortion leads to a dependence on it as a means of birth control. However, one can tentatively suggest that the fact a country has a Christian influence provides no guarantee of low abortion rates. It also gives rise to the question as to how far teaching and preaching in religious education are effective in spite of the massive resources placed at their disposal. Certainly there is a difference between theory and practice, between belief and behaviour; a point that Shakespeare describes in *The Merchant of Venice*: "If to do were as easy as to know what were good to do, Chapels had been Churches, and poor men's cottages princes' palaces."

In AID, IVF, surrogacy and embryo experimentation, Utilitarian attitudes prevail in Western society and even the theological positions of mainline religions, with few exceptions, are affected by this thinking. When comparing the West and Marxist countries in this area, I found one notable exception in the case of Professor Alipov of Leningrad who categorically rejected all embryo experimentation. Apart from this, the prevalent morality, both in capitalist and Marxist countries, was largely measured in the terms of getting results. If the results seem urgent enough, then paying the price is morally justified regardless of who or what gets manipulated or exploited in the process.

All the problems, therefore, which face Western research in

regard to bio-medical questions at the beginning of human life, as well as its transmission, are present in Poland, the USSR and East Germany. They reflect the feeling that now that science, as a whole, has the potential to control almost all aspects of human life, more rigid rules in some form or other must be developed against unlimited scientific freedoms. The more international, ecumenical and inter-cultural these laws are the better it will be for the global community, whose basic rights and liberties must be protected. This means abandoning the old and out-moded categories of nationalism and regionalism which are totally incapable of coping with these new situations. For example, there is little use in forbidding commercial surrogacy or genetic engineering in Britain if they can be continued in the United States. A new approach is, therefore, required and this entails helping all to see the world as *one* community rather than just a collection of nations. If this vision of unity – which is not only a vision but a hard inescapable fact – can become part of the common insight of the inhabitants of this planet, then we might begin to understand that beyond all our inevitable pluralisms and fragmentations, we can just about achieve enough unity of purpose to avoid genetic, nuclear and environmental disasters like Chernobyl and, therefore, defend our basic humanity; and the most basic good of humanity is life itself. Indeed, if this wider rationale of unity is under-pinned by the instinct of self-preservation and safety of the human race, then we could find, beyond all our pluralisms, just enough unity to convince us that the world community has to be protected *internationally* from manipulation, exploitation and destruction.

Bibliography

Acta Apostolicae Sedis (AAS) 41 (1949). Pius XII on rejection of masturbation and disruption of the marriage act. (For further comment on these matters, see also: AAS 43 (1951) pp. 849–51 and AAS 48 (1956) pp. 470–74.)

—— 66 (1974) "Sacred Congregation for the Doctrine of the Faith". In *Declaration on Abortion*, No. 13.

—— 75 (1983) "October address to biologists in Rome".

Alikhanin, S. (1976) "Success and Prospects for Genetic Engineering". In *Soviet Genetics*, Part 12. Translated and published by PL Consultants Bureau, New York, NY.

Allen, D. (1976) "Reply to Brenbert's *Marx and Utilitarianism*", *Canadian Journal of Philosophy*, Vol. 6, No. 3, September.

Allen, M. and Turner, U. (1971) "Twin-Birth: identical or fraternal twins?", *American Journal of Obstetrics and Gynaecology*, 37.

American Fertility Society (1984) Report on guidelines. *New Scientist*, 26 July.

Antoine, O. (1974) *The Month*, May.

Archbishop of Canterbury (1948) *Artificial Human Insemination*, SPCK, London.

Ash, W. (1964) *Marxism and Moral Concepts*, MR Press, New York, NY.

Baev, A. (1976) "Sovremennye napravleniya molekul yarnol genetiki: genetisheskaya inzheneriya" (Current Trends in Molecular Genetics: Genetic Engineering). Published in Moscow in the journal *Vestnik Akademii Meditsinkikh Nauk* SSSR, No. 7.

Baird, D. (1969) *Combined Textbook of Obstetrics and Gynaecology*, E. & S. Livingstone, Edinburgh.

Baptist Union (1985) *The Submission and Response*, Baptist Union, London.

Basmajian, J. (1976) *Primary Anatomy* (7th Edition), Williams & Wilkins, Baltimore, Md.

Batchelow, E. (ed.) (1982) *Abortion and Moral Issues*, Pilgrim Press, New York, NY.

Beirnaert, L. (1970) "L'avortement est-il infanticide", *Etudes*, CCCXXXIII.

Birch, C. and Cobb, T. (1981) *Liberation of Life*, Cambridge University Press, London.

Bishop of Augsburg (1979) *Theological Studies*, Vol. 40, No. 1, March.

Bloom, M. and Van Dongen, L. (1972) *Clinical Gynaecology*, Heinemann Medical, London.

Board for Social Responsibility of the Church of England (1984) *Human Fertilization and Embryology*, Church Information Office, London.

—— (1985) *Personal Origins*, Church Information Office, London.

Board for Social Responsibility of the Church of Scotland (1985) *Ethics and Medicine* 1:2, Rutherford House Periodicals, Edinburgh.

Bogdanov, B. (1978) "Iz istorii issledaniji filosofii gegelja" (The History of the Study of Hegelian Philosophy). In L. N. Suvorov *et al* (cited in Grier 1978) *Soviet Philosophical Science*.

Böhmer, W. (1981) "Etische Probleme der modernen Geburlsmedizin" (Ethical Problems of Modern Obstetrics), *Ziechen der Zeit (Signs of the Times)*, 35.

Bok, S. (1981) "Ethical problems of abortion". In T. A. Shannon (ed.) *Bioethics*, Paulist Press, Newark, NJ.

British Medical Association (1986) *A Torture Report*. Report of a Working Party of the BMA investigating doctors' involvement in torture. BMA, London.

Brown, D. (1983) *Choices: Ethics and the Christian*, Basil Blackwell, Oxford.

Bulmer, M. (1970) *The Biology of Twinning in Man*, Clarendon Press, Oxford.

Buster, J. (1984) "Tomorrow's Babies: The Warnock Report". Interview with Margaret Jay for BBC 2 television programme "Brass Tacks", 18 July. Transcript.

Callahan, D. (1972) *Abortion, Law, Choice and Morality*, Macmillan, New York, NY.

Cass, L. (1972) "New beginnings in life". In M. Hamilton (ed.) *The New Eugenics and the Future of Man*, Eerdmans, Grand Rapids, Mich.

Catholic Bishops' Conference of England and Wales (1980) *Abortion and the Right to Life*, No. 12, Catholic Truth Society, London.

—— (1983) In Vitro *Fertilization and Public Policy*, Report of the Joint Committee on Bioethical Issues, Catholic Information Service, Abbotts Langley.

—— (1983a) "Human fertilization: choices for the Future". In *Social Welfare Commission Report*, Catholic Information Service, Abbotts Langley.

—— (1984) *Comments on the Warnock Report*, Catholic Media Office, London.

Catholic Union of Great Britain (1960) *Artificial Insemination*, Catholic Truth Society, London.

Chamberlain, G. and Winston, R. (1982) *Tubal Infertility*, Blackwell Scientific, Oxford.

Chardin, Teilhard de (1959) *The Phenomenon of Man*, Collins, London.

Chetchot, D. (1984) *Brak, sem'ya zakon (Marriage, the Family and the Law)*, Leningrad University Press, Leningrad.

Connery, J. (1977) *Abortion*, Loyala University Press, Chicago, Ill. Connery also quotes Joseph Flavius and Philo, *The Annals of Tacitus*, 2, Oxford, 1891.

Corkery, P. (1983) Unpublished thesis ("Fabricated Man").

Corner, G. (1955) "The observed embryology of human single-ovum twins and other multiple births", *American Journal of Obstetrics and Gynaecology*, 70.

Council for International Organisations of Medical Sciences (1982) Geneva.

Council for Science and Society (1984) *Human Procreation: Ethical Aspects of the New Techniques*, Oxford University Press, London.

Craft, D., McLeod, F., Green, S. *et al* (1978) "Birth following oocyte and sperm transferred to the uterus", *The Lancet*, 2.

Curran, C. (1973) "Abortion, law and morality in contemporary Catholic theology", *The Jurist*, Vol. 33.

—— (1973a) *Politics, Medicine and Christian Ethics*, Fortress Press, Philadelphia, Pa.

David, H. (1970) *Family Planning and Abortion in the Soviet Countries of Central and Eastern Europe*, Population Council, New York, NY.

—— and McIntyre, P. (1982) "Eastern Europe: Pro-natalist Policies and Private Behavior", *Population Bulletin*, Vol. 36, No. 6.

Desfosses, H. (ed.) (1981) "Pro-natalism in Soviet Law and Propaganda". In *Soviet Population Policy: Conflicts and Constraints*, Pergamon Press, Oxford.

Division for Social Responsibility of the Methodist Church (1983) *Methodist Church Submission to the Warnock Committee*, Methodist Publishing House, London.

Donceel, J. (1970) "Animation and Hominisation", *Theological Studies*, Vol. 31, No. 1, March.

Dubinin, N. (1968) *Nekotorye metodologicheskie problemy genetiki (Some Methodological Problems of Genetics)*, Znanie, Moscow.

—— (1977) "Integriruyushchaya rol' genetiki v biologii i evolyutsionnom uchenii" (The Integrating Role of Genetics in Biology and Evolutionary Studies), *Vestnik Akademii Nauk* SSSR (*Bulletin of the Academy of Science*) No. 1.

—— and Gorodetskii, S. (1978) "Geneticheskaya inzheneriya: zadachi sovremmenykh issledovanii" (Genetic Engineering: The Problems of Contemporary Research), *Vestnik Akademii Nauk* SSSR.

Dunstan, G. (1984) "The Moral Status of the Human Embryo: A Tradition Recalled", *Journal of Medical Ethics*, March.

Dyban, A. (1978) "Schastlivyi zapret prirody" (Fortunate prohibition of nature), *Literaturnaya gazeta* (*Literary Gazette*).

Edwards, R. (1983) "The current clinical and ethical situation of human conception *in vitro*". In C. O. Carter (ed.) *Developments in Human Reproduction and their Eugenic Ethical Implications*, Academic Press, London.

—— (1983a) *Nature*, 208, pp. 349–51.

—— (1983b) "Test-tube babies: the ethical debate", *The Listener*, 17 October, p. 12.

—— (1984) "Tomorrow's Babies: The Warnock Report". Interview with Fred Emery for BBC2 television programme "Brass Tacks", 18 July. Transcript.

Engelhardt, H. (1983) "The viability and use of the foetus". In W. B. Bondeson (ed.) *et al*, *Abortion: The Status of the Foetus*, Reidel Publishing, Dordrecht.

Fagone, V. (1973) *La Civiltà Cattolica*, Vol. 2952, 16 June.

—— (1973a) *La Civiltà Cattolica*, Vol. 2953, 17 July.

Faversham Committee (1960) *Human Artificial Insemination*, Comnd. No. 1105, HMSO, London.

Field, M. (1956) "The Re-Legislation of Abortion in Soviet Russia", *New England Journal of Medicine* (August) No. 225.

Fleming, J. (1986) "Life in a Test Tube", Veritas Video Productions,

Dublin. A cassette with discussion between J. Fleming and Professor McAleese.

—— and Iglesias, T. (1985) "Human fertilization *in vitro* compared with nature", *The Lancet*, 19 January.

Fletcher, J. (1971) "Ethical aspects of genetic control", *New England Journal of Medicine*.

—— (1974) *The Ethics of Genetic Control: Ending Reproductive Roulette*, Anchor Press/Doubleday, Garden City, NY.

Ford, C. (1969) "Mosaics and chimeras", *British Medical Bulletin*, 25.

Fox, H. (ed.) (1984) *Haine's and Taylor's Obstetrical and Gynaecological Pathology* (4th Edition) Churchill Livingstone, Edinburgh.

Francover, R. (1970) *Utopian Motherhood: New Trends in Human Reproduction*, Doubleday, Garden City, NY.

Fritzhand, M. (1961) *Mysl etyczna mlodego maksa* (*Ethical Thoughts in the Marxist System*), Ksiazka Weidza, Warsaw.

—— (1982) "Etyczne aspekty wspolczesnej genetyki" (Contemporary aspects of moral genetics). In *Wartosci a fakty* (*Values and Facts*), Ksiazka Weidza, Warsaw.

Frolov, I. (1976) "Chelovek segodnya i zavtra" (Man Today and Tomorrow), *Nauka i zhizn* (*Science and Life*), No. 9.

—— (1982) *Global Problems and the Future of Mankind*, Progress Publishing, Moscow.

—— (1983) "Life, Death and Immortality", *Social Science*, Vol. IXV, No. 2.

Gasser, R. (1975) *Atlas of Human Embryology*, Harper & Row, New York, NY.

Geiger, H. Kent (1968) *The Family in Soviet Russia*, Harvard University Press, Cambridge, Mass.

Geissler, E., Hörz, H. E. and Hörz, H. (1980) "Zu Eingriffen in das genetische Material des Menschen" (Experiments on the genetic material of man). Lecture given at the conference on "Social Effectiveness of the Natural Sciences, Mathematics and Technical Sciences in the nineteenth and twentieth century", Berlin, 23–25 January.

Gill, R., (1975) *Social Context of Theology*, Mowbray, London.

—— (1977) *Theology and Social Structure*, Mowbray, London.

Glander, H., Graf, U., Piskazeck, K., Radow, G. and Theile, H. (1983) "Vorschlag für eine Richtlinie zue Durchführung der artefiziellen donogenen insemination" (Suggestions for a guideline for carrying out artificial insemination by donor), Deutsches Gesund-heitswesen (German Health Service), 38, No. 22.

Graham, L. (1980) "Reasons for studying Soviet science: The example of Genetic Engineering". In L. Lubrano and S. Solomon (eds.) *The Social Context of Soviet Science*, Westview Dawson, Boulder, Col. (Published simultaneously in England by Wm. Dawson, Folkestone.)

—— (1981) "Biomedicine and the Politics of Science in the USSR". In *Soviet Union*, Vol. 8, Pt. 2, Arizona State University, Tempe, Ariz.

Grier, P. (1978) *Marxist Ethical Theory in the Soviet Union*, Reidel Publishing, Dordrecht.

Grischchenko, V. and Parashuk, Y. (1984) *Akusherstvo i ginekolo-giya (Obstetrics and Gynaecology)*, 2.

Grisez, G. (1970) *Abortion: the Myths, the Realities and the Arguments*, Corpus Books, New York, NY.

Guild of Catholic Doctors (1984) Evidence to the Warnock Inquiry.

Hamilton, M. (1969) "New Life for old: genetic decisions", *Christian Century*, 86.

Hare, R. (1975) "Abortion and the golden rule", *Philosophy and Public Affairs*.

Häring, B. (1972) *Medical Ethics*, St Paul's Press, Slough.

—— (1975) *Manipulation*, St Paul's Press, Slough.

Harrison, R. and Romanes, G. (eds.) (1981) *Cunningham's Textbook of Anatomy* (12th Edition), Oxford University Press, Oxford.

Harvard Medical School (1968) "A definition of irreversible coma". Report of the Ad Hoc Committee of the Harvard Medical School to examine brain death. *Journal of the American Medical Association*, 5 August.

Healey, E. (1956) *Medical Ethics*, Loyala University Press, Chicago, Ill.

Hertig and Rock (1949) *American Journal of Obstetrics and Gynaecology*, 58.

Hewson, M. (1975) *Giles of Rome and the Mediaeval Theory of Conception*, Athlone Press, London.

Hick, J. (1976) *Death and Eternal Life*, Collins, London.

—— (1983) *The Second Christianity*, SCM Press, London.

Hillier, S. (1984) *New Scientist*, 27 September.

Hodges, D. (1974) *Social Humanism: The Outcome of Classical European Morality*, Warren H. Green Inc., St Louis, Miss.

Holland, B. (1979) "The Control of Reproduction in the Soviet Union, with special reference to the role of medicine". Masters degree, University of Birmingham.

—— (1980) "A Woman's Right to Choose in the Soviet Union". In J. Brine *et al* (eds.) *Home, School and Leisure in the Soviet Union*, Allen & Unwin, London.

Hollenweger, W. (1973) "Marxist Ethics". In *The Expository Times*, Vol. 85, T. & T. Clark, Edinburgh.

Hoyle, F. (1983) *The Intelligent Universe*, Michael Joseph, London.

Hume, B. (1984) *Briefing*, Catholic Information Service, Abbotts Langley.

Iglesias, T. (1984) "*In vitro* fertilization: the major issues", *Journal of Medical Ethics*, 1.

—— (undated) "*In vitro* fertilization: how far can we go?", Linacre Centre, London. (Not published.)

—— (1984a) *The Tablet*, 14 July.

—— (1984b) "Social and ethical aspects of IVF". In T. Iglesias (ed.) *Test-tube Babies: A Christian View*, Unity Press (Becket Publication), London.

—— (undated) "Questions concerning artificial insemination *in vivo* and *in vitro*". Report to the Committee on Legal Affairs and Citizens' Rights of the European Parliament. Linacre Centre, London. (Not published.)

—— (1985) *The Universe*, 24 May.

International Planned Parenthood Federation (1979) *Medical Bulletin*, Vol. 13, No. 4, London, August.

—— (1979a) *Medical Bulletin*, Vol. 13, No. 5, London, October.

—— (1981) *Medical Bulletin*, Vol. 15, No. 6, London, December.

—— (1982) *Medical Bulletin*, Vol. 16, No. 2, London, April.

James, W. (1970) "The incidence of spontaneous abortion", *Population Studies*, No. 24.

Jarovsky, D. (1961) *Soviet Marxism and Natural Science*, Routledge & Kegan Paul, London.

Jeffcoate, N. (1975) *Principles of Gynaecology* (4th Edition), Butterworth, London.

Jonas, H. (1984) "Biologia i Moralosc" (Biology and Morality). First published in Poland in the magazine *Miedzynarodowy Prezeglad Teologiczny*. Translated by Fr Lucian Bolter and published in *International Theological Review*, No. 6.

Joyce, G. (1948) *Christian Marriage: An Historical and Doctrinal Study*, Sheed & Ward, London.

Kant, E. (1959) *Foundations and Metaphysics of Morals*, The Bobbs Merrill Co. Inc., New York, NY.

Karpinskaia, R. (1978) "Mirovozzrencheskoe znachenie sovremennoi biologii" (Philosophical Significance of Modern Biology) *Voprosy filosofii*, No. 4.

Kass, R. (1972) "Making babies: the new biology and the old morality", *Public Interest*, Vol. 26.

Kennedy, I. (1984) "Let the law take on the test-tube", *The Times*, 26 May.

Kerimova, A. (1980) "Sotsial'no-eticheskie problemy genetiki cheloveka" (The Social and Ethical Problems of Human Genetics), *Voprosy filosofii*.

Keune, R. and Rothe, J. (1985) "Positionsbestimmung zur *in vitro* fertilisierung und zum embryotransfer beim menschen" (Defining an attitude towards human *in vitro* fertilization and embryo transfer), *Zeitschrift für Klinische Medizin (Journal for Clinical Medicine)*, 40, No. 24.

King, J. (1980) "New genetic technology: prospects and hazards". In R. L. Shinn (ed.) *Faith and Science in an Unjust World*, World Council of Churches, Geneva.

Klinger, A. (1965) "Demographic Effects of Abortion Legislation in some European Socialist Countries". In *Proceedings of the World Population Congress, Belgrade 1965*, Vol. 2, United Nations, New York, NY.

Körner, U. and Körner, H. (1984) "Ethische und methodische Aspekte der In-Vitro-Befruchtung beim Menschen" (Ethical and Methodical Aspects of Human *In Vitro* Fertilisation) Deutsches Gesundheitswesen (German Health Service), 29.

Kraatz, H. and Körner, U. (1984) "Schwangerschaftsabbruch und Ehrfurcht vor dem menschilchen Leben" (Termination of Pregnancy and Respect for Human Life). In *Grenzsituationen ärztlichen Handelns, Bd. 13: Medizin und Gesellschaft (Borderline Situations in Medical Practice, Vol. 13: Medicine and Society)*, Gustav Fischer, Jena.

Kyank, H. (1983) "Eztrakorporale Befruchung und Embryo-Transfer" (Extra-corporeal fertilisation and embryo transfer) *Spectrum: Monatzeitschrift der Akademie der Wissenschaften der DDR (Spectrum: Monthly Journal of the Academy of Science of the GDR)*, 14, No. 6.

Lader, L. (1966) *Abortion*, Bobbs Merrill, Indianapolis, Ind.

Lane, C. (1978) *Christian Religion in the Soviet Union*, Allen & Unwin, London.

Lapidus, G. (1978) *Women in Soviet Society*, University of California Press, London.

Lejeune, J. (1984) "Genetic Engineering: test-tube babies are babies". In T. Iglesias (ed.) *Test-tube Babies: A Christian View*, Unity Press (Becket Publication), London.

—— (1985) "Professor Jerome Lejeune". Interview for BBC Radio 4 programme "Today", 7 February. Transcript.

Life (1983) *Submission to Warnock*, Leamington Spa.

—— (1984) *Warnock Dissected*, Leamington Spa.

Llewellyn-Jones, O. (1978) *Fundamentals of Obstetrics and Gynaecology*, Faber & Faber, London.

Liseev, I. and Sharov, A. (1970) Neifakh's question was contained in the article by Liseev and Sharov, "Genetika cheloveka ee Filosofskie i Sotsial'no-eticheskie problemy" ("Human Genetics: its philosophical and socio-ethical problems"), *Voprosy filosofii*, No. 7.

Litvinova, G. (1981) "Pravovye aspekty iskuss tvennogo oplodotvoreniya" (Legal Aspects of Artificial Insemination), *Sovietskoe gosudarstvo i pravo (Soviet State and the Law)*, No. 9.

Lonergan, B. (1975) *Insight and Study of Human Understanding*, Philosophical Library, New York, NY.

Longman, J. (1975) *Medical Embryology* (3rd Edition), E. & S. Livingstone, Edinburgh.

Lucey, C. (1978) *Catholic Review*, 28 July.

McCormick, R. (1972) "Genetic Medicine: Notes on the Moral Literature", *Theological Studies*, 33.

—— (1981) *How Brave A New World?*, SCM Press, London.

McDonagh, E. (1972) *Invitation and Response*, Gill & Macmillan, Dublin.

McLaren, A. (1976) *Mammalian Chimaeras*, Cambridge University Press, Cambridge.

Mahoney, J. (1984) *Bioethics and Belief*, Sheed & Ward, London.

—— (1984a) "Warnock: a Catholic comment", *The Month*, September.

—— (1984b) "Tomorrow's Babies: The Warnock Report". Interview with Fred Emery for BBC 2 television programme "Brass Tacks", 18 July. Transcript.

Maleina, M. (1984) The original Russian text was published in Moscow by the Pravovedenie publishing house in 1983. An English translation appeared in 1984, in *Soviet Law and Government*, Vol. XXII, Winter, No. 3.

Marshall, J. (1960) *Ethics of Medical Practice*, Darton, Longman & Todd, London.

—— (1984) "Scientists and the embryo", *The Tablet*, 18 August.

Marx, K. (1933) *Capital*, Vol. 2. Translated by M. Eden and P. Cedar, J. M. Dent, London.

—— and Engels, F. (1975) *Collected Works*, Vol. 1, Lawrence & Wishart, London.

Medical Research Council (1985) "Response to the Report of the Inquiry into Human Fertilization and Embryology", *The Lancet*, 2 February.

Medvedev, Z. (1979) *Soviet Science*, Oxford University Press, Oxford, Appendix 1.

Mehlan, K. (1966) "The Socialist Countries of Europe". In B. Berelson *et al* (eds.) *Family Planning and Population Programs*, Chicago University Press, Chicago, Ill.

Messenger, E. (1949) *Theology of Evolution*, Sands & Co., London.

Mill, B. (1973) *Government, Politics and Society*, Fontana/Harvester Press, Hassocks.

Moltmann, J. (1979) *The Future of Creation*, SCM Press, London.

Moraczewski, A. (1983) "Human personhood". In W. B. Bondeson *et al* (eds.) *Abortion: The Status of the Foetus*, Reidel Publishing, Dordrecht.

Muller, H. (1967) "What genetic course will men steer?". In J. F. Crow and J. V. Need (eds.) *Proceedings of the Third International Conference on Human Genetics*, John Hopkins University Press, Baltimore, Md.

Murray, D. (1985) *A Question of Morality*, Veritas Video Productions, Dublin.

Neilson, K. (1971) *Reason and Practice: A Modern Introduction to Philosophy*, Harper & Row, New York, NY.

Nestorowicz, M. (1985) "Nation and Law" (Panstwo i Prawo), *Miesiecznik Polskei Akademii Nauk Instytut Panstwa i Prawa (Monthly Journal of the Polish Academy of Studies)*, Institute of Nation and Law, Warsaw, Vol. 2.

Nikitin, A. (1982) "Oplodotvorenie yaitsekletok cheloveka vne organizma i transplantatsiya zarodyshev (dostizheniya i trudnosti)" (IVF of human ova and transplantation of the foetuses (achievements and difficulties), *Arkiv anatomii, gistologii, embri-*

ologii (*Records of Anatomy, Histology and Embryology*), Vol. 83, No. 11.

Noonan, J. (1970) "An almost absolute value in history". In J. T. Noonan (ed.) *The Morality of Abortion*, Harvard University Press, Cambridge, Mass.

North, R. (1967) *Tielhard and the Creation of the Soul*, Bruce Publishing, Milwaukee, Wis.

Okolski, M. (1983) "Abortion and Contraception in Poland", *Studies in Family Planning*, Vol. 14, No. 11.

O'Mahony, P. (1977) "Where life begins", *The Month*, December.

—— (1978) "The beginning and end of human life", *The Month*, November.

—— and Potts, M. (1967) "Abortion and the soul", *The Month*, July–August.

Oparin, A. (1968) *The Origin and Initial Development of Life*, TFF 488, NASA, Houston, Tex.

O'Rahilly, R. (1973) *Developmental Stages in Human Embryos. Part A: Embryos in the first three weeks. Stages 1–9*, Carnegie Institute of Washington, Publication 631, Washington, DC.

Parliamentary Assembly of the Council of Europe (1985) DOC 5460, 17 September.

Pastrana, G. (1977) *The Thhomist*, Vol. 41, April.

Paul VI (1970) *Human vitae*, Catholic Truth Society, London.

Peel, J. (1973) *British Medical Journal*, Supplement, Vol. II, 7 April.

—— (1986) *Ethics and Medicine*, Rutherford House Periodicals, Edinburgh.

Philipp, E., Barnes, J. and Newton, M. (1977) "Early human development: from oocyte to implantation". In *Scientific Foundations of Obstetrics and Gynaecology* (2nd Edition), Heinemann Medical, London.

Philippe, P. (1985) "Genetic epidemiology of Twinning: a population-based study", *American Journal of Medical Ethics*, 20.

Pimenova, L. *et al* (1983) *Akusherstvo i ginekologia* (*Obstetrics and Gynaecology*).

Pohier, J–M. (1970) "Avortement et respect de la vié humaine", *Etudes*, CCCXXXIII.

Potts, M. (1969) "The problem of abortion". In F. J. Ebling (ed.) *Biology and Ethics*, Academic Press, London.

—— (1977) *Abortion*, Cambridge University Press, Cambridge.

(The) Practitioner (1947) Vol. 158, No. 946, April.

Quelquejeu, B. (1972) "La volonte de procréer", *Lumiére et vié*, 21, No. 109, August–October.

Rahner, K. (1965) *Hominisation: The Evolutionary Origin of Man as a Theological Problem*, Burns & Oates, London.

—— (1966) *Theological Investigations*, Vol. 5, Darton, Longman & Todd, London.

—— (1972) "The problem of genetic manipulation". In K. Rahner (ed.) *Theological Investigation*, Vol. 9, Hender & Hender, New York, NY.

Ramsey, P. (1973) "Abortion: a review", *The Thomist*, 37.

—— (1977) *Fabricated Man: The Ethics of Genetic Control*, Yale University Press, New Haven, Conn.

—— and McCormick, R. (1978) *Doing Evil to Achieve Good*, Loyala University Press, Chicago, Ill.

Ribes, B. (1970) Quoted in an article by J-M. Pohier (1970). (See above.)

Rock, J. and Menkin, M. (1944) *Science*, 100.

Rothe, J. and Henning, G. (1984) "Die artifizielle vorzeitige Schwangerschaftsbeendigung – soziale Funktionen und moralische Probleme" (Artificial pre-term Abortion – social functions and moral problems). In *Grenzsituationen ärztlichen Handelns, Bd. 13: Medizin und Gesselschaft* (*Borderline Situations in Medical Practice, Vol. 13: Medicine and Society*), Gustav Fischer, Jena.

Royal College of General Practitioners (1984) Evidence to the Warnock Inquiry.

Ryan, M. (1981) "Induced Abortion: Is it murder by the skilled?" *British Medical Journal*, Vol. 283.

Sacred Congregation for the Doctrine of the Faith (1987) *Instruction on Respect for Human Life in its Origin and on the Dignity of Procreation*, Catholic Truth Society, London.

Schaff, A. (1963) *A Philosophy of Man*, Dell Publishing, New York, NY.

—— (1970) *Marxism and the Human Individual*, McGraw Hill, New York, NY.

Schenk, R. (1968) "Let's talk about abortion", *Catholic World*, 207, April.

Scothorne, R. (1976) *A Companion to Medical Studies* (2nd Edition), Vol. 1, Blackwell Scientific Publications, Oxford.

Shannon, T. (1978) "The case against the test-tube babies", *National Catholic Reporter*, 11 August.

Singer, P. and Wells, D. (1984) *The Reproduction Revolution*, Oxford University Press, London.

Siskin, A. (1973) "Onekotoryx Voprosox issledovatel' skoj v oblasti etiki" (Concerning Several Questions of Research Work in the Area of Ethics), *Voprosy filosofii*, No. 1.

Skrzydlewski, W. (1984) "The Truth on Abortion in Poland", *Human Life International Report*, Washington, DC.

SOU (1983) "Children conceived by artificial insemination". Swedish government publication on AID. Two years later, a similar report (SOU 1985) on IVF and surrogacy was published.

Stojanovic, S. (1973) *Between Ideals and Reality: A Critique of Socialism and its Future*. Oxford University Press, New York, NY.

Suzuki, M. (1984) As reported in the *New Scientist*, 26 July.

Szawarski, Z. (1978) "Etyka i przerywanie ciazy" (Ethics and abortion), *Etyka (Ethics)*, 16.

—— (1983) *Studie Folozoficzne (Philosophical Studies)*, Nos. 8–9.

—— (1986–88) Letters to the author.

Thomson, J. (1971) "A defence of abortion", *Philosophy and Public Affairs*.

Tooley, M. (1971) "Abortion and Infanticide", *Philosophy and Public Affairs*.

Torrance, T. (1984) *Test Tube Babies: Morals, Science and the Law*, Scottish Academic Press, Edinburgh.

Towers, B. (1964) "Man in modern science", *The Month*, January.

Toynbee, P. (1985) *Lost Children*, Hutchinson, London.

Triseliotis, J. (1973) *In Search of Origins*, Routledge & Kegan Paul, London.

Trotsky, L., Dewey, J. and Novak, G. (1973) *Their Morals and Ours: Marxist Views versus Liberal Views on Morality*, Pathfinder Press, New York, NY.

Tuchmann-Duplessis, H., David, G. and Haeger, P. (1972) *Illustrated Human Embryogenesis*, Springer-Verlag, New York, NY.

Voprosy filosofii (Questions of Philosophy) (1972) No. 9.

Warnock, M. (1983) "*In vitro* fertilization: the ethical issues", *Philosophical Quarterly*, Vol. 33, No. 132, July.

—— (1985) *A Question of Life*, Basil Blackwell, Oxford.

—— (1985a) "The surrogacy scandal", *The Listener*, 24 January.

(The) Warnock Report (1984) "Report of the Committee of Inquiry

into Human Fertilization and Embryology", HMSO, London. The report was published in July 1984. It is widely discussed in this book and both the Inquiry and the Report are referred to throughout, sometimes in abbreviated form ("Warnock"; "the Inquiry", etc.).

Warwick, R. and Williams, P. (eds.) (1973) *Gray's Anatomy* (35th Edition), Longman, London.

Weibering, J. (1981) *Handeln aus Glauben, Grundriss der theologischen Ethik* (*Action from Belief, Outline of Theological Ethics*), Evangelische Verlagsanstalt (Protestant Press), Berlin.

Weiner, O. and Brit, J. (1978) *Journal of Obstetrics and Gynaecology*, 85.

Wetter, G. (1954) "Dialectical Materialism: The Philosophy of the Proletariat". In *God, Man and Universe*, Burns & Oates, London.

Whittaker, P., Taylor, A. and Lind, T. (1983) "The unsuspected pregnancy loss in healthy women", *The Lancet*, 1.

Wilder, H. (1904) "Duplicate twins and double monsters", *American Journal of Anatomy*, 3.

Wilken, H., Fliess, F. and Sudik, R. (1984) "Zu einigen Fragen der Ethik in der Forschung und Praxis der Reproduktionsmedizin" (Some questions on the ethics of research and practice in reproductive medicine) *Zentralblatt für Gynäkologii* (*Central Journal for Gynaecology*), 106.

Williams, G. (1964) "The legislation of medical abortion", *Eugenics Review*, 56, April.

—— (1979) "Religious Residues and Presuppositions in the American Debate on Abortion", *Theological Studies*, March, Vol. 31, No. 1.

Yavich, J. (1985) "Embryo quality and pregnancy rates in IVF", *The Lancet*, 2 January.

Ziolowski, J. (1974) "Poland". In B. Berelson (ed.) *Population Policy in Developing Countries*, Population Council, New York.

Index of Personal Names